Life with Breast Cancer Timing Medical Intervention

by

Sotiria Theoharis

DISSERTATION

Submitted in partial satisfaction of the requirements for the degree of

DOCTOR OF PHILOSOPHY

in

Department of Social & Behavioral Sciences

in the

GRADUATE DIVISION

of the

UNIVERSITY OF CALIFORNIA, SAN FRANCISCO

Approved:

Greg Bidell   *June 1, 2006*

Carrol J Estes

....
Committee in Charge

Deposited in the Library, University of California, San Francisco

....
Date   University Librarian

Degree Conferred:..

UMI Number: 3221175

INFORMATION TO USERS

The quality of this reproduction is dependent upon the quality of the copy submitted. Broken or indistinct print, colored or poor quality illustrations and photographs, print bleed-through, substandard margins, and improper alignment can adversely affect reproduction.

In the unlikely event that the author did not send a complete manuscript and there are missing pages, these will be noted. Also, if unauthorized copyright material had to be removed, a note will indicate the deletion.

Abstract

This dissertation studies breast cancer care historically and ethnographically to address four questions: (1) how breast care structures and normalizes the actions of medical scientists, care providers, and women, (2) how medical scientists make breast cancer facts, (3) how medical paradigms habituate in institutions, bolster professionals, and lived through the women affected by the disease, (4) what are the emerging parameters for women's participation.

Medical paradigms order lived experiences with the disease. They facilitate the building of durable medical/ clinical structures. They, also, can instigate social-scientific learning of how to cope. In medical paradigming, science making isn't the only parameter. Rather, an explicit alignment of laboratory and clinical science, of diagnostic and therapeutic action, of biology with society becomes a necessity. Medical paradigming requires finding ways to engage women in governance structures, to produce sustainable knowledge structures, as well as to direct more effective cure and care arrangements. The timing of medical intervention becomes a special feature of breast cancer therapeutic paradigms.

In breast cancer care, the timing question is profound. It is part of the condition for success and the definition of cure. It is part of the process of detection and the language that engages women in action. It is part of the logic for new therapeutics. With the emergence of bio-molecular indicators of the disease (like genetic testing) and new types of intervention (like chemoprevention), questions about timing became more forceful. Treatment turns into prophylaxis. Even as the timing of procedures before the advent of disease may provide hope for women at higher high risk, it may also lead to interventions that manage anxiety in the face of the disease with no certainty of the material benefits.

[signature] June 1, 2006

In memory of my Aunt Helene
And all who have suffered from this disease

Table of Contents

Acknowledgements

A dissertation is a first a process than an outcome. It is an educational journey through knowledge as production, profession, and institution. In my journey, events occurred that challenged me -- both my resolve and performance, and events occurred in the world that shook its democratic, modern foundations. In times of challenge, we turn to the basic structures of our life and world. We simplify. We adapt our tactics to new circumstances.

Being reflexive about my accomplishments, I wish to acknowledge the effort of members of my committee without their generous support and advice I would not be able to complete my studies: Prof. Shelley Adler, Prof. Gay Becker, Prof. Carroll Estes, Prof. Dorothy Porter. I also wish to thank my former advisor Prof. Adele Clarke for her insights and her instruction especially useful in writing chapters one and four. Prof. Donna Haraway for her comments on chapter one and her advice. Prof. Claudia Casteñeda for insights with regard to the structure of my project. Prof Judith Butler and Prof. Herbert Dreyfus for choosing me to attend their course on 'After Humanism: the subject and power.' This course was pivotal in writing chapter four. I thank the Advance STS Pro-seminar taught at UC Berkeley by Prof. Gene Rochlin and Prof. Jane Summerton. They gave me the opportunity to present chapter four. I thank the group for their comments. I thank Dr. Molly Sutphen for her feedback on chapter one as well as the opportunity to read original historical source materials. Prof. Warwick Anderson for his comments on chapter one. Fellow UCSF students who joined in the yearlong reading group: Chris Ganchoff, Cassie Crawford, Maya Ponte and who commented on work in progress.

In terms of funds, I would like to thank UCSF-SBS for fellowship moneys. Prof. Carroll Estes for employing me as an RA and GSI at IHA and SBS respectively. I wish to acknowledge the Stanford University/ University of Pennsylvania study Dr. Mildred Cho, Dr. Pamela Sankar, Dr. Paul Wolpe, Dr. Nora Jones, Dr. Antoinette Guerra, Berry Metzer, Cheryl Theis, Gwen Anderson for data collection, coding, and study design as well as the NIH grant R01 HG01576. I worked on this project to code and analyze the data and use some of that analysis for chapter five. I also thank Dr. Gayle Salamon and the Department of Women Studies at UC Berkley for hiring me as a GSI in Feminist Theory. I want to thank a fantastic group of students. I enjoyed teaching them and learned a great deal from them about undergraduate teaching. I would like to thank numerous students and teachers I encountered over the years the list is very long. I have learned the value of being an academic as well as the importance of being involved in the community.

I would like to thank my family for believing and supporting me as much as they could in moments of need. Their collective help was invaluable. I like to thank people who participated in the two studies I had the opportunity to work for or design. Through their willingness to participate I was able to illuminate how medicine works as a social institution. Understanding how we live with breast cancer is essential in structuring responsive and effective medical actions. I dedicate this dissertation to their lives and the life of my aunt Helene who passed from this disease.

Finally, I am grateful to the numerous Greek activists and organizations, who entrusted me with the opportunity to participate in the growing LGBTI rights movement in Greece and organize the online groups Forum and Omofylofilia. I will not list everyone involved but the people with whom I directly collaborated. Marianella Kloka and the magazine 'Antivirus: against the virus of violence and war' for hosting several articles and the organization *A World Without Violence and War*. The group and online website 'Sapphides' and Hermeia for publishing poems, thoughts, and for profiling me as an out Greek Lesbian. My participation and my attempts to organize the LGBTI community in Greece and in the San Francisco Bay Area however successful sustained me. My involvement gave personal meaning to my academic toil. My presence at the 'first' Greek pride last June filled me with joy in the possibility of a fruitful and open future. I wish to hold onto that hope

Introduction

Time is initially encountered in those entities, which are changeable; change is in time. How is time exhibited in this way of encountering it, namely, as that within which things change? Does it here give itself as itself in what it is? Can an explication of time that starts here guarantee that time will thereby provide as it were the fundamental phenomena that determine it in its own being? Or does the search for the grounds of the phenomena point us towards something else? --- Heidegger, 1992

Timing: Early/ Advanced

The concepts 'early' and 'advanced' are unique in breast cancer screening, diagnosis, and treatment.[1] Early indicates a medically manageable condition. Advanced designates an illness that surpasses the efficacy of current medical intervention. Early and advanced, also, denote a temporal dimension in the medicalization of breast cancer. As medicalized notions of timing action, early and advanced follow the idealized progression of cancer as a disease. Early and advanced become a function of cancerous spread throughout the body. Now we think of early and advanced in terms of stage one, two, etc. These moments mark the framework for successful medical intervention.

Physicians define this progression or staging in terms of (1) the kind of breast cancer-- its invasiveness, location, cell type, whether it is genetic; (2) its severity, the size of the tumor and the effect of how far cancer has spread throughout the body. Effective medical innovations, then, would improve how to cut and remove (surgery), see and localize

---

[1] Timing medical treatments as a theme shifts the focus away from war or epidemic metaphors. 'Early' and 'radical' describe the rapid mobilization of resources to handle breast cancer as a disease. (For an analysis of breast cancer and time from 1900-1970, See Aronowitz, 2001)

(mammography/ biopsy), define and diagnose (histology/ genetics) breast cancer. As a window of time, early and advanced demarcate successful interventions. Combined, they frame the coordination of medical action. Efficacy of medical action becomes a question of ordering appropriate procedures, involving women, structuring the decision-making process, and identifying techniques best suited for each case.

When ordering medical action becomes successful, it coheres into a treatment paradigm. These paradigms follow from consensus built among medical scientists, the adoption of regulations at local and state levels, and the successful participation of and intervention upon publics.[2] As medical paradigms congeal, researchers script both prospective and retrospective effects of known cases to delineate and account for the full range of possible effects and side effects. In the case of breast cancer, physicians and nurses construct treatment and diagnostic protocols that summon women's active and full engagement.

This is a moment where a mindfully biosocial arrangement of medical care becomes possible. Mindfully biosocial care shifts from structures grounded in social control to ones where decisions are collaborative and medical technologies transformative. These, then, enable individuals to make decisions and take actions. (See Clarke and al, 2003) Pitfalls are possible in both scenarios: medicine as social control led to massive sterilization campaigns of faulty individuals, even genocide, in the name of the population health and proposed social norms. Strategies of social control were most evident in Nazi Medicine. (See Proctor, 1999,

---

[2] To unravel the process of consensus building in scientific decision-making see Latour, 1987 and Latour and Woolgar, 1986. Medical science is more obviously biosocial. (See Epstein, 1996 for a look at how activists shape the production and direction of medical knowledge by altering the standard of the double blind clinical trial to gain access to potentially life saving drugs.)

1995b) Transformative medicine fuels the quest for enhancement driven by individuals and

society alike. This new kind of perfection enterprise takes hold of the human genome, the

modern body and life. (See Theoharis, *Birthing Pains*) Perfection has normative effects, but

highlights the rhetoric of choice from a set of prepackaged options to attain ideals.

Mastectomy as Paradigm of Practice

Radical mastectomy as paradigm became successful through the definition of a

duration cure.[3] Surgeons invented breast cancer as a curable disease by simplifying the

complexity of therapeutic intervention, by introducing a singular surgical procedure to

manage its complex bodily manifestations. (See Lerner, 2000 and 2001) This procedure

removed all suspect tissues *in toto*, with one surgical stroke for all cases alike. Radical

mastectomies became rigorous and comprehensive surgeries to eliminate the likelihood of

recurrence and to extend post-surgery life. (See Table 1 and 2 for definitions of current breast

cancer treatment and diagnostic intervention)

Radical mastectomy, as the centerpiece of medical practice, included a self or clinical

detection of a lump and a one step biopsy plus surgery procedure. Until the 1970s, these

surgeries tended to be radical or ultra-radical in scope. Turning away from radical

mastectomies, as the main therapeutic, followed the adoption of modified or simple

mastectomies. These surgeries are still extensive in scope, in reference to lumpectomies -- a

procedure targeting a particular lump and surrounding tissue. In medical practice, surgeons

---

[3] In breast cancer care similar debates over the relative success of surgical incisions occurred. The Halsted-Mayer paradigm sought to propose the most radical incision anatomically possible that would remove suspect tissue. Radical surgery removed breast and muscle tissues *in toto* avoiding contamination of healthy tissue during the operation, and eliminating local recurrence. Halsted targeted local recurrence as a preventable condition for the right incision and the right time. (See Chapter 1)

seem to retain some of the tenets of Halsted's treatment paradigm. Since Halsted, the operative statement for medical interventions has been: if surgeons treat cancer radically and early with meticulous expansive incisions that limit the recurrence of the disease, then a breast cancer cure is probable. (See Chapter 1)

Although a breast cancer therapeutic/ diagnostic paradigm formed around radical surgery as practice, later developments in medical science allowed limiting the scope of operations. Medical scientists introduced an alternative treatment model: less surgery and combination therapies. Even in proving that combination therapies were as effective, modified or simple mastectomies remained the main surgeries performed. Potential explanations for the persistence of extensive surgery in the face of alternative treatments include scarce insurance coverage and/ or costs of alternative procedures, professional availability and adequate expertise, the specificity of medical culture at each site and limited knowledge about alternatives. (See Shaffer, 2000 for an overview of breast care economics; Zones, 2000 for a political economy perspective; Weisman, 2000 for issues in policy)

A breast cancer cure still translates into supporting medical actions that facilitate women's survival over longer stretches of time and with fewer medical side effects. Under this logic, to be more successful, medical intervention had to occur earlier in the trajectory of the disease. The drive towards earlier intervention, then, fueled the invention of new technologies and techniques that could identify breast cancer sooner. In the domain of public policy, a call for earlier intervention mobilized more efficient and effective screening, diagnosis, and treatment. To be successful this campaign needed to raise public awareness of cancer as a social problem. (See Weisman, 2000; Aronowitz, 2001) The problem, however, might be less a question of timing radical treatment as the development of more efficacious treatments. These would potentially shift the definition of cancer from a tissue disease to that of the cell, gene, or environmental hazard depending on the type of cancer. (See Theoharis, "Gene, Germs, Sins, and Toxins" for a short history of medical definition of the disease and chapter 2)

Risk discourse has become the way to articulate the need for timely medical action. (See Baker, 1991) Risk discourse is temporal. It implicates women as they age; and it is connected to behaviors that avert it. So women become watchful. They are called act in accord with medical assessments and prescriptions to identify and survive the disease. In enrolling women, medical professionals project the likelihood of survival, the prospect of post-cancer quality and length of life. Building professional and infra-structural arrangements follow the direction of treatment/ diagnostic paradigming. Treatment/ diagnostic paradigming allows for institution building and profession growth. It, also, grounds and directs the efforts of public policy to contain the disease on a larger scale. Treatment paradigming is not a coherent singularity in practice. Yet, I imagine it follows medical treatment and diagnostic trends. In breast cures, it began with the acceptance of radical surgeries as curative. In this regard, breast cancer treatment paradigms establish the dimensions or shape of practice norms. These norms generalize through public policy, and habituate differently at each clinical site.

Medical paradigms structure both material and temporal inter and intra-actions.[4] The treatment paradigm of early radical surgical intervention facilitates the professional

---

[4] Intra-action refers to the ways the medical apparatus structures a phenomenon. Intra action is intra-apparatus and has to do with questions of disease ontology/ epistemology. (The term is taken from Barad, 1998 and applied to a medical settings) Interactions refer to the relations between and among people and infrastructures. Medical paradigms structure, are structured by both.

development and disciplining of surgery as a profession. Later, breast cancer paradigming grounded radical mastectomy as standard medical practice. It became entrenched in the management of this disease. Operationalizing a radical surgical paradigm came while Halsted was still alive. Surgeons continued for some time to develop more extensive procedures than Halsted proposed, but along similar lines to treat more advanced cases. Some sought to simplify the radical to decrease the size of the wound, but the principles were in tack. (See Chapter 1)

Medical practice throughout the US and Europe has not been uniform on the question of surgery, however. This variation followed many lines of influence as did lines of standardization. In the US, the government (both state and federal) as well as local medical authorities monitored medical practice and tended to have a homogenizing effect, as medical practice became outcome based. Local variation resulted from the medical culture at a particular site, the ways physicians, surgeons, and oncologists were trained, and the relative strength of advocacy groups to influence policymaking and actual practice. Even as the BRCA treatment/ diagnostic paradigm turned towards combination therapies and less surgery, local practices that called for modified mastectomy persisted.

Medical Institutions, Medical Action

The distinction between medical knowledge and practice requires an accounting of medical institutions as entities and women, providers, or medical scientists as individuals acting. Institutions, as entities, account for practice at a site. They account for the extent to which the standardization of treatments occurred, as well as how procedures structure particular medical interventions. In this regard, medical practice might follow 'habit' or the process of 'habituation.' (See Bourdieu, 1977 and 1998) In terms of medical practitioners, 'habituation' happens though medical education and training. In terms of medical institutions, normalization occurs through legislative/ administrative checks and balances, ethical standards and codes of conduct, as well as general requirements for funding.

The normative or habitual dimensions of institutions as collectives and individual professionals are not identical, yet follow similar processes. The persistence of a particular practice is an effect of individual and institutional 'learning.' (See Douglas, 1986) This 'learning' can account for the slow decline of modified and simple mastectomies even as radical surgeries are now rare (See Goldberg, 1996; Montini and Ruzek, 1989) As the radical scope of surgery came into question, the machinery of early intervention continued to ground the biosocial problem of identifying and treating breast cancer. In fact, the timing question has become more important with the questioning of radical procedures. (See Chapter 1) This questioning affected both the domain of treatments and the domain of diagnosis.

In the domain of treatments, early intervention materialized in altering the scope and style of surgery, permitting the option of combination therapies. Concerns with less surgery followed from the productive and disruptive coupling of medicine and activism. For some, 'cutting less' implied that radical surgeries are no longer paradigmatic in treating breast cancer. Armed with the legal right to select and negotiate a course of treatment, some women and physicians explored less radical protocols and advocated for them. Less radical procedures articulated different goals for operations turning away from the notion of 'surviving' cancer to include concerns over subsequent qualify of life: cosmetics, breast-conservation, and managing issues of disability. (See Montini and Ruzek, 1989)

The displacement of radical mastectomies to even modified ones necessitated earlier diagnosis and treatment. This necessity paved the way for a revolution in screening and diagnostic technologies. New imaging technologies made combination therapies more effective and a feasible alternative to radical surgery. Combination therapies modified the parameters of the surgical paradigm in the treatment of breast cancer. They became increasingly routine as part of an array of options to tackle this disease. This array became independent of a singular right tool, as was the case in the development and standardization of pap smears for cervical cancer. (See Casper and Clarke, 1998; Clarke and Casper, 1996) For breast cancer, no single right screening tool emerged: mammography earned this place for a while. (See Clarke and Fuijimura, 1992 for notion of the 'right' tool for the job) Rather a multiplicity of imaging or potential screening diagnostic techniques have gathered: mammography, MRIs, ultrasound as well as genetic testing; coupled with various forms of treatment: surgery in combination or not with chemotherapy and radiation.

Identifying breast cancer early, then, depended upon the development and standardization of seeing cancer in situ. (See Cartwright, 1995; Lowy and Krige 2001;) Seeing cancer is pivotal for early diagnosis and treatment. Seeing cancer involves technical innovations in equipment. These followed from and fueled the emergence of new fields of expertise such as radiology and imaging. Early diagnosis through x-ray mammography defines prevention as the identification of troublesome 'pre-cancerous' lesions that then can be located, classified, and removed. The utility of diagnosing breast cancer through x-ray mammography is controversial. Mammography allows for 'earlier' surgical interventions even as the extent to which these earlier interventions affect post-treatment length of life is ambivalent. (See Cartwright, 1995; Lerner, 2003)

Controversies in the use of mammography follow women's cumulative exposure to radiation, the accuracy of mammography to locate cancer, the optimal time to begin as well as the frequency of mammograms. The window of age between 40 and 50 is particularly controversial. (See Jatoi, 1997; Hann, 1996) Screening advocates argue the sooner mammography begins the sooner physicians can diagnose breast cancer at a manageable state. Mammography use became dependent on age because early intervention is optimal. However, the age dependence of mammography use becomes qualified because breast cancer incidence increased, as women grew older while breast tissue density decreases so growths are more visible on the x-ray film. The strategy of early intervention and diagnosis becomes troublesome with the emergence of genetic testing. This trouble forecasts the need for the development of new treatment strategies based on genetic and other 'causal' knowledge. Pharmacogenetics seems to be promising new treatment model for disease grounded in genetics. Breast cancer pathology points to a multi-causal/ multi-event disease process. (See Chapter 2)

Genetic testing emerged as a new risk assessment tool. (See Daves and White, 1995) Assessing the probability of breast cancer in a lifetime using genetic testing necessitates the constitution of a 'higher high risk' group. These women are subject to screening for breast and ovarian genetic markers. Genetic testing implies a shift from seeing and deciphering the earliest manifestation of cancer to alphabetizing our genetic probabilities of developing cancer as a particular life-event.[5] Before genetic testing, physicians used 'high risk' as a site

---

[5] Interconnected to the possibility of alphabetizing -- mapping and sequencing our genomes) -- is the use of genetic algorithms that can answer questions about the evolution of genomes. (See Helmeich, 1998) For the implications of the linguistic metaphor is prevalent in the production of genome. Scientists portray genomes as

where the conjunction of several co-factors (behavioral, environmental, occupational, or hereditary) became possible. In this array of factors, genetic testing is the latest scientific tool used to assess the probability of cancer and identify women who may be subject to more extensive screening and prophylactic surgical, chemo, or hormonal interventions.

In the context of genetic testing, breast cancer interventions shift from seeking the earliest detectable moment of disease, to identifying and treating 'higher high-risk' individuals in advance of the disease. With the aid of genetic testing, prevention becomes prophylaxis: treatment in advance. However, genetic testing is premature as a screening tool because genetic knowledge is not precise enough to effectively screen without error the general population. This population is not necessarily at an elevated hereditary risk for the disease. BRCA 1 or 2 mutations increase the likelihood of breast, ovarian and colon cancers in persons with extensive family histories. (See Nicoletto et al, 2001) Mammography, thus, retains its status as the screening tool of choice coupled at times with more experimental perhaps more precise imaging technologies such as MRIs and ultrasound. Imaging technicians and radiologists calibrate these technologies to effectively read breast tissue.

Core Questions

This dissertation traces the social-historical dimensions of the therapeutic/ diagnostic paradigm for breast cancer. The question is not simply about a particular technique such as radical mastectomy. Rather, it is about understanding the effect women and medical professionals have on past and current cure/care arrangements. I seek to illuminate the

---

a sting of text written in four letters (A, C, G, T), where expressed genes become intelligible words to be decoded with mutations being alternate spellings. (See Hilgartner, 1998; Keller, 1994; Hayes, 1991)

process of creating durable structures of cure/care, of building medical institutions, and of understanding how these institutions are inhabited. Medical paradigming grounds institutional and professional growth. It also structures specific relations between women and physicians.

First, medical paradigming supports the adaptation of particular diagnostic and therapeutic tools or procedures. Second, the efficacy of these tools facilitates the emergence and credibility of professions and professional cultures that endure, adapt, and create a home, a material place to reside. Finally, they bring forward an opening where women can have a role in their medical decisions. In summary, I seek to establish how medical treatment paradigms are lived and practiced, how they affect emerging social worlds and worldviews. The main questions are fourfold.

- What are the parameters of therapeutic/ diagnostic paradigming for breast cancer? The surgical cure seems to have a distinct temporal dimension that seeks to consolidate the efficacy of operations, to gather social support and legitimacy, and to bolster women's participation. Breast care paradigming is biosocial. It intersects biomedical knowledge with life lived. The process of paradigming is not only about the creation of knowledge structures and operative fields of perception. It is, also, the construction of stable observable things, which can act, or upon which actions are directed. Paradigming is about the creation of durable institutional structures able to handle and witness the contingencies of life events. These institutional structures become better able to foster communities where disease experience becomes part of collective and interpersonal meaning making. Paradigms, as practice/ knowledge arrangements, become filters where truths or essences can be borne with care.

- How do medical scientists and practitioners negotiate and solidify breast care facts, strategies, expertise, to then mobilize them in local and trans-local settings? The interconnection between the lab and the clinic, between experimental and applied comes to the foreground. Recent studies of science privilege the lab as a site of investigation. (See Latour and Woolgar, 1986) How does the lab extend into the clinic, into the lived world, and vice versa? How does medicine act not just as a social and political instrument or institution but also as a scientific one? Without its social, political, institutional, community, and scientific underpinnings, a picture of how medicine legitimates its study and cures/cares for breast cancer, how medicine works and acts to define biosocial problems as having medical solutions is incomplete.

- How do controversies arise in the development and application of breast cancer technologies, practices, and expertise? Boundaries between professions -- surgeons, pathologists, anatomists, and the emergence of new disciplines that make knowledge claims and develop new techniques such as imaging, radiology and genetics are sites of controversy. Disciplines require boundary work to settle them and vie for resources. (See Gieryn, 1995; Clarke, 1998) Emerging disciplines also develop boundary objects that cut across established fields. (See Starr and Griesemer, 1989) For breast cancer, such boundary objects are mammograms, breasts as organs and sites for cancerous cells that become research materials, lab rats, even novel technologies, classifications, and procedures as they are standardized and arranged. (See Clarke, 1995 as an example of the importance of studying research materials)

- How does medicine map breast cancer and construct women as agents and patients? The logic of risk-safety circumscribes breast cancer as a hazard; it directs women when navigating breast cancer care; and it orders breast care as a medical field or domain. This logic rationalizes and governs the deployment of medical resources. Biomedical expertise translates into the public domain though the logic of risk and safety. The application of knowledge, then, becomes part of a precautionary strategy set against an ill-defined disease. (See Sunstein 2005) How does medicine wield power and influence the social? How do social and political movements affect the direction and development of medical technologies and expertise, the construction of medical institutions and professions? (See Koenig, 1998)

Historical and Theoretical Contexts

To address the questions proposed in the dissertation, I explored existing literatures that address the following issues. (1) How do the development, deployment, and configuration of medical perception affect the structure of medical institutions in a historical and social sense? What are the effects on the scientific apparatus and on treatment paradigming? How do changes in the structure of medical perception relate to framing breast cancer as a problem subject to medical action? (2) How does medicine consolidate disease ontology and epistemology? After the advent of scientific medicine, what are the parameters for grounding medical and governmental action? (3) What are the parameters for breast cancer treatment paradigms? At which point are paradigms simply hegemonic entrenched into orthodoxy and habits of practice? When do institutions cease to learn? What roles do women, health movements, and medical counter-hegemonic strategies play in settling or unsettling treatment paradigms, fueling disputes and constructing new evidence, in facilitating learning? How can we effectively manage breast cancer as a disease, as a biosocial phenomenon? What roles do the discourse of precaution play in settling or heightening some of these disputes?

Medical Perception

Medical perception is not static. It has a trajectory. I traced the historical development of medical institutions, tools, knowledges and knowledge practices, while I also focused on moments of change and transformation. The emergence of scientific medicine occurred in the 19th century. Scientific medicine impacted the structure of medical institutions for most of the 20th century. The emergence of scientific medicine followed from the construction of the hospital not only as a site of care for the infirm, but also as a site of knowledge, experimentation, and new technologies. These technologies are both therapeutic and diagnostic. (See Porter, 2002; Risse, 1999; Foucault, 1994; Bynum, 1994) In the hospital, medical knowledge found a home and bloomed. Initially, this knowledge simply cataloged diseases and symptoms: the discourse of Nosology. Later, this knowledge became empirical and experimental, grounded first in cadavers, then in living beings and processes. Finally, this knowledge became scientific requiring particular standards for evidence and argument before ascertaining efficacy of treatment.

With gross anatomy, the cadaver became a site of interest to establish cause of death and later determine disease process. Understanding the material dimensions of disease process lead to the development of appropriate diagnostics and therapeutics. The scientific turn in medicine followed from three trends. First, cadaverization: that is, the material location of cause of death as an effect of disease in the cadaver, in the dead body. Second, localization: that is, disease process became rooted in specific organs, tissue or cells, in the body of the living. Third, mechanization along two dimensions: one following the use of scientific tools and two the mechanization in terms of scientific style.

Scientific methodology as adopted by medical scientists benefited from the structure of the hospital, and its conjunction to the university. In the university new technique, knowledge, and innovation emerged. The university/ hospital became the site of experimental knowledge and higher learning. It was the site where new laboratory techniques coupled with medical care, where medical scientists developed, learned, and applied new disciplines and tools, as opposed to medical practitioners who based their judgment solely on experiential yet untested accumulated knowledge.

In the 20th century, scientific medicine expanded its focus from experiential and clinical to experimental and laboratory. Three central trends fuel the direction of scientific medicine. Those are imaging (See Kelves, 1997; Cartwright, 1995 for mammography see Lerner, 2003), molecularization (See Chadervian and Kamminga, 1998; for germs theory and vaccines see Rosenberg, 1992 and Porter D. 'Tyranny of Salvation'; for viral hypothesis of cancer see Creager and Gaudilliere, 2001), and genetization (See Keller, 2000; Daves and White, 1995). Each trend grounds disease in the body, reconstructing the live body as a site for medical intervention.

In terms of late 20th century, computerization becomes especially important. It allows for the processing of massive amounts of information relevant in understanding the biomedical factors punctuating disease process. It shapes the informational structure of medicine: the dissemination and structure of information as well as its availability. These trends illuminate the multi-locality of medical practice. Medical action shifts from lab, university, hospital, clinic, and home. (See Graph 1)

Medical paradigming allows for the sedimentation of successful medical action into medical practice. Medical inter and intra action becomes essential in delineating how medical paradigms order health situations. Medical actions figure around three modes: observing, witnessing, and caring. These situations structure medical subject/ object through technical arrangements and expert discourse. These modes congeal within sites such as the lab, clinic, and home, but also among them as well. Each mode establishes a particular subject/object dynamic dipole in the situations it structures or normalizes the most. These situations are complex at times stinging together various types of action, various techniques, and professions. An active medical paradigm solidifies into a practice paradigm when that paradigm coheres across observational, witnessing, and caring arrangements. A medical paradigm cuts across subject/ object arrangements at the sites where medical inter and intra action is effective. (See Table 3) So medical paradigms are not just about knowledge production. They are also about maintaining efficacious medical practice, of creating standards and norms.

In my dissertation, breast cancer care serves as a site to explore medical institutions and knowledge. The shifts in medical perception and the ordering of medical intervention ground and are grounded by knowledges and practice. Medical institutions as social actors that halt disease play an important role in establishing paradigms and professions and in fostering progress.

Disease Ontology/ Epistemology

Understanding the process of disease causation and classification is important. Disease causation and classification lead to particular ordering of diagnostic/ therapeutic intervention. These interventions implicate populations and individuals alike. Disease agents, then, are the biological and ontological essence of illness stripped from flesh, stripped from social, political, religious environments and discourse. (See Fleck, 1979; Canguilhem, 1991, 1994; Gaudilliere, 2001; Bowker and Star, 1999)

Disease ontology and epistemology ground medical knowledge and practice. They direct medical institutions. Targeting disease derives from (1) accumulating the knowledge of kind and scale for disease agents as distinct entities (disease ontology), (2) describing the effects of disease agents as it is known in symptoms (disease epistemology), (3) and then, establishing appropriate therapeutic interventions aimed to halt disease progression (disease management). (See Table 4, for a sketch of particularly historical disease formations) In this regard, a disease formulation is an effect of a knowledge structure: the logic of attributing causes, delimiting disease effects, and establishing the potential for practical intervention. (See Chapter 2 for breast cancer implcations)

Specific disease ontology, epistemology, and intervention have distinct historical and social parameters. A medical paradigm, then, is always geared towards particular kinds of intervention. Illness/ disease is socio-cultural and biological without a primacy of one or the other. In the process of delineating the bio-sociality[6] of illness/disease: genes, germs, sins/ behaviors, and toxins emerge as pivotal nodes when we sort appropriate beliefs, facts, and actions about our construction of disease. Diseases ordered through notions of germs, genes, sins/ behaviors, and toxins produce particular lived topologies – individualized but also

---

[6] Paul Rabinow (1992) first used the term biosociality. He has used the term specifically in the context of genetization. I feel that the concept can be equally extends to other formations of disease such as the logic of germs, that biosociality refers to the conditions inherent in the exercise of social medicine.

shared psychic terrains of discourse in action and discursive deliberative actions. (See Chapter 4)

Breast cancer is a site of medical and social controversy and innovation. As a disease, breast cancer is evasive. It is neither the effect of germs, genes, environmental hazards, or particular behaviors, nor even the general aging process. Breast cancer threatens the health of women from wealthier nations. Breast cancer is a disease that increases in incidence as women age. Preventative strategies do not, yet, concretely affect breast cancer. Breast cancer, still, affects the body and remains undetected because it is difficult at times to diagnose 'early' enough to effectively cure.

Thus, the fear of death and disability permeates women's experience with a breast cancer diagnosis even in managing the prognosis of high risk for the disease. Medicine armed with newer technologies has sought better ways to understand, define, and treat beast cancer, better ways to inform and educate women. Our current breast care arrangement reflects as much our lack of knowledge as it does our understanding. (See Proctor, 1995)

Women and Breast Cancer

Breast cancer causation is not clear. Breast cancer is a cluster of diseases with multiple triggers. This multiplicity of causation implicates women as agents responsible in averting this disease. The sense of responsibility for care can exacerbate inequities. Women of color, poor women, and women who are older have differing levels of skill and access to care to be able to successfully manage this disease or the potential of this disease. (See Zones, 2000)

Women are responsible for diet, exercise, regular screening depending on their age and risk assessment, as well as frequency and onset of pregnancy, menstruation, timing of menopause -- for estrogen dependent cancers, the use of hormone replacement therapies. (See Lock, 1998; Jasen 2002; Fosket, 2004; Kelly, 1991) Recently, genetic markers seek to establish bio-molecular markers for women at higher high risk for the disease. (See Davies and Whites, 1995) This responsibility for care and care choices is new for women as patients.

In the domain of treatment, radical surgery, combination therapies, and prophylactic treatments are the main therapeutics. (See Table 4 for definitions) In terms of diagnostics, breast exams, biopsy, imaging and genetic testing seek to identify breast cancer at a treatable state. (See Table 3 for definitions) These procedures follow along two main strategies: one aggressive intervention including in some cases prophylactic procedures or two watchfulness and breast conserving interventions. (See Graph 2 for a Breast Cancer Care Map)

Women's health and social movements changed the place of women as patients in medical decision-making. Medical institutions opened up to collaborative and deliberative decisions. Medical practice shifted. It also became more flexible and interactive. Women became both objects of disease, subjects of illness, and agents in care decisions. Their opinions began to matter. Medical interactions became biosocial if still asymmetrical in effect. This mindful biosociality marks a new era of participant medicine.

Sources

Historical

For chapter 1: 'March of Cancer,' I collected relevant articles that addressed breast surgery as a cure at the turn of the century (1870-1920). Those included the Annals of Surgery and the Journal for the American Medical Association. For European references, I relied on a collection of seminal papers by Robbins, (1984). The Robbins (1984) collection translated seminal German, French texts, and collected US surgical papers (some I found independently). The editors addressed this volume to surgeons interested in the historical context of their everyday practices. The editors, also, recognized a shift occurred in surgical thinking and practice with the introduction of radical breast surgery as a cure. The goal in this chapter was to detail how surgery became the main therapeutic and set the therapeutic parameters for breast cancer care paradigm in the 20th century.

For chapter 2: 'Defining Breast Cancer,' I looked at shift in the definition of breast cancer as a disease during the later part of the 20th century. I researched the current scientific literature to see how scientists contested cancer causes as hormonal, viral, generic, and environmental. The method was an overview and analysis of current scientific literature to establish the links between definition of disease and treatment models. Multi causal test animal models (mice and rats) and language (risk/ probability) play an important role in negotiating new treatments of a biological level (animal models) and on an interpersonal level risk models. The definition of cancer was relatively fixed during the time when radical mastectomy was considered the paradigm of practice. So more recent literature shows the definition of cancer in flux consolidating pathways of events that lead towards particular kinds of genetic instability characteristic of cancer.

For chapter 3: 'Women and Breast Cancer,' I overviewed breast cancer care as a field. I started from the present and moving at times backwards to draw selective histories, at times sideways to anticipate new developments. I again relied mostly on an analysis of primary and secondary sources to sketch the evolution of breast cancer diagnostics and therapeutics as well as the experience of women with the disease. The goal is to establish trend lines in breast cancer care (both diagnostic and therapeutic) that later can illuminate the development of structures of thought with regard to breast cancer care and experience. This chapter, then, becomes the ground for the qualitative analysis that follows.

Qualitative

For chapter 4: 'Breast Cancer Care Topologies,' I interviewed six (five as part of my pilot study and one to develop the questions) women who had at least one mammogram. The interviews were open-ended. The questions focused on the role of screening technologies such as mammography as an obligatory point of passage in breast cancer care. My questions gathered on how women conceptualize experience breast cancer risk. I sought to map the juncture between experience and science, women and medicine, high and low risk. Even though the sample was small, the interviews were quite detailed and allowed for an initial conceptualization into breast care practices/norms that I better elaborated in my analysis of the last chapter.

For Chapter 5: 'Timing Medical Intervention,' a team of researchers located at Stanford University Bioethics Center and University of Pennsylvania conducted and analyzed sixty-eight interviews of women who considered genetic testing as part of their BRCA decision-making. These interviews were both semi-structured and open-ended. They focused on the impact of genetic testing on women's health care decision-making process. I use grounded theory methods to analyze the process of medical decision-making for women who consider genetic testing for breast cancer.

Methods and Design

This project uses several methods and modes of analysis. It combines historical and qualitative methods and sources to the research questions at hand. I did not use these methods indiscriminately.

I used discourse analysis in historical chapters to illustrate the context, content, and direction of medical scientific ideas about breast cancer as a disease and its treatment. I used combination of grounded theory (See Strauss and Corbin, 1998) and phenomenology (See Holstein and Gubrium, 1998) in qualitative chapters to develop appropriate coding and reflect on theoretical questions at hand. Such questions involved subject/ object formation in medicine as a social field. The fissure of subject/ object is produced though normative forces and the actions of larger scale actors such as institutions upon smaller ones. A social field is distinct from a social world. A social field places the emphasis on the conditions of emergence for subjects and objects. A social world is descriptive of existing arrangements, where meanings can be found and actions become practice.

Each method has strengths in illuminating social phenomena and allows for more sophisticated analysis of the question of timing treatments and diagnostics. The question of timing becomes key. It becomes heightened with the introduction of new treatment/

knowledge and women's health movements that support change. However, I argue that these so far have not altered the core parameters of the surgical treatment paradigm set at the turn of the century. Bio-molecular advances may.

Outline of Chapters

Chaper1: 'March of Cancer,' I traced the circulation of surgical practice and knowledge about breasts and cancer when radical mastectomy became the scientific cure. I read pivotal surgical papers between 1870s and 1920s spanning Germany, France, England, and the US. Then, surgeons began to propose that radical breast surgery was a potential cancer cure. Surgical knowledge and practice traveled across national boarders and consolidated differently in each local. I traced how surgeons sought to define early radical surgery as its scientific cure, while highlighting within their writings how women presented as willing patients and docile bodies. As the surgical cure interfaced with institutions of care, the temporality of early radical intervention supported a precautionary narrative. This narrative mobilizes and normalizes women's timely and complete participation and compliance.

Chapter 2: 'Defining breast cancer,' I looked at current biomedical literatures for emerging molecular, genetic, viral or environmental definitions of breast cancer as a disease. It seeks to understand the implications of the biomedical definition of breast cancer on women and the treatment options available to them. As medical scientists better understand breast cancer, new treatment and diagnostic tools emerge that promise to better manage the disease.

Chapter 3: 'Women and Breast Cancer,' I reviewed current breast cancer treatment and diagnosis apparatus, how that apparatus is experienced by women, how women began to alter it. It is a pivot point between historical and qualitative research and analysis. It also illustrates how women create meaning find voice through collective gatherings, how then these gatherings become movements and impact medical care, the perceptions of disease, the parameters of the experience with the disease.

Chapter 4: 'Breast Care Topologies,' I mapped the contemporary juncture between women and medicine. This chapter concentrates on how that naming effects, affects and mediates women in medical practice. It asks how to problematize and open the process up for negotiation and interrogation to enhance women's agency in breast care. Interviewing six women about their experiences with breast care aided me in understanding how biomedicine works. Specifically I asked about how biomedicine frames women, breasts, and cancer, and how women perceive and embody an agency that constitutes their sense of self and their understanding of what they need to do in breast care.

Chapter 5: 'Timing Intervention, ' I highlighted the question of timing breast cancer intervention with the increasing adaptation of genetic testing for BRCA 1 and 2 markers. This chapter explores the impact of considering genetic testing upon women's decision making, her perception of the disease, and her subsequent choice of screening and therapeutic or prophylactic treatment. BRCA testing allows women who are at high risk for hereditary breast-ovarian cancer to shift the emphasis from early detection (reliance on frequent screenings) to prophylactic surgery and chemo or hormone prevention.

The March of Cancer

This terrible foe of suffering mankind, this dread especially of the female sex, become oftener silenced and made more submissive to the surgeon's knife, provided the operation is done early, before remote parts of the system have become infected.

--- Meyer, 1894

Introduction

At the turn of the 20th century, surgeons defined success in curing breast cancer. This cure consisted of timely radical operations. In the US, the Halsted/ Mayer operations settled the parameters for this operation. (See Halsted, 1894; Mayer 1894) These papers sought to define the style and scope of surgical intervention to curtail cancer as a disease, and a timeline for success necessary to mobilize the public, professional organizations, and the government. In the years following their initial publications, radical operations became standard treatment for breast cancer. Key was the definition of success. This definition was the duration cure. It became the grounds for hope to extend the life of affected women, even if that hope was qualified. The radical cure, also, benefited surgery as a profession. It sat well with the vision of modern scientific medicine. The combined result was a new kind of institution: the specialized hospital that supported the conjunction of laboratory technique and surgery as a medical practice. (See Risse, 1999)

In this chapter, I will focus on how radical mastectomy defined the cure for breast cancer as a disease. When and how did radical mastectomy become standard treatment? What practices and principles guided its prominence and defined its success? By asking these questions, I will illumine the work of surgeons in structuring breast care institutions as well

as contemporary thinking about the disease. The task is to sketch the context of

mastectomy's rise to prominence in curing breast cancer between 1870s and 1920s and to

examine the conditions that enabled modern scientific forms of surgery to triumph over

breast cancer. The terms modern and scientific became polemical, contesting what types of

surgery qualified as cancer cures and in what situations. The meaning of modern and

scientific shifted though discussions on the role of surgery in the cure for breast cancer.

Surgeons benefited by use. The implication was that the proposed new surgical strategy

would be successful in the face of previously untreatable conditions like breast cancer.

Modern and scientific helped in articulating the need for collectives able to build institutions,

to convince publics, and other medical professionals of the medical efficacy of surgery.

Assembling Collectives

Within modern hospitals, surgeons lead a team of experts to tackle this disease. The

team expanded with the development of specialized knowledge and technique. The team of

experts adapted with surgical knowledge and the needs of emerging institutions. During the

19th century, pathology and anatomy became central disciplines in developing a surgical

paradigm: pathology to identify the disease and anatomy to define its boundaries in the body.

Anatomy, also, provided a ground for the incisions used to treat the disease. Surgeons

developed sub disciplines like surgical anatomy and surgical pathology to facilitate the cross-

pollination of knowledge and technique. In the 20th century, the team expanded to include

oncologists, radiologists, and more recently geneticists and genetic counselors. (See Chapter

II) New experts offered benefits at times challenging, others supporting the surgical cure, its

institutional, or social credibility and authority.

Today, surgeons continue to play a leading role in breast cancer therapeutics. Surgeons continue to define mainstream parameters for therapy even if their role has changed along with the scope and style of operations performed. Radical mastectomy, as a procedure, held a central place in breast therapeutics for over half a century. Radical mastectomy -- Halsted style -- was *the* radical cure. Surgeons no longer perform this procedure. Modified and other tissue conserving operations have taken its place. Radiation and chemotherapy supplement these operations. Surgery, however, has become a prophylactic strategy for women at genetic risk, who are now determined to be at higher high risk for the disease. (See Chapter III, Lerner, 2001, 2000; Olson, 2002) Current trends towards prophylactic and aggressive treatments of 'early' or pre cancers raise questions of over-treatment. Questions of over-treatment refer to high dose chemo as well. (See Goldberg, 1996; Zones, 2000)

Trajectory of Cure

The success and duration of radical mastectomy supported surgery as a profession and bolstered Halsted prominence. It became a signature operation often referred to as the Halsted radical. Attitudes towards this practice shifted in the 20th century. The procedure offered hope in the face of the dread disease. Radical mastectomy became a disfiguring but necessary operation. It is now equated with an authoritarian style of medicine that perpetuated, an unnecessarily brutal practice in the face of conflicting evidence. These attitudes were not universally held. They marked shifts in reference to new evidence, to new attitudes towards medicine and physicians, and responded to cultural, scientific and political changes in the status of medical professions and social norms. (See Montini and Ruzek, 1989)

The turn towards less surgery is not simply medical. It is biosocial:[7] a product of women, who became patient activists, of surgeons and researchers, who questioned and sought alternatives, and of new standards for medical knowledge -- the clinical trial. (See Lerner, 2001; Montini & Ruzek, 1989) The bio-sociality of medical paradigms illustrates that medicine is necessarily both a social and medical actor and institution that the relations between medicine and society must be better understood to direct and anticipate changes in the basic structure of disease (as knowledge and treatment) and illness (as experience).

Radical surgery, as the cornerstone for breast cancer treatment, marked five moments. Each is a turn and re-arrangement of breast cancer therapeutics. These moments are dynamic and overlapping. A brief list follows: its definition as modern practice -- early to mid 19th century; the controversy surrounding the failure of initial operations-- middle 19th century; more effective definition -- late 19th early 20th; prominence -- mid 20th; and trial and readjustment-- late 20th early 21st.

Moments of Flux

Surgery came under fire during the mid 19th century because it did not effectively curtail cancer. Operations were successful even as the patients shortly after perished. In the 20th century, radical surgery came under fire because of its perceived limitations. Issues such as postoperative quality of life such as disability, the effective extension of life beyond a defined duration, and the limitation of recurrence beyond a certain cancer free interval came to the fore.

---

[7] The term biosocial emerges in Foucault (2003) and is taken up by Rabinow (1992).

In the second instance, women and allied surgeons, who sought to limit the scope of radical operations. The challenge required a new theory of how cancer spread and a different array of therapeutics that included surgery, chemotherapy, and radiation. (See Chapter 3) Timing breast cancer interventions, then, became even more important for successful and a more lasting cure than was previously thought. Molecular and genetic research began to pose anew the question of when is the best moment e.g. earliest to intervene. (See Chapters 2 and 5) The temporal dimension of cancer intervention has disputed and contingent upon the fact that we have not yet identified a cure. The temporal dimension is key in describing the shifts that occurred through time with regard to the treatment of the disease.

Surgeons have been resilient in the face of trial. At times, they incorporate the most useful of these practices, to assemble a team of experts and a new medical toolbox to tackle this disease. At times, they might have obstructed the development of these technologies, arguing that they may not be relevant or beneficial (for example mammography). In the mid 20th century, the challenge of earlier diagnosis supported by mammography required a different vision of cancer spread. The theory that cancer metastasized sooner and required chemo or radiation some times before cancer was palpable combined to derail the rational for Halsted-like radical procedures and surgery as the sole therapeutic intervention. This logic argued that cancer remained local long enough for surgery to be an effective cure. Surgeons, at the turn of the 20th century, believed (1) that cancer was primarily a local disease until late in its trajectory and (2) that cancer flows primarily through the lymph nodes meaning that node negative cancer were necessarily local.

In response to these two sets of challenge, surgeons had initially expanded the scope of the operation to produce what appeared as a viable cure and later limited the scope of surgery: simple mastectomies, lumpectomies and combination therapies where appropriate while they proposed preventative surgery for those deemed at higher high risk. The late 20th century array of breast cancer therapeutics and diagnostics showed that the challenge to the surgical cure persisted because surgery did not provide a definitive cure, because cancer as a disease is just beginning to be understood. (See Chapter 2)

Historiography

Writing history means speaking of temporally and/or geographically distant events, persons and institutions. In writing history, I have struggled with the presence or evidence of the historian as witness and thinker. The temptation is to erase the historian as to avoid any anachronisms or the production of history as ideology. In my writing of history, however, I came to must reflect upon the present and the presence of the historian. I have sought to make visible the writer in the written. In the juncture of social-historical, the weighty structures of institutions become fluid. They become an assemblage of multiple underdetermined situations where actions of smaller sized actors take place. The sociological quandary of structure/ agency becomes a function of the relative duration and scale of events, the life cycle of structures, actors, actions and situations.

What is the relation of present to past? What continuities and ruptures unfold in the present as the present- recedes into past or pasts- strengthening into presence both combining in the emergent possibles? I use chronogeography as a tool to show the diachronic fluidity of terms and the synchronicity of past and present in contemporary use. It helps me be mindful of the underdetermined nature of the past, not just the present or the future. We tend to think of the past as already determined. But the past, as we understand it, is a reference only to a particular unfolding present. The nature of the past reflects the nature of the present.

Thus, I can avoid at least two frequent yet unsatisfactory solutions in the writing of history. (1) The history of heroic figures and grand actors, which produce an unproblematic yet powerful dynasty or continuity of presence. The history of grand actors becomes the property of successful institutions that govern, rule and 'win' in the process, consuming women's lives and bodies when we speak of specifically female patients and masculine medical institutions. (2) A history of grand causes or origins, where a few key tropes seem to stage the primary scene from where all historical developments emerges and where a new beginning might spring after a noble return to basic facts and premises.

Each is a narrative strategy. Each accounts for and appropriates the complexities of change. The narrative points forward though notions of progress, modernity, success or loops to a return, retreat, perhaps even a defeat or disillusionment. Discourse: the spoken and written, opens a place, where the undercurrents of institutions and large or small actors reside. The key to unearthing the complexity of events is to define compound situations, to ground a careful analysis of the complex flows of discourse, action, and presence. Then, a dense vortex of eventuality resides in and tangles past - present – possible on the march.

In this chapter, I will trace the traffic of surgical and medical science innovation in the field of breast cancer treatment across time and place. My focus gathers both upon scientists' writings and women's experience. This dual focus allows me to begin to unearth their interrelationship. This relationship is embedded first in the production of medical knowledge as it reifies woman as body-object, second in how knowledge is reproduced through medical practice and is reflected in medical decision-making.

Chronogeography, as an analytical tool, demarcates the flow of historical events. It highlights not only scientific knowledge as the grounds for care that structures illness experiences, but also the temporal and geographic distribution of that knowledge and practice. The flow of knowledge/ practice itself is a product of institutional growth, policy decisions, and public awareness that points towards and away from ethno-medicine. In looking at these flows, I maintain that the temporal and geographic are not separable in this analysis, that they together form the situation under study. Chronogeography enables me to trace historical time-geography in non-sequential fashions, to meditate upon dead ends and successes -- both valuable in an analysis of what follows.

Historical time is bounded by the surgical knowledge and practice. When did radical mastectomy begin to be thought of a curative? What did radical mastectomy entail? It is not restricted geographically for a very important reason. The place varies seeking the denser locales of development. In the process, I realized that ideas are not immaterial substance. Ideas as discourse -- spoken and written, articulate an understanding, set the parameters for situations and actions, and circumscribe potential effects in an effort to manage the contingency of illness. Discourse in the hands of institutions becomes rule; actions become practice. Practice need not always follow rule, but it becomes normalized through it especially as rules guide the building and planning of infrastructure. Institutions as collectives and authors of rule become the site of origin for the modern application of power over life events. (See Foucault, 1994, 1979)

In a chrono-geographical sense, I analyze how surgical knowledge and practice developed and traveled across locales and research sites and across national borders. The flow of knowledge/ practice facilitates breast treatment paradigming. Once operational in the treatment paradigm takes the structure of rule. Then, the structure of treatment became normalized by rule. (See Kung, 1970) Journal articles, I gathered, also traced the flow of evidence and concept. I can trace the emergence of surgical thinking through the use of citations. (See Latour, 1987 for examples of citation analysis) In journal articles, a nexus of knowledge/ practice also emerges where the socio-historical dimensions of medico-scientific ideas and institutions are set in action. Surgical articles are complex. They contain argument and data used to frame results in reference to treatment and experiences with disease. The illness narrative of patients is rarely evoked. The data appears to be both resource and reference. It garners validity for particular applications. At the same time, its potency exceeds the intended use.

The material speaks a different tale to a different reader – different to a feminist academic situated in the beginning of the 21st century than to a surgeon a century ago. In faithfully representing the materiality of women's lives and bodies, that materiality is preserved in a time capsule irrespective of the ways we perceive them. These articles then weave beings, bodies, case histories, cells, surgical practice and knowledge, incisions, statistics, in ways responsive to time, place, and curious eyes. Their material is not just a referent. It is not free-floating and circulating. It captures moments. It produces stills that then presence and become witness to a new set of statements. These, in turn, become new practice or critique.

Seeing journal articles as a nexus of practice/ knowledge, material/ semiotic, woman/ doctor allows me to highlight not only the structure of surgical thinking at the time, but also begin to show how women as patients and bodies engaged and co-produced surgical knowledge/ practice. Women's lives and actions are present as participants in the creation of knowledge even as the surgeons staged their participation. Women's voices or direct experiences are absent from surgeons' accounts. Their bodies (tissues and organs), their photographs at times abstracted illustrations, their experiences as case histories, all combine to construct evidence. Their status in the journal articles was that of mute presence. This status (between thing, animal, human) allowed surgeons to speak in their place, to manufacture evidence and treatments. Mute presence also signifies the place women occupied in medical institutions as predominately male surgeons structured them. Two key tropes emerged in my analysis: early and radical.

Key Tropes

The notion *radical* qualifies the style and scope of surgery: aggressive and extensive. The notion *early* qualifies the timing of diagnosis to sustain successful surgical outcomes. Surgical authority depends on this definition of success. The construct early also enables women to act promptly in the face of the disease. (See Table 1)

The relationship between diagnosis and treatment has modified with the content of radical and early. Combined, these concepts also normalize women's illness experience. Early and radical are still influential in the trajectory of technological innovation in breast cancer detection as well as the experience with illness. Their meanings have shifted in terms of what timing constitutes early or what combination of practices is radical. The modifier 'early' contrasts to the notions 'late' or 'advanced.' The modifier 'radical' contrasts to 'conservative.' (See Brieger, 1992)

Three surgical traditions outside the US appear to influence the consolidation of radical surgery as a paradigm of practice at least within the United States. In the United

Kingdom, surgeons seem interested in gross and pathological anatomies of the breast. In Germany, pathology and surgical practice combined to detail the lymphatic flow of cancer in the breast. In France, surgery was first outlined as a likely breast cancer cure. (See Table 3) I outline the work that early and radical did as concepts for the surgeons who began to employ them. The first question is a 19th century question.

Can Surgery Cure Breast Cancer?

19th Century Surgery

At the turn of the 20th century, a breast cancer diagnosis roused dread and despair. The negative feelings would proliferate not just among women but physicians. (See Paterson, 1987) Until the 1870s, surgeons were unable to cure breast cancer successfully. Most surgeons performed breast amputations as operations of last resort with the main goal being palliative, to minimize pain. Some questioned the wisdom of surgery as a practice in breast cancer care, suggesting that surgery exacerbated the condition. The experience of early surgery was very painful. Anesthesia was rare. Antisepsis had not yet made surgeries a viable treatment option. (See Porter, 2002; Risse, 1999)

However as early as 1818, some surgeons like John Butler in "Practical observations on the compression of cancerous breasts" suggested that surgery might yield better results. He describes and negates compression as treatment for breast cancer. He argues that compression might deal with tumors that are not cancerous by nature that compression itself fails to ask the question of the nature of cancer. Is it a local or systemic disease? Butler argues for prompt surgical intervention, "the sooner that tumor is removed the better" because "with cancer it is always dangerous to tamper and unsafe to procrastinate." Butler recommends "Freedom with the knife" to eradicate the disease. However, these formulations had not the specificity that would crystallize a century later into the radical breast operation proposed as a surgical cure.

Despite the initial assurances for the potential of a surgical cure, most of the 19th century breast operations were not successful. These outcomes discouraged surgeons because they failed to cure cancer, and most women died shortly after painful operations. For example, Sir James Paget questioned whether surgical interventions added enough length of life or comfort to justify the risks of the operation. (See Paget, 1853) Surgeons seeking to better the odds sought to redefine the parameters of breast cancer through the study of breast anatomy and pathology.

Sir Astley Cooper became renown as a surgical anatomist. He published a comprehensive treatise on the breast and was the first to show the existence of supportive breast ligaments. He invented ways to illustrate and die breast tissues. His work mapped the contours of the normal and pathological breast. He also compared human and animal mammary glands in terms of function, anatomy, evolution, and milk nutritional value. (See Cooper, 1845) Innovations in anatomical and pathological techniques, which incorporated microscopic investigation, lead to a cellular focus for breast cancer diagnosis and grounded the question of subsequent surgery. Van Volkmann was the first to propose a cellular definition of cancer. (See Porter, 2002) In terms of surgical practice, techniques such as antisepsis and anesthetics, made breast surgeries into better medical treatments.

By the end of the 19th century, all parameters were in place for a cure: a cellular definition of the disease, an understanding of the spacio-temporal flow of cancer, and sufficient developments in surgical practice -- antisepsis and anesthetics. The rhetoric shifted accordingly. Surgeons deemed radical breast operations to be scientific and systematically recorded women's postoperative survival to establish the conditions for the best operation. As women survived the operation long enough, they argued, surgery became more apt in curing cancer. Becoming scientific, modern, and successful enhanced the status of surgery in its quest for curative incisions and surgeons' professional ambitions. The perceived success enhanced surgery as a profession. The university hospital brought together the necessary new techniques and knowledge to make these successes possible.

Breast Cancer Treatments

Before surgery became prominent in curing breast cancer and various treatments captured medical and popular attention, surgeons would extract cancerous breasts conservatively. Velpeau, a French surgeon, described the most comprehensive surgical operations on the breast before cellular pathology and microscopic investigations better defined cancer. In his *Treatise on the Diseases of the Breast and Mammary Region* translated into English in 1859, Velpeau characterized an array of breast cancer treatments both internal and external. These treatments included bleeding with leeches, purging with emetics or hunger, ingesting hemlock and other substances such as arsenic, an ammonium solution of copper, or mercury, and the compression of the breast a mechanical cure.

Among these treatments, Velpeau situates the surgery of the mamma without privileging it or calling it more scientific. In terms of surgery, Velpeau proposed a dual operative modality: extirpation for extracting a portion of the breast where the tumor was located and amputation, when surgeons removed the whole breast. Velpeau preferred tumor growth extirpation to amputation if it was feasible given tumor's growth and location.

Velpeau considered breast surgery to be a serious operation. He questioned the nature of extracted tumors and called upon general pathology to aid in establishing criteria of difference between benign and cancerous growths. Frequent recurrence and high operative as well as post-operative mortality plagued early surgeries of the breast. If women survived the operation, surgeons considered it a surgical success.

As women survived the operation, surgical thinking focused on the extent of surgery that would target and prevent the recurrence of the disease. Surgeons sought ways to identify the boundaries of the disease in the live body. In 1867, Moore read a seminal paper before the Royal Medical and Chirurgical Society titled "The Influence of Inadequate Operations on the Theory of Cancer." For Moore, recurrence followed when surgeons did not completely remove all cancerous tissue with the operation; cancer recurred, diffusing from the primary site instead of spontaneously re-growing. The difference between spontaneous re-growth and diffusion speaks to the nature of cancer. Spontaneous re-growth referred to an inherited condition that led to little hope of complete recovery. Diffusion meant that surgery could play a role in better eliminating cancerous tissue before it spreads. Moore observed that cancer often recurred near the scar of the initial operation, and that recurrence affected skin, lymphatic, and proximal tissue. This suggested diffusion rather than re-growth of new cancers.

These observations about the nature of recurrence led Moore to urge a more extensive operation than practiced before. These operations required excising whole breasts rather than parts as Velpeau preferred and most surgeons practiced. For Moore, the remaining skin and tissue near the chest wall was suspect and needed extraction. Moore cautioned surgeons must incise with care into breasts or when exposing tumors during the operation as to prevent cancer from contaminating healthy tissue. The proposed operation included the removal of the whole diseased breast along with adjoining tissue affected by the disease especially skin, lymph nodes, fat and in some cases the pectoral muscles. An inability to sever healthy from diseased tissue in one surgical stroke was established as the main source of ineffectual operations.

Palliative/ Curative

In the middle of the 19th century, some surgeons thought extensive breast surgery was unscientific and/or barbaric. The practice became infrequent. By 1882, Professor Banks argued for the return to an older method of operation. Such as method and reason proposed by Moor. Surgery failed, Banks argued, because it did not remove all of the cancer from the body. Women died of breast cancer after operations not because they had surgeries, but because they did not have enough surgery. Banks charged that surgeons were timid in treating breast cancer and thought that extracting small elliptical portions of the breast with the nipple would not rid women of the disease.

This attitude was responsible for the lives of some women who would benefit from a "free removal of cancerous growths." Reminiscing of earlier technique, Banks continues as when "the breast is laid hold of with great pincers; and having been cleanly cut off, the surface was rubbed over by a red-hot poker." (Banks, 1882: 1138) Surgery's inability to cure cancer fueled this return to a bold, total, and brutal operation. Banks lamented that few women died from this operation, but all died of the disease just a short while after. Regardless, surgeons advancing a more radical or free removal of the breast as a cancer cure were negotiating their claims against the notion that breast cancer was not yet treatable through the knife. Most surgeons believed that extensive surgery was dangerous to women, inelegant, and not in tune with more modern methods.

In its pursuit of a cure, scientific surgery became more radical. What constituted success was not a given. Examining earlier practice from a perspective situated at the end of the 19th century, surgeons redefined the ends of less radical surgeries or surgeries on advanced cancers to be palliative. The distinction between palliative and curative allowed the conceptual space for a shift towards radical breast surgeries to occur as the solution. Palliative as an adjective contrasts to curative. It worked in two ways. First, it marked past surgical efforts that failed to produce curative effects even when women lived 4 to 5 years after the operation. Second, it still described contemporaneous scientific surgeries done when cancer was too late to hope for a cure.

The separation between palliative and curative is fuzzy. It shows how surgeons utilized the distinction as a rhetorical tool. This tool opened the space for a conditional definition of success and for further utilization of surgery and experimentation with the style scope and manner of incisions. Surgeons negotiated when a procedure was palliative or curative. Most times this was decided after the operation, recurrence of the disease, or the death of the woman. The definition of a cure, then, became increasingly depended on length of time women survived from the operation or before the disease recurred. Even in cases where cancer was too advanced or too late for a cure, surgeons operated to alleviate pain. Sometimes the surgery expedited the end. With the distinction of palliative/ curative, we can see how an extensive cancer-free interval after the operation became an operational marker of surgical success. Surgeons did not adapt this definition until Halsted.

By the end of the 19th century, whether or not surgery was successful, removing cancerous breasts became an integral part of modern medical practice. The name used for the operation within surgical papers to reflect a shift from palliative to curative ends. At first, surgeons called the operation breast amputation, or extirpation. This name was used during the time of failure to achieve a cure. As surgery became curative, surgeons labeled it radical. Later in clinical practice, surgeons called curative radical surgeries mastectomies and lumpectomies. The logic of postoperative survival, as a *duration cure*, guided the extent of surgical interventions. (Table 2)

Surgical Paradigming

The knife could cure cancer, Halsted claimed. At the turn of the 20th century, identifying the conditions of cure became the job of surgeons, anatomists, and pathologists. Surgeons vested the breast in claims of treating cancer. The breast was well suited for developing a surgical cure for cancer because the breast was "among the most frequent and easily accessible body surfaces offering relatively little difficulty for investigation." (See Heidenhain, 1889) Even as the surgical means to cure breast cancer gained evidence and support, how to cut, which cuts were best and under what circumstances, remained contested, subject to surgeons' style, to the peculiarities of each woman's breast and its disease. Successful breast operations would transform the theoretical hunches of Moore into practice by overlaying pathological, anatomical, and surgical expertise.

The term overlaying implies an active process of superimposing heterogeneous knowledges about breasts, cancer, and surgical techniques even if this process did not achieve alignment. This overlaying of anatomy, pathology and surgical technique defined the dimensions for surgical success and sought to illuminate how/ when cancer marched through tissue. At the turn of the 20th century, surgeons determined, which breast and muscle tissue cancer affected more frequently. This tissue became subject to recurrence or metastasis. Recurrence and metastasis seemed to be the main obstacle for the surgical triumph over this disease. So the solution seemed obvious, remove all suspect tissue *in toto*. Expertise and technique at the boundaries of surgery, anatomy, and pathology modified the criteria for successful breast surgeries. Situated at such intersections, surgeons proposed more scientific, systematic, and successful operations. These operations aimed to stop the flow and re-growth of cancer with better surgical cuts.

Surgery, Anatomy, Pathology

At the turn of the 20th century, a curative operation became a more radical operation. For surgery to be successful, cancer had to be local thus evaluated to be 'early.' Early meant that the tumor was localized in the breast, muscle and adjacent removable tissue. Surgeons would remove this localized growth along with sufficient breast, muscle, and connective tissue. Pathologists entered to identify the parameters of malignant tumors. Surgeons sought to see tumor in the flesh and to understand when/ if tumors were localized enough to be treated. In their joining, surgical pathology differentiated between operable and inoperable lesions. Inoperable cases were still subject to surgery not for curative, but for palliative ends. Surgeons decided these ends at times on the operating table or while writing up, reviewing their case studies and reports.

Actors, from what became different disciplinary angles, worked together to configure the parameters for successful breast amputations. Surgical pathology delimited the boundaries of curative operations. Surgical anatomy defined the least debilitating operations. Surgery as a therapeutic discipline became successful and able to define better curative operations when some surgeons trained and adopted techniques of pathologists and anatomists. For example, Heidenhain was a pathologist and a surgeon working in the Küster Surgical Clinic in Berlin; Banks was a professor of anatomy and a surgeon. Cross-disciplinary fertilization fueled research and practices that promised to curtail the flow and re-growth of cancer, to enhance post-operative healing, to reduce scarring and subsequent disability. Surgeons having constructed evidence that showed some promise, developed strategies to persuade other physicians and women of their efficacy.

Surgical pathology and anatomy as hybrid disciplines adapted techniques to accommodate surgeons targeting morbid growths. A communication and authority problem followed. Pathology and anatomy dealt with tissue and extracted organs. Surgeons dealt with live bodies, specific morphologies and pathologies. Surgery posed applied problems for pathology and anatomy. Each discipline mustered expertise, techniques to tackle these problems, but only surgeons in the end presented themselves as best qualified to decide applicability. In this context, Halsted argued that the surgeon was the ultimate arbitrator of claims about breast tumors, about their severity and operability: "There is a gap between the surgeon and pathologist, which can only be filled by the surgeon. The pathologist seldom has the opportunity to see diseased conditions as the surgeon sees them. A tumor on a plate and a tumor in the breast-- how different!" (Halsted, 1898: 558)

Surgical pathology classified cancer through histology. Malignancy clustered in classes. Surgeons sought to link these classes to operative outcomes and surgical techniques to establish rates of cure, rates of success. By utilizing anatomical and pathological expertise, surgeons identified specific criteria that differentiated between benign and malignant tumors, to identify the extent of the malignancy, and to decide when a lesion was operable and by extension 'curable' with the knife. Breast cancer taxonomies aided surgical prognosis and became the grounds for continued surgical success. Thus, breast surgery became more scientific when it linked its outcomes to cancer taxonomies. Micro techniques like preparing tomes, locating, and staining tissue to differentiate between cancerous and healthy were also the techniques that surgeons like Heidenhain (1889) mobilized to describe the lymphatic flow of cancer.[8]

In 1889, Heidenhain focused on the intersection between surgery and pathology. He supplemented and solidified the surgical success with microscopic investigations that traced the cellular roots of cancer spread through the lymphatic system and recommended removing the connective fascia between gland and muscle. In most cases, cancer involved the connective fascia. Surgeons did not remove the fascia when they excised the breast and this was a source of lingering recurrence, some argued. Heidenhain proposed that separating the fascia from the pectoral muscle was difficult and that lymphatic vessels flowed from muscle to breast. In some cases, cancer might already involve the muscle tissue, so surgeons would consider the need to cut into it. (Heidenhain, 1889)

Pathology had influenced surgeries of cancer on a larger scale not only for breast, but also for cervical tumors. In this context, Ruge and Veite (1881) developed biopsy as a technique to diagnose cervical cancer more accurately. Bloodgood (1914) would modify biopsy to identify the nature of borderline breast lesions. Surgical pathology through the

---

[8] Classification of tumors becomes an active and actionable matrix for organizing not just cancer as a disease, but medical intervention, as well as the therapeutic environment. This is how classification as discourse comes to structure both disease and illness experience as Topology. For more on the notion of topology see chapter 4.

technique of biopsy became an obligatory point of passage for operations, in the diagnosis of cancer. It circumscribed when a surgical cure was necessary. Pathology overlaid the cellular and lymphatic flow of cancer within the framework of breast anatomy. If surgical pathology was concerned with when and how much to excise, surgical anatomy was involved in how much and how to excise to limit recurrence, disability, the duration of the operation, and any cross-contamination from diseased to healthy tissue.

Specifically, surgical anatomists delimited the horizon of the breast as an organ. Stiles (1892) described three types of tissue: gland proper, connective (blood and lymphatic vessels, nerves), and fat. Particularly important to surgical success was mapping the lymphatic flow within breast and pectoral tissue. Lymphatic capillaries were difficult to study microscopically because they collapsed during preparation. Anatomists described the location of lymphatic vessels to understand how they permeated breast and muscle tissue to circumscribe the extent of the operation, and to identify how cancer cells disseminated through the lymphatic system. Stiles (1892) argued that recurrence resulted from the failure to remove foci of cancer that resided along the lymphatic track. Identifying where cancer cells lurked remained a problem for surgeons arguing for a surgical cure of breast cancer.

Classification

Cancer classification at the time juxtaposed surgical, anatomical, and pathological breasts to define the severity of the disease and the operability of growths. Variations in how cancer affected breast tissue led to classifying growths along two separate paths: cellular and clinical.

Along the cellular dimension, pathologists identified several varieties of cancers: *calloid, scirrhus, medulary, Paget's disease, duct cancer*, and *adenocarcinoma*. The prognosis and operative possibilities for each of these varied not only by type, but also by location. The spread of cancer within the breast and lymph nodes depended of the virulence of cancer. How much a cancer had spread and how quickly defined its operability. Sometimes surgeons defined operability during the procedure. Sometimes larger tumors were a sign of advanced disease, but that depended on the duration of the condition and its spread. Some tumors were slower growing, less invasive and dangerous because they did not spread easily. In terms of severity of type, *medulary carcinoma* was more lethal than *adenocarcinoma* or *calloid* cancers. Outer quadrant cancers were more frequent and deadly than inner quadrant as with upper over lower location. Early onset cancers tended to be more invasive and deadly. (See Halsted 1898,1907; Pilcher, 1903)

Clinical diagnosis of cancer was complex and spacio-temporal. It followed along the lines of early-advanced, benign-malignant, invasive-slow growth, outer-inner and upper-lower quadrants. Whether the tumor was in the outer/inner or upper/lower quadrant of the breast led to different severity because lymphatic vessels flowed differently within the breast and sometimes could spread cancer more rapidly. Cutting cancer early meant to capture cancer when women reported a problem and when clinicians could first palpate or diagnose it. Earlier diagnosis became a necessary prerequisite for surgical success. The temporal 'early' of diagnosis was different in each case. Breast surgery was curative when it limited cancer recurrence, when it arrested the march of cancer through tissue with more radical surgical incisions. Today cancer classification refers to both grade and stage of disease. Grade one means that cancer cells resemble breast tissue. Grade two and three both refer to cancer differentiation into unrecognizable cells. Stage refers to spread of cancer through the body. In combination stage and grade capture the notions early or late diagnosis and attempt to predict outcomes. (See Stoppard, 1998)

Radical Cure

Limiting recurrence grounded a successful turn from palliative to curative ends for breast operations. Heidenhain showed how cancer disseminated through the lymphatic system. Mapping the flow of cancer would mark the scope of the operation. Recurrence followed when, despite the best efforts of surgeons, cancer lurked within the body undetected. Remaining cancerous foci provoked recurrence. Stopping cancer from recurring predominately at the chest wall or near the scar indicated surgical success. Recurrences were either local (on the chest wall near the scar) or metastatic (when cancer cells spread to the lungs, bones, or liver). Surgeons thought local recurrences were directly associated with errors in surgical technique while metastases marked advanced disease. Surgeons characterized their cancer diagnosis as being 'too late,' when they could not fully remove the disease on the operating table and a surgical cure was unlikely. Some palliative operations accelerated the trajectory of the disease, yet surgeons continued to perform these operations to ease pain.

Surgeons sought to define the scope of tumors to identify whether they had excised enough tissue, or if they could have removed more with relative safety. Surgeons thought that finding the best incisions would stop the re-growth of cancer after the operation. Whether a postoperative growth was a result of spontaneous reappearance or if it related directly to the removed cancer, limiting recurrence indicated the parameters of surgical success. Surgeons, then, sought to differentiate between postoperative growths that were due to their potentially moderate operations and those that were not. Surgeons defined postoperative growths that were due to inadequate operations to be local recurrences -- when the new growth was in close proximity to the original one. The notion of proximity is analytically important. Proximity could be spatial, temporal, or both. For Halsted, in his 1894 paper, proximity became spacio-temporal. A recurrence was proximal in reference to both the duration of its emergence after the time of the operation and its location near the original operating site. Halsted proposed that local recurrences within a 3-year postoperative interval were due to an inadequate operation.

Overall then, Surgeons negotiated between anatomy and pathology to target cancer and to obtain an earlier diagnosis. Surgeons tied success with early intervention defined through Halsted's notion of proximity. Cutting radically and early reduced the incidence of local recurrences and defined recurrences as the results of surgeons' inadequate incisions. Surgeons traced the scope of breast cancer to settle which tissues were involved and to decide the extent of the ideal operation. The goal was to remove enough tissue to eliminate the malignancy. This cutting was both regional in how it traced the breasted body and temporal in how it configured cancer as operable. An extensive line of cut defined the means to cure cancer. A spacio-temporal 'early' or 'late' became a designation of surgeons' imminent success or failure.

Style and Scope

The lymphatic spread of cancer implicated the whole breast and sometimes part of the pectoral muscle as suspect cancer tissue. Volkmann (1882) meticulously separated the breast and connective fascia from the muscle. Volkmann, however, removed the whole breast even for the smaller tumors. Surgeons sought to develop checks that defined how much to incise into the breast and muscle. Stiles (1892) described dipping the amputated breast into a nitrous solution to show if cancer foci remained on the amputated surface, which would indicate whether to incise deeper. Since the spread of cancer as a disease varied, identifying how much to cut in each case could not be standard. If cancer affected the connective fascia, surgeons would excise the breast and sometimes the pectoral muscles *in toto*. Whether to remove the pectoral muscles became a serious question. Checking the auxiliary and supraclavicular glands could determine if cancer had advanced too far. Sometimes surgeons cleaned these areas first. A surgical cure became equivalent with the removal of a substantial chunk of tissue, a radical cut, and a radical wound.

Halsted (1894) and Meyer (1894) independently proposed operations boasting effectiveness in stopping recurrence and increasing post-operative length of life. These surgeries were both more radical and complete, than before for all breast cancer cases alike. They were also independent of the severity of the disease. Halsted agreed with the scientific analysis of von Volkmann, but feared that surgeons were being too delicate in separating cancerous and non-cancerous tissue, running the risk of cutting into affected areas and contaminating healthy ones. This contamination occurred during the operation, he argued, and was a stoppable source of cancer recurrence.

One incision of both breast and muscle would suffice to treat most breast cancers if they were operable, Halsted argued. "The pectoral major muscle, entire or all except the clavicular portion, should be excised in every case of cancer of the breast, because the operator is enabled thereby to remove in one piece all of the suspected tissue." (Halsted,

1894: 507) Halsted illustrated how a more radical, complete operation could eliminate early local recurrences in most breast cancer cases, but continued to check lymph nodes in the sub-clavicular, neck, and axilla sometimes operating more extensively.

At the same time, Meyer (1894) proposed his radical surgery. He removed the breast, the contents of the auxiliary and sub-clavicular region, and both major and minor pectoral muscles in one stroke without exposing the contents of the breast and muscle. When the muscle was involved, a more radical operation would be better, he argued. He argued that his surgery was more radical and more properly anatomical than Halsted's operation. Meyer hoped to eliminate breast cancer through his radical incisions. Thus, he would stop cancer. Making cancer more submissive to the knife however translated into women submitting to radical surgeries for breast tumors earlier and in increasing numbers.

Success for Surgeons and for Women

Surgical Definition

Limiting early local recurrence within three years after the operation became Halsted's measure of surgical success. Halsted proposed that later recurrences were infrequent and less relevant because cancer recurred at a pace similar or faster in speed as when it first occurred. He radicalized not only how much breast and muscle tissue needed to be excised to cure cancer, but also the manner of incision, urging surgeons to treat the appearance of the disease promptly, radically, and thoroughly. As radical surgery defined the scientific approach to breast cancer, notions of surgical success became clearer. Surgeons modified their incisions to fit particular contingencies guided by the parameters of radical excision. Most surgeons began to extract more rather than less and to excise tissue *in toto.* Surgeons competed with one another with different incisions that produced and qualified 'better' outcomes seeking to modify or negotiate a better surgical treatment for breast cancer.

Halsted (1894) argued that operational success depended on reducing relevant recurrences -- early local recurrences. Continued surgical success hinged upon increasing the duration of cure, on incisions that follow along anatomical and surgical aesthetics, and facilitate postoperative functionality. Surgeons measured 'duration of cure' through post-operative survival. Anatomical and surgical aesthetics delineated the dimensions, directions, and curvatures of incisions to reduce extensive scarring and minimize the length and complexity of the operation. Attending to functionality would limit subsequent disability, such as the disuse of the arm, extensive scarring, or lymphadema from poor drainage of the wound. The criteria -- post-operative survival, surgical-anatomical aesthetics, and functionality--were secondary to eliminating early local recurrence, and having women live cancer free for a 3-year interval after the operation.

Surgeons tabulated women's survival to illustrate the success of breast surgeries, and women purchased surgical success with their lives. After surgeons established cutting as a cure for cancer, finding better ways to incise along the lines of the secondary criteria came to the forefront. Warren (1904) argued, before he proposed his operation, that "all other considerations, which enter into so many operations, should be disregarded, with the single exception of the safety of life. Anatomy and aesthetics should always play a secondary role. This having been conceded, there is still much that can be done to make the operation less exhausting and disfiguring than some of the 'complete methods'." (864) Stopping recurrence involved not only demarcating the best incision, which was to cut more rather than less, but also finding ways to cut cancer early. Cutting cancer early implied finding cancer when it had not yet dispersed through the whole breast and other connected organs and structures. Curing cancer with the knife meant women had to self-monitor, to learn to identify and report the first indications of cancer, and then to submit to surgery more rapidly, readily, and frequently.

Curative Radicals

Radical, therapeutic amputations of the breast included the pectoralis major sometimes minor, lymph nodes and glands in the clavicular or auxiliary region, extensive amount of skin, and a substantial amount of healthy-looking tissue. Jackson (1920) summarized the requirements of radical operations: remove a sufficient chunk to avoid cross-contamination during surgery. The extent of the operation, he argued, involved the following regions: extensive skin; mammary gland; pectoral muscles; auxiliary glands, fat, and fascia; supraclavicular space; abdominal fascia. Surgeons began to incise more along aesthetic, functional, and anatomical lines to avoid debilitating effects of extensive scarring or skin grafts.

The move towards a standardized surgical cure also concerned post-operative disability not only eliminating recurrence of cancer. Surgeons photographed women after the operation minus a breast and their arms held high-- statues of liberty-- to signify reduced disability and the surgical triumph over cancer. Surgeons argued that an anatomically correct operation would not disable the arm and that a radical operation would cure cancer. Disability, they argued, resulted from extensive scarring due to the direction and extent of the wound, unnecessary skin grafting, or the retention of the pectoral minor. These concerns were secondary to radically removing cancer and having women live.

With their separate publications in 1894, Halsted and Meyer framed the parameters of radical curative surgery and surgeons began to debate them more rigorously. Most surgeons saw Halsted's method as more definitive. Meyer's operation recommended removing the pectoral minor as well as major and cleaning out the supra-clavicular region. By 1918, Meyer (1918) was concerned that Halsted's operation, a less radical operation, was more popular. He countered charges that his operation was unduly mutilating, substantially weakening the arm after the operation. Meyer disputed that excising the pectoral minor as well as major would not disable the use of the arm rather allow a freer range of motion. Then, women would have achieved the statue of liberty pose in every instance. Something that Halsted's operation did not guarantee. (Meyer, 1918) Meyer (1920) argued that Halsted's operation resulted in a substantial loss of blood due to the direction of the incision from the chest to the to the clavicular portion and the axilla. Meyer's method started at the axilla and allowed the division of blood and lymph vessels before extracting the cancerous breast. Overall, Meyer bolstered his surgical techniques, as being more efficient, less bloody, less disabling, and more radical than Halsted's operation.

In 1894, Halsted had proposed a radical operation that moved from the clavicular portion to the axilla, leaving a flap near the armpit to close the wound. He was not against skin grafting. Sometimes he urged excising a sufficient amount of skin because it could save women's lives. In 1907, Halsted warned against cosmetic operations that would sacrifice the lives of women to better close the wound and decrease convalescence. He proposed modifications that implied a more radical operation than suggested in his 1894 paper. In some instances, he would require removing part of the chest wall, checking the neck to identify if the sub-clavicular region was affected, and at times excising the pectoral minor and major. He urged that the surgeon be mindful of the lymphatic flow of cancer and operate extensively. He focused his energy on diagnosing cancer earlier. Any sign of imbalance between the breasts was a potential sign of malignancy. Halsted praised his staff because they began developing the clinical expertise to identify even the slightest possibility of disease. (Halsted, 1907)

How to cut and how much remained a contested topic for the early part of the 20th century even as surgeons agreed upon the general principles for curative radical operations.

Skin Grafts

During the first decades of the 20th century, radical surgeries had prevailed as breast cancer cures. Radical as a principle captured the surgical imagination and defined what a surgical cure for breast cancer would be. Radical surgeries for the first time had significant results to back curative claims. Radical became increasingly tempered by concerns with aesthetics and functionality even as surgeons insisted on timely extensive operations to 'extend' post-operative life. The rhetoric of 'saving' lives draped surgical action. How to close the wound and eliminate enough skin were the main questions many surgeons still asked.

For example, Rodman (1901) proposed that lingering recurrence of tumors was an effect of remaining affected skin. Surgeons spared the skin to close the wound properly and avoid scarring. He argued that wound closure was less important, that surgeons and women had an undue bias against skin grafting. Remaining skin could be cancerous, he warned. "The mistake is always presumably due to the natural and proper desire to secure immediate union on the one hand and avoid undue scarring on the other. There is, I believe, a prejudice against skin-grafting, as a supplemental step in this operation, which is shared by the operator and the patient; the first because it prolongs the operation and not infrequently fails to accomplish it's intended purpose; and second because it leaves unsightly scars" (Rodman, 1901:138). For Rodman, the best incision is the one that removes potentially al cancerous skin despite needing a graft.

Conversely, Warren (1904) discouraged skin grafting as it adds an unsightly scar as well as length to an already demoralizing operation. He proposed an operation that moves from the axilla towards and around the breast and creates a flap on the outer side of the pectoral region to help close the wound. Collins urged incising "from without inward in a direction exactly opposite to that carried out in Halsted's operation, so that the entire mass to be removed is thrown towards the median line" (Warren, 1904: 828). This incision left a wound that closed more easily. It also allowed for a dissection of the sub-clavicular triangle before excising the breast. The operation was speedy. Surgeons completed the operation within a period of 30 to 40 minutes. It also reduced post-operative infection because surgeons did not expose the wound for a long time (Warren, 1904).

The question of skin grafts was not easily resolved because in some cases the spread of breast cancer required removing an extensive amount of skin. Elsberg (1915) claimed that for these cases "the abdominal skin-flap" incision would help cover the wound and not require a skin graft. He argued against skin grafts because sometimes necrosis of the skin followed. His incision used skin from the abdomen to cover the amputated area. So "the size and shape of the abdomen skin flap will depend on size and form of the raw surface on the chest wall" (678). He argued that this incision was not original, but would become standard in operations where surgeons needed to remove a large amount of skin.

Ideal Incisions

Radical defined better incisions, curative incisions. Radical incisions tempered surgical and anatomical aesthetics to facilitate wound closure, to diminish scarring, and to retain the use of the arm, which was significant in enrolling women. The ideal incision was radical then. It eliminated breast cancer and its recurrence. It reduced blood loss and the time spent in the operation. It minimized temporal exposure of the wound and any cancerous contamination of healthy tissue. Stewart (1915) summarized his criteria for a better incision in supporting a transverse incision for breast cancer surgeries. He thought that the axilla must be attacked first to establish the feasibility of the operation, to secure blood vessels at their origin. Securing blood vessels would minimize hemorrhage, and save time. Then, he sought to suppress lymphatic drainage, and to cover the thorax with the breast until the final stage. Horizontal sutures easily closed the wound, minimized the scar, and facilitated the movement of the arm.

Thus, curing breast cancer with radical cuts had a positive relationship with identifying the disease early. The temporal sequence early-advanced underpinned when cancer was surgically curable. Early-advanced became a structuring dynamic supporting the predictive nature of surgical actions.

Deploying the Surgical Cure

Early Diagnosis/ Detection

Early diagnosis mobilized, ordered, and aligned actors, various techniques, and technologies in the clinical setting. Early diagnosis illuminated the conditions for the engagement and participation of women and their breasts. Surgeons sought to recognize cancer not only under the microscope, but also by touch and sight to gauge the need for an operation (Halsted, 1907). Warren (1907) warned that the surgical treatment of benign tumors must keep up with the improvements in operations for mammary cancer. Benign tumors became suspect sites for eventual malignancies and some surgeons removed them less radically before they turned malignant.

As women began 'presenting' earlier for surgical consideration, surgeons sought ways to identify the earliest possible cancerous lesions. Palpation alone could not differentiate between benign and cancerous lesions. Early cancer diagnosis depended on biopsy. Biopsies became key because they defined if a lesion was cancerous, the type of cancer, and sometimes the scope of a cancerous growth. The margin of error in diagnosing breast cancer became slim. In 1914, Bloodgood defined borderline lesions as pre-cancerous and surgery followed. He linked better surgical results with the earliest possible diagnosis. (Bloodgood, 1914)

Even for advance or hopeless cases, surgery provided an answer. For advanced cancers, surgeons operated more extensively, removing lymph glands and tissue in the neck, the clavicular region, the axilla, and even the abdomen. Diagnosing early was possible if the surgeon noticed "this almost imperceptible suggestion of pull, which, when the faintest possible, is of course elicited by dislocation in one direction only. This sign, however, slight is all that is needed for diagnosis." (Halsted, 1907:14) Halsted has just referred to the process of clinical breast exams before they had begun to be standardized.

Women's Participation

Through the notion of early, surgeons identified ways to connect cancerous body space with duration of cancer spread. This linking of duration and body space helped pin down a fuzzy disease like cancer. Cancer was slippery. Sometimes it was local but it could become systemic. Causes remained mystified. Cancerous tissues were breast cells run amok. When breast cancer became a surgically treatable disease, it became spacio-temporal in specific ways. It was local and not yet metastasized. (See Chide, 1907, Theoharis, "Genes, Germs, Sins, Toxins")

Surgical anatomists wondered about the location of the tumor in relation to the chest wall. Surgeons connected a cancer cure with the conditional statement: if surgeons excise the disease early. The temporal early was inextricable from the spacio-temporal localization of cancerous cells marching through the breast. Surgeons linked a spacio-temporal flow of cancer to a temporal consolidation of women's active participation. The temporization of cancer as a disease challenged and mobilized women to become subject to surgery, to accept a surgical cure, to be ever more vigilant, more responsive to and responsible for detecting the earliest signs of cancer

Even as women became aware of breast cancer as a risk, surgeons did not include their self-reports within the scientific domain. Surgeons dismissed women's self-reports as well as most physicians' reports of the disease. They believed these reports had little accuracy about the trajectory of the disease, especially since palpating a cancerous lump began already to define the disease as advanced. Early diagnosis became an authorial marker for surgeons. Early diagnoses demarcated whether a particular breast cancer was operable. Early diagnosis defined the condition for more successful surgical interventions and paved the way for standardized surgical cures. Early diagnosis required that women act in accord with surgical norms and knowledges about breast cancer as a disease.

Defining Breast Cancer

The anger I felt for my right breast last year has faded, and I'm glad because I have had the extra year. My breasts have always been so very precious to me since I accepted having them it would have been a shame not to enjoy the last year of one of them. And I think I am prepared to lose it now in a way I was not quite ready to last November, because now I really see it as a choice between my breast and my life, and in that view there cannot be any question.
--- *Lorde, 1980*

Introduction

What is breast cancer? The question appears to be simple enough, but the answer is not. Over the course of the 20th century characterizing benign or malignant breast cancer tissue and cells became key in defining what are the appropriate parameters for a cure. The later part of the 20th century saw specific advances into the causation of breast cancer as a disease following from genetic instability. Those causes can be genetic and viral, hormonal and environmental. Questions about the causation of cancer were not new, but the status of medical science had not allowed those questions to be fruitfully answered. The need was molecular biology. Molecular biology bridged chemical, genetic and cellular process. Key, also, became the successive definitions of cancer from a disease of specific organs, to a disease of tissue, cells/ cellular processes and lately genes.

Breast cancer causation became genetic with markers like BRCA1 and 2, viral with HMTV, molecular in terms of (1) internal environment – hormones/ enzymes/ catalysts: the effects of estrogen and progesterone, the effect of enzymes that correct DNA, the effect of epigenetic processes e.g. catalysts for methylation that we think silences/ activates gene and (2) environmental with the discovery of chemical agents (mutagens/ other hormone like agents) or radiation that may cause mutations and suppress natural defenses to lead to breast cancer. The question remains whether and when these causes are internal, inherent or external and what particular combinations leads to a chain of events that manifests this disease. In this regard, it is important to ask if breast cancer and cancer in general challenges the medical definition of disease where a single pathogen leads to a distinct and singular pathology. (See Theoharis, 'Genes, Germs, Sins, Toxins') Recently however, the pathways that cause cancer have become clearer. These pathways are molecular and genetic.

In chapter 1, I looked at the 19th and early 20th century questions about breast cancer as a disease. Those questions were descriptive. They sought to account for the success of the surgical cure by inventing a new kind of cure: the duration cure and cancer as chronic disease. This cure allowed surgeons to claim success while still investigating the parameters of this disease. Surgeons articulated the parameters of a surgical cure though the notions: radical and early. Those notions became cemented in practice for part of the 20th century.

In the process of settling the surgical cure, the questions asked were many. But one question led to another in a suggestive fashion. This reasoning sought to forestall outcomes within the logic set by principle arguments around the translation of medical knowledge into medical action and practice. Such a circuit in rationality produces closure in argument that may not be settled by the facts either because such facts cannot be yet known or because dispute about facts does not lead to clarity or a composite viewpoint. Closure occurs through on one side the accumulation of credit, on the other discrediting. For example, radical mastectomy became known as the Halsted procedure even though several surgeons performed similar operations. It was the way in which he articulated his reasoning that mattered. (See Chapter 1) The closure of argument in medical science/ practice and clinical science/practice follows different pathways. Both however follow the norms for when the interests of knowledge are in conflict with and are subsumed by the interests of care. This is a judgment call. This question, also, came to the fore with issues surrounding AIDS drugs and clinical trials. (See Epstein, 1996) In the case of cancer, late 20th century advances in molecular and genetic science began to clarify the nature of disease and thus begin to impact the nature of treatment.

The closure of arguments is essential in the production of knowledge as it becomes operational into action. This translation should not be mediated solely by scientific norms but by the norms of the community that cares for the needy. However, such closure need not be righteous. It needs to be mindful that in action it becomes force and force not tempered by knowledge and thought has profound side effects. One of the solutions is to account for error and not produce a coherent singularity when treatment action translates into practice. This needs to occur without facilitating malpractice. Government plays a role here. In medical paradigming, the shifts occur along the pathways of novel understanding about the structure of the body and the nature of disease. It is in essence about the birth of a new medical/ clinical juncture that would follow new knowledges and practices.

In breast cancer, the logic early/ advanced cemented the surgical cure at the turn of the 20th century. This logic from our standpoint veiled the nature of surgical operations, the nature of cancer, and the nature of what cure is. The question 'is cancer local or systemic?' would link to the question, 'is subsequent surgery curative or palliative?' or 'is a growth early or advanced?' The question 'Is cancer recurrence spontaneous or diffused from the initial site of the disease' would connect to the question: 'was the surgery performed radical enough to cure or not really appropriate as the condition was likely congenital or too advanced?' These questions began to be answered through the microscope where the mystic of cancer began to be lifted. Can continuities be identified between the cellular and later genetic composition of an earlier growth with the newer one or with a metastasis in other parts of the body? How did cancer diffuse and metastasize? Was there a way to establish the extent of diffusion and continuity?

Trajectory of Treatment/ Diagnosis

In the 19th century, surgical pathologists first looked at establishing the nature of the respective lesions. Second, they sought to identify the extent of cancer spread prior and/ or during the operation, by examining adjacent lymph nodes. Heidenhain established that cancer spread through the lymph nodes. Halsted and earlier Moore postulated that 'sloppy' surgery facilitates the spread of cancer, defeating the purpose of the operation. He and others also examined lymph nodes in the clavicle and armpit to establish the extent of cancer spread. Bloodgood formulated biopsy as a procedure to identify cancer on a cellular and tissue level as well as establish 'borderline' growths what we would call 'pre-cancers' that could warrant surgical intervention. (see chapter 1)

Biopsy was an important procedure especially as it became distinct from the actual operation. Biopsy subsequently became an accepted obligatory point of passage for the definition of breast cancer. Subsequent treatment did not vary dependent on the type of cancer, but more so in terms of the extent of spread. Initially, surgeons subjected women to surgery immediately upon a biopsy diagnosis as to avoid any contamination from the procedure. However, such urgency changed as biopsy as a technique evolved. This allowed women the time to contemplate a cancer diagnosis and set a course of treatment. The nature and paradigm of surgery is no longer to remove every cancerous cell possible and thus cure cancer. Rather, it is to remove enough cancer that the body's immune system is able to cope and handle the disease along with appropriate chemo and hormonal therapies.

Biopsy as a procedure was able to minimize any contamination of surrounding tissue and allow for a better sampling of a tumor for an accurate diagnosis. The hypothesis that cancer was a local disease until late did not prove to be entirely accurate as in certain instances cancer cells traveled through the brood stream and in earlier moments then previously imagined. (See Chapter 3) Sometimes surgeons perform a lumpectomy as part of a biopsy. Sometimes they sampled the tissue of tumor to establish its nature. Today the nature of a growth is staged through biopsy. Biopsy takes on many forms: Surgical -- incisional (part of a lump), excisional (a whole lump), core biopsy when a thick needle is used to sample tissue, or fine needle, when fluid is removed. If a lump is detected on a mammogram and cannot be felt by a clinical exam, techniques such as ultrasound, stereotactic, and needle biopsy are used to localize the area in question.

Staging of cancer is particularly important. In 2002, the American Joint Committee for Cancer (AJCC) updated staging criteria for cancer on recommendation of the Breast Cancer Task Force. This new staging system was put in effect in 2003. This tumor, node, metastasis (TNM) scale rationalized staging of the disease but may also improve outcomes. This improvement, however, may be due to the new labeling rather than to actual effects on patient lives. (See Singletary et al, 2003) The new TNM scale had improvements for breast cancer treatment because as a result of screening new cancers were diagnosed sooner and were of smaller size. (See Singletary et al, 2002)

Lately a cancer diagnosis also includes questions over whether or not a cancer is gene positive (BRCA 1 and 2), estrogen receptor positive, or her2-neu positive. Her 2- neu is a particular gate on the cell membrane of monoclonal cancer, which stimulates a particular protein (tyrosine kinase) responsible for DNA synthesis and/ or a protein responsible for angiogenesis. Grading refers to the type and clarity of cancer cells. Pathologists do an accurate grading of cancer after a mastectomy. Surgeons establish the staging of a cancer as it relates to the type of treatment pursued. (See Love, 2001)

Late 20th century early 21 century questions concern the location and character of 'pre-cancers' as well as how to treat them. Treating pre-cancer is a way to forestall a cancer diagnosis. It follows the logic of earliest intervention. The timing of interventions, thus has become essential. An array of procedures emerges where women have choice over the direction, timing and type of treatment. In the late 20th century early 21st, we discovered that the body's defenses against cancer-genesis are essential. These defenses are endocrine and immunological: endocrine in that hormones and enzymes have a role in cell life; immunological in that immune cells monitor cellular proliferation and any cells infected with viral DNA. To understand the development of medical science in the late 20th century and the treatments of the disease as well as women's role in changing medicine, I will look to how cancer as a disease became clearer, how it was redefined on molecular, genetic grounds. I, also, look at how the emerging definitions of breast cancer link up to new diagnostics and treatments, as well as a new paradigm for the relationship of medicine and society.

Breasts as Body Parts

Breast cancer is specific in that it carries with it the ambiguities of cancer as a disease and the complexities of breasts as social and medical objects. Breasts are subjects and objects of fascination. Even in medical practice, they are saturated with the significance of sexuality, femininity, motherhood, and aging. The implications permeate the treatment and science of breast cancer. Managing the health of breasts enters into a dialogue with the discourse and precautions associated with being an aging woman. When is it best to have children? What should women do with aging ovaries, hormonal events like menstruation and menopause?

Breast as medical objects, then, carry with them the significance of being woman subject to medicine, and an object of medical practice. That significance however has positive and negative implications. Breasts implicate the medical 'condition' of being a woman as one prone to particular kinds of diseases and as an effect of particular choices. These life choices have a moral undertone. For example, some physicians recommend that 'women should not put off childbearing until their 30s or 40s because they are more prone to breast cancer.' Placed in the context of regulating women's reproduction such statements sound as moral dictums of an earlier century. Regulating sexuality is a matter of science and a matter of society. Fundamentally, however, it is a matter of women's choice and right. Reproduction and by consequence the expression of sexuality has been a domain of activity where women's lives become subject to social norms and pressure. (See Clarke, 1998)

In defining breast cancer, then, one comes across how to manage and define a genetic/ molecular/ cellular disease and to sort through the meanings of breasts for aging women. In a sense, we are dealing with a double narrative: one of women's relationships with their breasts and bodies; one of medicine entangled with the management of its deadly disease as well as societal norms. Each narrative has multiple threads and follows many lines of action. Sometimes these narratives clash. Sometimes they intersect with or constructively influence the other. Sometimes they are disconnected.

In this chapter then, I will concern myself with late 20th/ early 21st century definitions of breast cancer and it's implications for screening, diagnosis and treatment as well as the implications for women. The definition of normality and pathology of the breast: its cells and tissues becomes key in how medicine organizes a response as well as the ways women become implicated in reproducing medical practices or forwarding medical science. Then, I will trace various cancerous actants (molecular, viral, genetic, environmental) as well as risk and animal models that attempt to answer the intricacies of breast cancer as a multi-event/ multi-factor process.

Normal and Malignant

Breast Organ

The breast gland is composed of ducts, lobules, and connective tissue. The glad is enclosed in a fat layer and suspended by breast ligaments. For humans, the breast rests on top of the chess muscle. The breast gland may have 5-7 duct/ lobule systems that lead to the nipple and form a lobe. The main biological function of the breast is to produce milk after pregnancy as to nourish the offspring. Breasts can be lumpy, yet clear of cancer as a disease. Breast tissue is dense and responsive to hormonal changes. These are marked through menarche: period of breast growth, menstruation: period during which breasts produce milk, and menopause: period during which breast tissue becomes less dense and more fatty. Cancer is not the only disease of the breast. Breasts can be cystic and prone to certain kinds of inflammation or infections.

Two main technologies are used to establish breast cancer as pathology. These techniques grasp the breast as a whole organ. They are imaging technologies and breast exams. (See Love, 2000; Naas et al, 2001) Mammography is the main imaging technology joined with others. I will briefly talk about how both mammograms and breast exams seek to map out the breast as an organ to identify pathology.

Mammography seeks to illuminate breast pathology. Timing becomes key for mammograms not only in terms of frequency, but also in terms of age. During menopause breast tissue becomes less dense. It becomes more translucent under x-rays and visible on the mammography film. It becomes able to yield lumps or other abnormalities. Mammograms virtually cut across breasts to create dense 2D cross-sections. By looking at these plates, radiologists seek to visualize breast tissue in a multi-dimensional manner. Advances in mammography such as CAD and digital technology have helped in making breasts imaging multi-dimensional.

Standard angles for plates are horizontal and vertical. Radiologists usually take these during a routine mammogram. Other angles target specific problem areas. Mammograms, then, image breasts as squishy dense spheres. Yet, that density may prohibit their efficacy. Other limitations relate to size: too large or too small breasts are hard to grasp with existing equipment. Breast implants cause complications for imaging. In reading mammograms, radiologists look for variation between serial mammograms taken at a six-month, year or two-year interval. These variations can be shadows, the appearance of micro-calcifications, or other irregularities/ asymmetries in relation to the other breast or prior plates.

Mammograms can also be painful experiences. They squeeze the breast to flatten it out along defined angles.

Mammography, however, became part of an array of tool we have for the job of breast cancer screening. There are other tools that are complementary like Ultrasound and MRI. This arrangement of tools challenges the logic that one tool is effective for breast cancer screening and diagnosis. This may be due to the density and complexity of tissue. Combined these imaging techniques are efficacious in detecting breast cancer. The efficacy results from early detection of abnormality, which leads to more effective treatment. Mammograms couple with biopsies for non-palpable masses to ensure that the right location is sampled for abnormal cells. These cells may not yet form a sizable or dense enough lump to be detected by self or clinical breast exams.

However, the efficacy of imaging techniques is subject to certain biases: one, over-treatment of abnormalities that may not lead to serious pathology if left unchecked; two, the selection of slow growing cancers which are less deadly; three, self-selection of women who are more at risk; four, lead time from when an abnormality in a mammogram will become a detectable lump: this time is more significant in slow-growing tumors. (See Love, 2000; Naas et al, 2001)

In breast exams, the principals of size and symmetry matter. The texture of skin and the size or quality of the detected lumps matter. Larger breasts are more prone to disease. Asymmetries are also problematic if not congenital. Any swelling felt in the breast, armpits or clavicular lymph nodes is a sign of trouble. Examining breasts involves palpation of lump that can be cancerous. Figuring out which lumps are cancerous and which are not is not easy by touch. Breast exams have not proven to be the best means of identifying breast cancer. So breast exams couple with biopsy, mammography, and clinical exams. Usually when a lump is large enough to be palpable, this is taken for a sign of more advanced disease. However such statement is not completely accurate as some growths are benign in character or slow growing.

In clinical studies, self-breast-exams seem not to have a significant impact on an earlier breast cancer diagnosis. (See Love, 2000) Rather, they seem to cause for more vigilance and frequent biopsies. Self-breast exams (SBEs) , however, empower women to look for signs of disease. SBEs are more effective at an earlier age when no adequate screening technique is available. SBEs are also an educational tool about the risks and signs of the disease. Also, some women I interviewed reported that they were able to detect questionable lumps that physicians or mammograms did not detect and valued this procedure. (See Chapter 4) Breast exams had become the screening tool of choice before mammography was adopted. Breast exams still play a role in breast cancer detection though its relative value is hard to quantify.

Breast Tissue and Cells

Breast ducts and lobules branch throughout the breast. The branching doesn't fit into neat quadrants. Breast ducts and lobules are sites of precancerous change: Ductal or Lobular Cancer in Situ (DCIS or LCIS)/ Hyperplasia with atypical cells/ hyperplasia. Each is a description of a pre-cancer form more serious to less. Each characterizes breast epithelial cells as a point along their path to cancer. At some point, intra-ductal cancer bursts out of ducts becoming invasive or low-grade cancer. Two theories exist on how that happens: one that there is some property of precancerous cells that break down the duct walls; the other that an enzyme that prevents the cells from breaking down the duct walls stops working. Estrogen may weaken duct walls. Estrogen, also, works as a fuel to proliferate cell growth. From this finding, the distinction between cancer that is estrogen receptive positive and ones that are negative emerged. Estrogen receptive positive cancers are potentially preventable. Hormone therapies like Tomoxifen act as estrogen blockers in some tissues and as estrogen in others. These selective hormone receptor modulators (SERMs) can help stop cancers in tissue affected by hormonal change. (See Love, 2000)

Not all cancers relate to lobules and ducts as particular sites. The list of types of cancer grew from chapter 1. It includes the following as well as their combinations: Infiltrating ductal, Invasive Lobular, medulary, mucinous or colloid, tubular, adenocystic, papillary, carcinosarcoma, Paget's disease, inflammatory, in situ ductal and lobular. Any depiction of cancer as a percentage across each quadrant is misleading. When a duct becomes cancerous, the cancer may be in one duct/ lobule system, but cross many quadrants. (See Love, 2000)

Dr Love and others have developed a technique called ductal drainage that may allow for a targeted detection of certain kinds of pre-cancers. (See Love, 2000) This technique draws from the work of Dr. Papanicolaou who pioneered the technique in 1958. He, however, was not able to diagnose cancer using this technique and no one knew how to use this technique effectively until more recently. Ductal drainage could potentially be something like a pap smear for the breast. (See Papanicolaou, 1974) In 1917, Dr Papanicolaou first developed the technique of a smear in sex research. He used the vaginal smear of guinea pigs to stage their estrus cycle. (See Clarke, 1998)

What causes cancer is not fully clear. We do know that the causes are molecular and genetic in nature. We think that cancer is caused by a series of mutations. A cell will then become atypical and eventually abnormal or cancerous. There is a natural process meant to protect cells through an enzyme that corrects DNA. An abnormal cell will be killed if it cannot be corrected. This process is called apoptosis. However due to environmental or other reasons this enzyme may not work. All in all, cancerous cells are those with mutations in few key areas of DNA. One is the area regulates cell life and reproduction. Enzymes and hormones generally regulate cell life and reproduction. Irregularities in endocrine events may then secondarily impact cancer as it impacts immunity to the disease. So the primary causes are events that alter specific sections of a cell DNA to cause it to proliferate and/ or events that impact the body's ability to distinguish and kill abnormal cells. The second is the area that regulates chromosomal structure or genetic organization.

Cancerous cells are distinguished under the microscope by their nucleus size and cell shape. The nucleus becomes enlarged. The cell shape becomes irregular. These are rough indication of malignancy. Recently, the question of ploidity/ aneuploidy (e.g. abnormal number not diploid but triploid, tetraproid.... or general arrangement of chromosomes) as a cause of cancer has resurfaced. This would shift the focus for some cancers from a disease particular to genes that regulate cell life to that of genes responsible for genetic organization: the number and length of chromosomes. This hypothesis is still not completely worked out e.g. what genes are involved, but may account for the abnormal size and shape of the nucleus visible in many cancer cells.

Researchers have identified a few nodes of cancer causation: one changes to DNA through heredity (the inheriting of active DNA); changes to DNA due to viruses (external

DNA that is inserted through infection or silent DNA that was viral and became activated by hormones, stress, toxins...); changes to cell function that are hormonal (due to alteration in the internal environment: the ways that hormones activate particular cells); or toxic changes (external environment: the acts of mutagens or radiation that impact the DNA molecule and lead to the creation of atypical cells and/ or hormone like substances that impact cell growth and life). These events can be linked in a chain or sequence. Age is a compounding factor in cancer genesis. With age, cells loose their reparative qualities. More errors accumulate. These errors lead to the abnormal expression of genes. I will briefly elaborate each node of causation as well as how it potentially affects women and future treatment.

Causation: Viral/ Genetic

Viruses

Some sections of the genetic code are not articulated in each cell of the body. These sections may function as back up sites, cushions for mutations and or old viral DNA that managed to infect the human germ line. The DNA molecule is exceptionally long about 2 meters long and is packed in each chromatin and then linked to an identical copy. The DNA is composed of 4 different base molecules, which are linked in pairs (Adenine-Thymine: A-T/ T-A, Guanine-Cytosine: G-C/ C-G); a phosphate molecule and a sugar form the backbone. Each base pair across the two DNA strands has a distinct polarity in each direction so (A-T is different for T-A). The base pairs are linked together by hydrogen bonds. Across the length of DNA, we find the genetic code consists in 3 letter words composed of the four bases. The sets amount to 64 codons, which combine to form genes, which encode for proteins.

Some of the DNA code we inherit is silent. This silent DNA may be DNA that we do not understand. Some silent DNA we think is viral in origin. Viruses have DNA or RNA for sections for encoding information. These short strands are inserted into the human genome through infection. If viral DNA becomes inherited through the generations, it seems not to be expressed, e.g. not active in cell life. Silent DNA cushions active DNA from errors due to mutations or other random events as the likelihood of error at a particular site reduces along the length of the DNA molecule.

Viral code inserts into the human germ-line and may be inherited through the generations. This code is not active in cell life unless and until environmental or other factors interfere. Then a cell enters into a lysogenic cycle. Cancer may be the effect of activated viral DNA. Some of this DNA may have been retroviral in origin. A retrovirus is a virus that is encoded in two RNA strands that translate into host cellular DNA through reverse transcription. This DNA may be latent and remains silent, yet encapsulated in human DNA through the generations. HIV is an example of a retrovirus. We know that this virus crossed species barriers from primates to humans. There are also questions about the nature of HIV and if it is the primary cause for AIDS. Some questions have arisen as to whether HIV viral strands cause in and of themselves the diseases associated with the syndrome of AIDS, e.g. opportunistic infections. (See Papadopoulos et al, 2004; Duesberg, 1988)

Some cancers, then, may be caused by infection of viruses or pathogens. This infection follows two paths: one from an external virus and two from the activation of silent viral DNA. The viral model for breast cancer causation has not been widely explored. Some results are promising. A specific virus that causes breast cancer in the mouse is a site of interest: mammary tumor virus (MMTV). (See Bingren Liu, et al, 2001) MMTV is known to transmit from parent to offspring through two routs: endogenous and exogenous. The first is the effect of viral DNA that inserted itself in the germ-line of the parent. The second passes through the consumption of mother's milk.

The human version of this virus (human mammary tumor virus-- HMTV) is found in about 40% of breast cancers. (See Holland and Pogo, 2004) This virus is said to originate from the mouse which caries the disease. It crosses species barriers and it is much more frequent in areas that are abundant in mice with MMTV, which may explain the prevalence of breast cancer in certain geographic populations. The viral hypothesis for cancer causation held sway in the 70s and 80s, but the evidence was inconclusive.

In the 90s, research shifted to the genetic components of the disease. Inheritance, however, accounts for a small fraction of breast cancers. Thus viral, hormonal and environmental factors need to be fully examined to determine their relevance. Recent literature re-examines the role HMTV (human mammary tumor virus) in human breast cancers in light of new molecular and genetic techniques. If HMTV hypothesis holds sway, there is a solid a possibility for developing specific vaccines to treat/ prevent the subsequent breast cancers. (See Garry, 2004) The virus is shown to be causative for breast cancers as infections and antibodies precede the cancer. The virus connected with cancers that may occur during breastfeeding. A question remains whether a re-infection of the mouse virus occurs or whether the Human strand, which is similar, developed long ago. (See Holland and Pogo, 2004) Because of the nature of viral infection, women may fear breastfeeding their children. This is true for mouse tumors, but has not been shown to be true for humans.

If HMTV is transmitted through breast milk, women may hesitate to breastfeed. We know breastfeeding passes maternal antibodies to children and may be key in their fight against childhood infections. Finally, we have not found a vaccine capable of stopping any viral causation of breast cancer. Vaccines have been developed to successfully deal with most cervical cancers that follow from the Human Papillomavirus (HPV). Controversy has followed the development of the vaccine as Christian scientists feel that it would undercut the abstinence message to adolescent girls. (See Cohen, 2005) Vaccines based on immune recognition of cancer show promise. (See Riddell, 2001)

Hereditary and genetic modes of cancer causation can be true in different cases. Both inherited mutations and pathogens can lead to genetic dysfunction within a cell that we come to characterize as cancer. Viral DNA does not have a particular function within the human body other than to insert itself in a host cell and replicate. An infected cell will be silent or it may reproduce the virus. In the first case, it follows the lysogenic cycle. In the second it follows the lytic cycle. The two are not necessarily distinct modes of viral reproduction. The human body mounts an immune response to viral infections and sometimes is able to stave off infection. Some organ systems may be infected even though the host appears to be healthy. The virus tends to be in a latency stage. Some never exit latency except in moments of severe stress. Hereditary mutations are clear in their effect if we think of them as misspellings to existing functioning genes, but these misspellings may also be a secondary byproduct of infection or toxins. Such clarity is put into question the relation of viral and host DNA. This relation becomes less determined over the long durations of evolutionary time. Finally, gene expression plays a role.

BRCA 1 and 2 genes, which are actually classes of mutations at particular sites within the genome, associate with high rates of cancer mortality and link with intermarrying populations. In intermarrying populations, the hypothesis is that mutation load increases in future generations. In other cases, a mutation may be a result of a carcinogen or a viral infection or be latent and then articulated by other epigenetic processes. These changes may not be heritable, but they may impact the germ-line of the next generation. Epigenetic, viral, toxic or mutation effects results in genetic instability and may in the long haul have adverse consequences for human populations. The questions about cancer causation reflect gene/ parasite/ environment (internal/ external) interactions. We seek to discover the sequences of events that lead to cancer. These questions are at the core of life and evolution. They also help us begin to understand the birth of neoplasms in modern societies.

Genes

In contrast to viral DNA, that can cause cancer infection or through activation of silent DNA, genes implicated in cancer are inherited mutations, and active or expressed in cell function. That is, they are mutations inherited in the human germ-line through the generations and expressed in particular tissues that compounds abnormalities in cell life leading to cancer. Since the body has natural defenses against abnormal cells, the key areas of cancer genesis are the area of the DNA that regulates cell life and death and the area that encodes for enzymes that recognize or correct cell error. The genetic composition of cancer cells is 'unstable.' This genetic instability in some instances means mutations in the area that is responsible for maintaining chromosomes. Aneuploidy is a particular phenomenon of abnormal number and organization of chromosomes that is common in cancer cells as well as other inherited genetic diseases.

We know that BRCA 1 and 2 are inherited mutations leading to breast cancer in families with a history of the disease. These genes are recent discoveries. They lead to particular kinds of genetic instability. The BRCA 1 gene is located on the long arm of chromosome 17 at position 21, which is the tumor suppressor area and in the breast it inhibits the growth of milk duct epithelial cells. The BRCA 1 protein is shorter. It interacts with other proteins that regulate DNA repair leading to genetic instability. Both BRCA 1 and 2 genes impact the function of other genes as well as suppress tumors, which are the two checkpoints towards tumor causation. (See Venkitaraman, 2002) The BRCA 2 gene is located on the 13th chromosome at the 12.3 position. BRCA 2 functions similarly BRCA 1 though it is different. Genetic polymorphisms characterize both genes. BRCA 1 -- 600 mutations. BRCA 2 – 450 mutations. These genes are inherited through an autosomal dominant fashion that means that one copy is enough to cause the disease.

These 'genes' have differential penetrance. This means that not every woman or man with the BRCA 1 or 2 genes has the same probability or type of breast, ovarian or colon cancer. So the initial postulation that all women with this mutation are at extremely high levels of risk is not necessarily as true if it is not followed by the statement that these women belong to a family at high risk for the disease. The BRCA 1 'gene' in particular came to be known as the 'Jewish gene' or more specifically 'the Ashkenazi gene' as it is frequent within this population. This is a misnomer. We have associated this gene with populations that have high rates of intermarriage. (Love, 2000) However, we do not know the exact probability of one particular cancer-causing event in a lifetime, bar the genetic mutation for high-risk families. Hereditary forms of breast cancers are about 5% to 10% of all cancers. BRCA 1 and 2 mutations account for 75% of heritable breast cancers. Other genes may play a role as well.

Variable penetrance means more changes must occur in the DNA code for tumor formation to begin. These events can be other mutations, hormonal, dietary or lifestyle events. Methylation may be an epigenetic process responsible for some variable aspects of tumor genesis. This process holds promise in braking down the sequencing of events that lead to non-hereditary cancer-genesis. It, also, may show the ways that gene/ environment interact through inflammation due to radiation or toxins. The genetic risk for the disease lends itself to the logic of an event probability. As a probability, its relation to outcomes is different from an accumulated risk of extraneous factors that lead to the disease.

Prophylactic oopherectomies are specific treatments, which may alter the risk for breast cancer in women. (See Chapter 5) However BRCA1 cancers tend to be considered estrogen-receptor negative cancers. So the logic of oopherectomy as their treatment is not all that clear. Some indications that Tomoxifen may in fact improve the outlook for non-receptor estrogen cancers, also, puts into question whether there are other pathways for estrogen to have an effect on tumor genesis in the breast. Genetic testing, then, is a potentially useful tool in that it establishes the grounds for estrogen receptor negative cancer though estrogen may still play a role.

In the cases where a definitive inherited mutation is at play in the chain of events that lead to cancer, pharmacogenetics may play a role in therapy as well as retroviral gene vectors/ viruses. Pharmacogenetics seeks to make drugs specific to tumor characteristics and shared biologies. (See Pusztai et al, 2005) or gene vectors to supplement the functions of BRCA genes. (See Khalili, 2006) Decisions based on genetic information must be tempered with the knowledge that we are not clear about cancer causation and heredity. Probability should not be treated as eventuality. For women at hereditary risk, two troublesome situations occur. One is that women are afraid of having children for fear of passing on the curse of breast cancer. The other is that they feel hopeless with regard to treatment. So they end up having radical treatments from prophylactic operations and preventative hormone therapy to allay anxiety and risk. (See Chapter 5)

Recently, epigenetic processes seem key in tumor genesis. The process of methylation is essential in the expression or silencing of the human DNA. (See Rodenhiser and Mann, 2006) Methylation refers to a molecular process that adds a methyl group to the CpG (Cytosine-Guanine) di-nucleotide in a DNA strand. This di-nucleotide occurs in rare 'islands' within chromosomes. These regions promote gene expression or silencing. Methylated Cytosine, then, functions like the fifth molecule in the four-molecule DNA chain. Gene expression may be the key to understanding environmental/ hereditary interactions in the articulation of the disease.

Epigenetic processes are also connected with the expression of BRCA 1 genes. In particular, hypermethylation may prove to be a pathway for intervention. For ovarian cancers, molecular techniques have opened a window to study the early trajectory of the disease. No adequate biomarker exists. Ovarian cancer is detected late to warrant good prospects for survival. The question of timing is embedded in the science of 'precancers' and early cancers for both breast and ovarian cancer, where now intervening on a precancerous condition means finding a pathway to arrest the process of disease at a molecular level.

Causation: Hormonal/ Toxic

Hormones

Hormonal causation of breast cancer has become clear. Estrogen plays an important role in tumor growth for tumors that are not hereditary in nature. Hereditary cancers (BRCA

1 positive) tend to be estrogen receptor negative while BRCA 2 positive cancers have an estrogen effect and others yet have estrogen receptors. Estrogen is the growth fuel for breast cancer cells. Estrogen may also weaken the duct and lobule walls liable then to release abnormal cells into breast tissue to form a lump. Hormonal causes of cancer affect women in particular because they have implications for childbirth decisions. Lesbians are a group at higher risk for cancer. This may be due to diet, lifestyle and childbirth decisions. (See Saunders, J. M. 1999) These issues should not run a woman's life however. Women need to be mindful and make choices that best suit them. Lets' take each potential hormonal risk one by one.

One, hormonal events in a woman's natural lifecycle can cause an increase in cancer risk. These are early onset of menstruation or late onset of menopause. They are not events that a woman can alter. Women on birth control pills may increase their chance of breast cancer. However, some studies suggested the opposite. Women who have children early are apparently less at risk because during pregnancy women do not have periods which means that they are not subject to hormonal variations of the estrus cycle. Having children late might increase breast cancer risk. We do not know how much. What is the tangible value for all these risks?

Two, hormonal events related to lifestyle choices. Diet high in saturated fats can increase breast cancer risk. An adolescent sedentary lifestyle may lead to breast cancer risk in later years. Also, weight gain due to sedentary lifestyle in general increases risk as does alcohol consumption. Certain foods like soy protein in a low saturated fat diet may actually reduce risks for heart disease and breast cancer. However, soy as a phytoestrogen supplement may increase breast cancer risk. (See Usui, 2006) Three, hormonal events related to medical decisions such as taking estrogen supplements at menopause. HRT is known to increase breast cancer risk, but it also decreases the incidence of osteoporosis and heart disease. Tomoxifen and other SERMs serve as a way to grant a selective estrogen effect to certain tissue. In other words, SERMs act as estrogen blockers in the breasts, but still have the positive estrogen effects on the heart and bones. In this way, SERMs may prevent breast cancer.

For women, the hormone effect on breast and ovarian cancer causation makes them weary of certain life decisions. Some medical and public health officials have used increases in breast cancer morbidity as a way to advocate that women lead a particular lifestyle. This requires early motherhood when most are simply not mature enough to take care of the young or take care of our selves. Delayed motherhood has the advantage of allowing women to develop a career and a strong sense of self before taking on the responsibility of childbirth. Also not all women must be required to marry and have children. Some have genuinely different sexual orientation and should be allowed to live a healthy productive and full life within the parameters of that choice. Some also may choose to have children.

Toxins

Toxins such as pesticides, organochlorides, dioxides may have an estrogen effect, or act as mutants to sensitive areas of DNA. Excessive radiation also affects the body and may cause breast cancer. Toxic and environmental carcinogenesis may lead to tumors that are harder to understand and predict as the ways that these toxins affect the body may produce cells that are difficult to identify, harder to destroy, and less predictable than ones that result from known viral or genetic elements. Toxins, acting as hormones, may fuel existing or compound potential carcinogenesis. Toxins, acting as mutants, impact existing DNA structures leading to instability. Toxins, enhancing the process of (hyper or hypo) methylation, impact gene expression. Inflammation due to radiation or toxins may be responsible for some epigenetic effects in cancer genesis.

Toxicology and environment/ gene interaction are an important piece, but so far we think of toxins acting along the side of biological pathways for the disease. We do not have a clear sense of dosage and length of exposure to have any meaningful sense of the actual effect of a particular toxic agent. Some are present in the environment in low dosages. Studies into cancer clusters have so far been unable to yield particular connections between exposure and disease like the Long Island study or similar studies of cancer cluster elsewhere. Environmental exposure tends to have a class effect in so far as people of low income/ racial-ethnic minority communities have less choice but to accept hazards in their back yards or live in areas that are near industry.

Let me give an example. A byproduct of DDT can be found in the breasts of women with environmental exposure to such pesticide. How toxins affect the body is not totally clear. Research into toxins and their cancer consequence is difficult as onco-genesis takes a long time. However, a mutation due to exposure to a chemical agent is common. The best cure is the removal of the environmental toxin. The body has natural processes to induce cell death so in most instances such mutations on their own do not lead to cancer. (See Love, 2001)

Toxins as a cause for breast cancer are understudied. This is in part a byproduct of the medical model where illness is defined as an individual responsibility and is an effect of a particular biological agent. Toxins are more defused in the environment and may differentially affect women, depending on their proneness to disease as well as their age. Research into the toxicology of cancer-genesis has been stunted. The government and industry are not inclined to deal with this cause of cancer. (See Proctor, 1995)

Pollution, pesticides, food additives, some cosmetics and excessive radiation from the depletion of the ozone layer may all be contributing to neoplasms, which down the line are harder to diagnose and treat.

Causation: Multi-factorial

Animal Models

Mice are specifically apt lab animals because their reproduction cycle is short enough to allow for breeding many generations, but also mice are genetically close to humans. Mice may be the origin for a trans-species viral infection. The mouse became an ideal (e.g. practical and profitable) animal model for research into both causation and treatment of breast cancer. (See Malakoff, 2000) Mice became a cottage industry raking in money and leading scientists to produce new and enticing breeds to compete for the science makers of tomorrow!

There are a few ways that mice or rats are used in breast cancer research. One is through the xenograph model. The transposition of human tumor cells on mice. The other is through developing specific stands of mice. These mice have biological markers, which mimic the pathways of human breast cancer. In this regard, research proceeded in vitro and in vivo as well as across species. Two kinds of strategies for using mice: one targeting the molecular mechanisms of the disease trying to identity 'early' biomarkers and treatments; the other targeting advanced cancers, the process of matastasis. (See Heppner et al, 2000)

Mice and other animal models have come under criticism as not being entirely accurate in terms of the trajectory of the breast cancer in humans. (See Wagner, 2004) Still, they have became the animal counterparts even 'companions' to human suffering in the development of bio-scientific research of cancer and in the development of current therapies. (See Haraway, 1997; 2003) In our understanding of biomedical knowledge production, we must also account for the costs in human and animal life in biomedical advancement.

Eliminating animal cruelty in medical research is important while not prohibiting essential research into human and animal disease. Improving in vitro technique and establishing standards for reducing/ eliminating animal suffering is the second step. (Gruber and Hartung, 2004) In cancer research, investigators are now obliged to limit tumor growth at a certain size and to avoid unnecessary distress to the animal before sacrificing it. Such standards are put in place by regulation. (See ILAR, 1996) At the moment, animal models are still needed for the progression of cancer research. The use of animal models helps to test both the molecular causation and therapeutic basis of cancer. Mice and rats account for 77% of animal used. (See Baumans, 2004) With a better understanding of molecular and cellular processes, research will likely move to in vitro systems and focus on the early biomarkers for the disease. In such a case, animal models will be less prominent and essential in future cancer research.

Risk and Probability Models

In trying to balance several co-factors that contribute to the development of breast cancer, Dr M. Gail developed a computer risk model. This model uses demographic variables like age and race; life style issues such as age at first live birth and age at menarche; as well as personal and family history: number of biopsies, history of atypical hyperplasia and how many first-degree relatives had breast cancer. A score above 1.7 was considered high risk and subject to further scrutiny and treatment. (See Gail et al, 1989)

This model is not a good measure for genetic risk for breast cancer because it does not account for second-degree relatives. It, also, does not account for other important lifestyle and hormonal effects such as exposure to toxins and radiation or age of menopause, and birth control use. All in all it is a good model to measure risk for white women with access to mammography. (See Gail and Constantino, 2001) There is evidence to suggest that race/ ethnicity is an important factor in breast cancer incidence and morbidity. (See Chlebowski, 2005) However, the exact implications of such findings are not clear. Some are attributed to lifestyle and diet changes. Some might be environmental. Some are a question of access to high quality care.

Dr. Clauss has developed a risk model that would account better for hereditary cancers by including second-degree cancers in a computation of risk. His model focused solely on hereditary cancers and age of onset. His model did not incorporate other risk factors or breast/ ovarian cancers associated with paternal line of inheritance. Better probability models for predicting a gene carrier emerged. However, they had limitations with regard to race and ethnicity. (See Domcheck et al, 2003)

Genetic testing establishes the probability of hereditary cancer in a lifespan. This is an estimate of a probability not a risk estimate. Even though in common usage risk and probability are conflated, risk and probability have slightly different meanings. Risk implies the definition of potential harm that follows from a present process, which may be governed. Insurance is built to measure and govern such risks using the precautionary principles by actions or knowledge grounded in a cost/ benefit analysis. (See Sunstein, 2005) Probability is not subject to such analysis because one, probability reflects the concrete likelihood of a discrete event (negative or positive) to occur which follows a natural or random process and because two, probability reflects the uncertainty embedded in what can be known about such process.

For example, being BRCA 1 or 2 positive implies an estimated 40 to 80% probability of breast cancer in a lifespan. This probability is an estimated absolute value for breast cancer as a particular individual hazard. Such number reflects a particular natural process that leads to a particular outcome. This probability is subject to scientific uncertainty or error and the random process of genetic recombination through the generations. On the other hand, being at risk for breast cancer implicates the actual harm that follows as a result of an accumulation of behaviors, situations, and decisions, which may be governable, whose outcome then is much less certain, measured, or determined. The logic of risk then holds each of us accountable for a particular outcome.

Medical/ Clinical Juncture

Breast cancer diagnosis and treatment moves between three phases: one risk assessment and genetic testing, two screening and diagnosis, and three treatment and prevention. During those moments the intersection of medical science and clinical practice is visible.

A breast cancer prognosis follows from risk assessment. In contrast to risk assessment, genetic testing is a new way to define the hereditary probability for breast cancer. This probability will take the form of an 'absolute risk value,' which may be less subject to events. Computational models of risk take into account other variables. They are recent means of dealing with chronic disease such as breast cancer. These models built in biases about health seeking behavior. So they are not as accurate across ethnic or race populations. Genetic testing seeks to supplement existing risk assessment for hereditary markers of the disease. These tools are new. At best, they are used to 'educate' women about breast cancer and what can be done with the available tools and science to manage it.

Diagnosis and screening in our current arrangement highlights mammography, breast exams and biopsy. Not all women are able to follow the regimen of frequent mammography. Mammograms miss some types of tumors: one in young women or women whose breast are dense, two tumors that are too fast or slow growing. Breast exams are a buffer. They allow women some control over their breast health even though their efficacy is not proven. They supplement mammograms and clinical exams.

Biopsy combines with mammograms to identify the kind of lump at hand. When speaking of Lobular or Ductal cancer in situ both breast exams and mammograms are not effective. Breast drainage may be a way to identify the earliest signs of disease in a duct system and it may well serve as a breast pap smear. Classifying, the nature of breast cancer cells in more concrete ways than simply the shape of the cell and size of the nucleus may clarify some of the causation issues with regard to the disease. Clearly, cancer is a multi event process where our cells and our cellular defenses break down.

Treatment follows along the lines of slash-surgery, burn-radiation and poison-chemotherapy. (See Knopf-Newman, 2004) Surgery removes the tumor and most affected tissue. Radiation shrinks the size of a tumor to an operable state. Chemotherapy deals with loose cancer cells. These cells have the quality of reproducing frequently so they are more readily targeted. Specific chemotherapies are now developed for specific kinds of cancer cells. Targeted chemotherapy, then, will not affect the rest of the body and its regeneration process. As better chemotherapies develops. Surgery becomes more conservative in its scope. Its target is to facilitate the health of the immune system and its response against the disease.

Prevention follows along the lines of early detection of pre-cancers or very early cancers. Now prevention has taken a new meaning for estrogen positive cancers. That is, the preventative use of SERMs. Tomoxifen, roloxifen and now herceptin are drugs, which are more targeted to certain kinds of breast cancer. Roloxifen showed promise initially, but that promise has not been born out. These drugs may increase the risks for other diseases such as heart disease. (See Love, 2000)

In terms of future trends, pharmacogenetics/ genomics shows promise for breast cancers that are due to specific mutations. Such drugs might actually retain normal cell cycles for women who inherited a genetic mutation in the tumor suppressor area of the genome. The development of vaccines for breast cancer that is due to infection is also probable. Vaccines also are developed to help stimulate an immune response to cancer: e.g. immuno-therapies. For estrogen positive cancers, hormone prevention with SERMs is likely to yield strong results as these types of drugs better target the estrogen flow in breast tissue.

For cancers resulting from environmental stimuli, no clear answers are present as the cells, which follow, seem more atypical.

The question of timing becomes even more profound as treatment moves away from surgery. In the early radical surgery model, all cancer cells must be removed with the operation for a chance at success. Now it has become clear that surgery may become important in more 'advanced' growths. Loose cells are targeted with chemotherapy. With the genetization and further molecularization of cancer as a disease, the goal of research was to develope specific biomarkers to establish the potential for cancer, the pathways for disease progression, and ways to intervene before the actual advent of cancer cells.

New interventions are molecular agents that supplement the function of faulty genes (mutated or inherited) or retroviral viral vectors that add sections of healthy DNA, or vaccines that provide anticancer antigens. The paradigm of slash, burn and poison will yield its place to new and better tools. The paradigm (slash, burn, poison) took over the radical debilitating surgeries of the beginning of the 20th century. Advances in molecular and genetic science coupled with a better understanding of immunology and basic cancer genesis may in fact spell the end of the dread for the dread disease.

For women embedded in current medical science/ practice, many new possible solutions to the disease emerge. Until those materialize women still have to make choices about surgery, chemo and hormone therapy. Navigating breast cancer is not easy. (See Chapters 4 and 5) In addition to dealing with a potentially deadly disease that has been synonymous with a painful prolonged agonizing death, modern women are embedded in multiple at times contradictory narratives of emancipation, work, motherhood and care giving.

Being at loss for losing a breast is serious. The loss is multiple: a loss of a site of pleasure, a loss of a site of nurturance, a loss of feminine identity, and for some a loss invested with a different personal or polemical identity. Breast reconstruction then becomes contested in how women begin to manage such loss. Some prefer to retain the scar as a rite of passage into a life where breast cancer becomes an active personal concern, a life measured through the narratives of survival. Some prefer to be made into a new 'whole' through cosmetic surgery. The choice needs to be respected.

Conclusion

Defining breast cancer is key in understanding the emerging array of new treatments. These may cure and better define particular instances of this disease. The question of whether a particular breast cancer is a combination of viral or genetic alterations and environmental or hormonal effects is important in determining appropriate directions for future research and treatment. Radiation or toxins, which may not act like estrogen, may cause mutations that lead to cancer. These cancer cells may be too abnormal to predict how they would act in the body or to identify and kill. The environmental aspects of breast cancer need particular attention now that molecular science has began to unravel the pathways for the disease. They have not received its due in part because the studies have been inconclusive.

Defining breast cancer is not simply a biomedical question. It is a social question, a political question, a personal question, and a woman's question. Women participate in the development of scientific knowledge about the disease. They are particularly interested in a positive conclusion to the condition of living with the risk of breast cancer. As this disease has been better defined, and as better treatments have begun to be developed the duration of life with breast cancer bettered in quality and quantity. In this regard, breast cancer as a disease has shifted from being acute, when women died a painful death to being chronic where women began to meaningfully live with the disease. Not all medical diseases follow such trajectory towards cure. Antibiotics and vaccines were able to halt and eradicate the spread of other diseases much more rapidly. When we are speaking of cancer, which is the effect of a multi event process, or AIDS, whose viral cause shape-shifts, the medical solution is not simple. A shift from an acute disease to chronic one allows for the time to sort out the pathways of the disease and establish a meaningful a cure.

At the moment, other infectious diseases have become perplexing due to drug resistance. This results from improper administration of drugs where cells infected with a virus such as TB learn to survive the treatments meant to eliminate them and the virus. Drug resistance is a problem with certain forms of cancer that are not responsive to existing treatments as well as AIDS. The days of sanatoriums, of AIDS or cancer wards seem long past, yet in a society threatened with incurable, deadly contagious diseases such practices may enjoy a return. It is in the interests of all to establish responsible and responsive structures to manage existing and emergent diseases especially when we face the threat bio-terrorism, the threat of disease used as warfare. These structures, then, must take into account individual liberties such as the right to life and privacy, as well as shared interests of maintaining public health.

Our biomedical notions of disease structure the paradigm of cure and the direction of future research. These notions reside in the nexus between medicine and society. Understanding the timing of medical actions and interactions requires understanding and mapping out contingencies, uncertainties and probabilities that otherwise get eroded in the historical narratives of progress, right, and triumph. Clearly medical action needs to take into account both the needs of knowledge, the needs of cure and care.

Animal models have filled the gap between what is plausible in human trials with the disease and the needs/interests of medical knowledge. Medical knowledge comes at a price. This price is paid in suffering, in blood and tears. Animals in the case of breast cancer: mice and rats are bred to fill in the gap left from what is possible in human research and are scarified for the purposes of our knowledge and health. The use of animals in medical research needs to be regulated to ensure that animal suffering is limited. In vitro systems and techniques show potential in taking over most scientific needs for in vivo models.

Sometimes research into the human inconsistencies with treatments needs to be pursued. Human inconsistencies to medication and treatment are the subject of both the particularity of disease progression for that individual as well as the distinct biologies that are produced by ancestry, ethnic, racial or geographic groupings. We are finding that biological differences matter in medicine, in the development of appropriate therapeutics. However, those differences must not be politicized, subject to the explanation of social inequity. In other words, biological difference should not be racialized and be converted into the justification for social and political inequity or adverse public policy. At the same time, an operational medical paradigm must allow for corrections and reframing of its positions with new insight even if that means re-ordering of the relation between medical and clinical. Medical paradigms at times become entrenched in their norms and practices. These norms and practices need to ensure that new and promising formations of disease and new arrangements of treatment emerge.

In the case of breast cancer, the question of professional dominance is key. Surgeons have played a primary role in defining and treating this disease for most of the 20th century. Emerging professions similarly vie for the definition of disease and its treatment to gain credibility. Disease becomes redefined on the grounds of new chain of causation, with new sites for intervention. In the case of breast cancer, it would be viral, genetic, hormonal and toxic. An operational autonomy yet interdependence between medical and clinical science/ practice will ensure that the emerging order does not preclude the conditions of betterment and change.

The medical-clinical-social arrangement becomes clearer as new factors, actors, technologies, and facts emerge. To govern them, we must understand the complex nature of biosocial medicine: the roles that women as patients, consumers, and communities play; the decisions of lawmakers, employers and insurers; the practice/ knowledge of biomedical scientists and caregivers. Medical institutions in particular become the contested sites of knowledge, law, and hope. Medical institutions settle actors/ actants/ and interactions. Their relatedness becomes visible if one is mindful of the scale and power of events and collectives to define disease, treatment, and target populations at risk.

Women and Breast Cancer

Every one of the 180,000 American women diagnosed each year is still individually responsible for getting herself screened, biopsied, treated, and monitored. And those lucky enough to escape a positive diagnosis (this time) are, equally, burdened with the responsibility to maintain their disease-free state (through so-called lifestyle modifications like diet and exercise). These are the symptoms of an implied social policy that, in the absence of an effective cure, emphasizes the individual rather than the social control over the disease.

-- Leopold, 1999

Introduction

When we are born, we become citizens of this world. Our illness, health, or disability shapes our status as citizen. (See Sontag, 1977; Ong, 1998) It, also, structures how we imagine our lives. Breast cancer as a medical disease effects the structure, quality and lifespan of women at risk. Being at risk for breast cancer, women[9] tangle between health and illness. They navigate uncertainties of screening, diagnosis, and treatment. Women become cautious. Even if managing breast cancer grows easier, women shoulder the risk and onset of this disease alone, at times in silence. This began to change with an emphasis on the psychosocial aspects of a cancer diagnosis, which begins to deal with the fear of the disease. The lives and bodies of women who handle breast cancer become pioneers. These women may help re-structure medical practice through their participation in research and activism.

The modern condition of breast cancer is defined through notions such as risk and responsibility. These notions are lived as norms. They instruct women in their response to

---

[9] Rarely, men experience breast cancer about 1% of cases treated and 2% of those are subject to bilateral mastectomy. Men seem to be diagnosed later in the disease trajectory because men are not regularly screened. The treatment of male cancers is different as well as they require mastectomy at times removing muscle due to the general small size of male breasts. (See Kahla et al, 2005)

medicine as an institution of care and knowledge as well as cancer as a disease. Women subject to breast cancer are also members of communities learning to cope with uncertainties of health and illness and new medical techniques.

Being at Risk

If women are born into a cancer prone family, they might find support and comfort there. If at high risk, breast cancer becomes an added concern. It becomes a life-long task of maintaining awareness and developing personal strategies to handle a rapidly changing care environment and a potentially deadly disease. Defined as a personal responsibility, breast cancer becomes independent of communicable agents (environmental toxicity, viruses, radiation, or additives in the food or water supply to name a few). Breast cancer as a disease, then, is neither subject to targeted prevention efforts nor environmental accountability.

Prevention equates with the earliest possible detection of the disease and intervention upon women. The discourse of precaution plays a role in individualizing breast cancer. Women's participation, conformity, and vigilance, then, become requisite for their survival. Being at risk implies dealing with multiple uncertainties. These are: (1) breast cancer causation is not clear; (2) treatment, detection, and cure are not certain; (3) the disease is debilitating/ traumatizing in the least and potentially deadly. Being at risk, also, has begun to organize women into collectives, which may have more say in the future of the structures that handle this disease.

First, breast cancer is a disease with multiple causation pathways. (See Chapter 2) This multiplicity of causation places a burden on women to avert this disease. Second, depending on their levels of risk -- perceived and assessed -- as well as personal styles of managing risk and uncertainty, women choose to follow different treatment trajectories. (See Chapter V, Becker and Kaufman, 1995) Sometimes women adopt a more aggressive stance towards risk with prophylactic surgeries and chemoprevention. (See Table 4 for an array of treatments, and graph 2 for a map of the breast care arena)

In current medical practice, genetic technologies and knowledge allow the targeting of breast cancer risk in advance of its occurrence. However, it does not alter the style and content of medical interventions as of yet. Rather, genetic technologies affect their timing. With genetic testing, treatment becomes a question of prophylaxis. Prophylactic surgery is the main treatment option available independently or with the addition of chemoprevention. The extent and combination of these treatments depends on the style of treatment: aggressive, prophylactic, breast conserving, watchful waiting. These are the current options for governing the risk of the disease. Finally, being at risk translates into dealing with issues of death and disability. Recently, the psychosocial dimensions of managing breast cancer have become prominent. Support groups for patients and family members help in alleviating some of the stress, alienation and hopelessness felt in facing this disease. Supports also establish the grounds for survival, for buffering uncertainty!

Survival and Hope

In most cases today, we evaluate breast cancer treatment along the lines of survival. The language of cure has been used, but its effect is largely rhetorical. That is, to recruit, energize, and mobilize women around a particular medical construct of a treatable disease. (See Lerner, 2001 and 2000) Survival is the number of years lived from the moment of treatment. The 'survival' line denotes a cancer free interval of at least five to ten years depending on the classification of beast cancer and its stage. In contrast to the notion of survival, a medical cure would establish conditions of full recovery -- with the end of life being a different cause altogether independent of the stage of the disease. Our breast cancer paradigm, then, produces a conditional cure for a defined duration.

As survival rates increase and extend, the quality of life lived after treatment must also become better. With extensions in survival, breast cancer shifts between acute and deadly to a potentially chronic condition and concern. With the advent of better diagnosis/ detection, physicians identify breast cancer sooner, allowing women and families more time to manage it. Before surgery (palliative or therapeutic), deaths from cancer tended to be long in duration, highlighting the *ing* in dying. Cancer was marked with prolonged pain and suffering not just for the individual, but also for the family responsible for caring. That is why even today attitudes towards cancer reflect dread for the disease. (See Patterson, 1987)

The narrative of hope is essential to the medical management of the disease. Today, physicians and women do not associate cancer with a horrible prolonged death or with unbearable suffering. Today some women can survive one and even two bouts of breast cancer. After surviving their first cancer episode, women live with an increased likelihood of disease recurrence at higher high risk. The advent of genetic and other risk assessment tools have made cancer into a chronic concern. Diseases like cancer subvert the logic of chronic and acute and replace it with long-term strategies of managing being at risk. (See Baker, 1991; Hann, 1996)

Being at increased risk defines the parameters for a treatable disease as well as the kinds of interventions available to manage it. Managing risk, dealing with the likelihood of recurrence, or even a second cancer diagnosis disrupts the logic of chronic and acute (as well

as the care arrangement that follows this division between the clinic/ hospital). (See Graph 1)
Centers specializing in cancer care have emerged to provide adequate up to date care for both
clinical and specialized laboratory or surgical interventions. A similar shift from acute to
chronic occurred with AIDS. The drug cocktails extended both length and quality of life of
persons with HIV and subsequently displaced the survival line for this illness. The result is a
re-definition of the condition from an immanent untreatable threat to one that we manage
with some level of success over time. AIDS drugs begin to provide that time, but also drug
resistant strains threaten this success. (See Monette, 1988)

Risk and Inequality

Inequity in breast cancer outcomes is a complex phenomenon. Inequality is cultural,
social, political, and economic. It is the unintended effect of policy, of building medical
infrastructure, of wording, and circulating information, as well as of personal styles in
managing risk, treatment, and detection.

The logic of being at risk appears benign, yet can reinforce inequality. It
individualizes breast cancer since it becomes an added responsibility that requires the time,
know-how, and access to navigate available cure/care arrangements. Women of color, poor
women, and women who are older have differing levels of skill and access to care. They are,
thus, less able to manage this disease or the potential of this disease.

This implicit requirement can explain differing outcomes along with other more
obvious inequalities. Although breast cancer incidence is more frequent in white women,
black women are diagnosed later and have increased mortality/ morbidity. (See Zones, 2000)
Structural inequities of current medical practice exacerbate poor outcomes. Those

inequalities result from the availability and use of medical infrastructure, the sensitivity of medical professionals to care and work with culturally, sexually (gender and orientation), and racially different persons and styles of managing risks and illness.

Understanding the medical framework for breast care is important to understand any inequities that it produces or reinforces. At the interfaces between women and medicine, medicine and inequality two questions come to mind: how did our current care arrangement emerge? In what ways has the structure of care influenced women's actions and their experiences with the disease and arranged them so unequally? To answer these questions, a historical trajectory of therapeutics (breast surgery, chemotherapy, radiation) and diagnostics (biopsy, breast exams, mammography, genetic testing) is necessary.

This sketch shows the sedimentation of the current care environment. It, also, shows the development and modification of treatment paradigms. There, I stage the interplay between women's experiences with this disease and how its care structures these experiences at times structures them differently. To examine the interface of women's collective action upon medicine, I will look to woman's breast health movements and the development of breast cancer societies. Health movements have shaped institutions of care in ways that meet the needs of a diverse group of women. Important is to take advantage of emerging technologies, and to invest in structures of care that empower women in the process of handling this disease.

Treatments

At the turn of the 20th century, surgeons set the parameters for breast cancer care and cure. (See Montini and Ruzek, 1989; Leopold, 1999; Lerner, 2001; Olson, 2002) Claiming success in curing breast cancer, surgeons were able to accumulate credit and transform medical practice and science. Reforms of medical science in terms of instrumentation/ experimentation and profession/ institution building allowed surgery as a profession to dominate the juncture of medical, clinical, and social thought/ action in handling breast cancer as a disease.

The surgical cure structured the medicalization of women at risk and 'socialized' tools -- treatment and diagnostic -- used to supplement surgery in managing this disease. The surgical cure was not successful however in eradicating this disease. Thus, women still experience the contingencies associated with medical knowledge making in breast care. Learning how to live with breast cancer risk and medical uncertainties in terms of treatment and knowledge is necessary for most women as they age and become subject to breast cancer risk. By managing risk, women establish a level of control over their body and health. New strategies to manage disease risks and uncertainties then become a necessity for any progressive movement. Doctors, then, sought to propose alternatives to the treatment model set at the turn of the 20th century. (See Lerner, 2001; Becker and Kaufman, 1995)

Breast Surgery

Radical mastectomy flourished in the United States at the turn of the 20th century where it became paradigmatic and normalized. The relative success of radical breast surgery as a cancer cure facilitated the professionalization of surgery. (See Lerner, 2003, 2001; For the history of surgery see Lawrence, 1992a; For the professionalization of medical knowledge Friedson, 1986) Surgery defined not only what the appropriate kinds of interventions were, but also began to delimit what needed to be done for the surgical cure to cross the threshold from palliative to curative. The qualifiers surgeons used in defining

curative scientific breast surgeries were 'early' and 'radical.' 'Early' and 'radical' marked the

transition from palliative to curative goals for operations and set the conditions for a surgical

paradigm of practice. (See Chapter 1; Table 1) A radical procedure specified the removal of

the whole breast and muscle in one surgical stroke for most operable cancers even for the

smallest tumor.[10] (See Table 4 for a definition of treatment options)

A surgical cure for the first half of the 20th century translated to radical and super-

radical operations with little or no influence of women on the course of treatment. The style

of heroic surgery, which venerated Surgeons and their actions to save lives, would latter be

understood as the effect of surgical arrogance resulting in surgeries that can be described as

mutilation. (See Olson, 2002; Lerner, 2001) After the world wars, some physicians and

women challenged radical surgery opening the road to combination therapies (surgery plus

radiation and/ or chemotherapy). These therapies allowed for less extensive operations. With

the acceptance of mammography as a screening tool in the 70s, radical surgery eclipsed in

medical practiced; the numbers performed dropped precipitously being replaced by simple

mastectomies. (See Montini and Ruzek, 1989) Women, who afforded frequent screenings

and knew about their family history/ cancer risk, could take advantage of these innovations.

Radiation and Chemotherapy

The use of radiation began as an alternative to surgery. It became an addition to

surgery. Chemotherapy began as a combination treatment. Both techniques initiated a

conservative trend in breast operations. This trend was concurrent with questions over radical

---

[10] See Chapter 1. The qualifiers of early and radical set the surgical paradigm for breast care.

operations: how they affect women's health; what was the timing of cancer metastasis; whether extensive operations were curative. The women's health movement fueled this breast conservation trend. This movement claimed a role for women as patients in medical decision-making. The efforts of physicians, who were sensitized to women's concerns to alter the care environment, benefited from and fueled this movement. Women began to avoid radical mastectomy because this procedure adversely affected their quality of life leading to questions of disfigurement, loss, and disability. (See Montini and Ruzek, 1989; Lerner, 2001)

Radiotherapy targeted advanced or inoperable tumors. It was used as a palliative procedure to avoid super radical surgery. As early as 1935 in Great Britain, Keynes compiled five-year data using radiotherapy alone that were comparable to Halsted's results. However, surgeons at the time were not convinced. (See Olson, 2002) For patients who refused radical mastectomy and were staged as 'early,' radiation therapy was an experimental alternative. Peters (1967), a Canadian women physician, applied radiotherapy, and yielded again comparative results to Halsted. Her results faced hostility from the medical establishment. (See Lerner, 2001)

Surgeons dominated the care of cancer -- male Surgeons. They were committed to saving lives through extensive radical procedures. They saw Peters as an outsider and a woman whose data and methods where not rigorous. At the time, women had difficult breaking into the medical procession and to be taken seriously when presenting results. (See Morantz-Sabchez, 1985; Lerner, 2001) She published her findings and persisted with her data. Her stance gave impulse to question Halsted's procedure and move towards experimentation with more conservative managements of breast cancer even as her results were peppered with controversy and profound skepticism. (See Lerner, 2001)

Lastly, Fisher (1968) proposed a new model of treatment: chemotherapy-plus-surgery. The new treatment model suggested that breast cancer diffused (became multi local) early in the trajectory of the disease, so even radical surgery was not sufficient enough to cure it. For him, medical knowledge was not tested. There were no comparisons between contradictory clinical claims. He urged that medical claims be rigorously tested through clinical trials: a new standard for medical knowledge. (See Fisher, 1985) His model for cancer suggested (1) that cancer spread through other means not just the lymph nodes; (2) that cancer spread more quickly into bloodstream than Halsted proposed.

If medical intervention targeted cancer sooner, than the pectoral muscles would not be involved. Their removal would not be necessary. (See Lerner, 2001) The idea that the cancer became a systemic disease sooner and probably before cancer was palpable required intervention at the 'earliest' moment of possible detection. Chemotherapy would be able to eliminate loose cancer cells and combine with less extensive surgery. The combination could effectively cure cancer. This strategy allowed for less disfiguring operations: a simple or modified mastectomy and lumpectomy.

Fisher proposed rigorous scientific investigations to compare research findings and establish the best possible outcomes for a combination of procedures. He followed Halsted's example in proposing a new medical paradigm for breast cancer. He introduced a new medical arrangement, a theory of cancer, and a new method to check the findings: the randomized clinical trial. Halsted had relied on statistical results, but his data no longer seemed rigorous because it was not comparative and independently tested.

Fisher argued that prior medical knowledge was not as scientific in that it did not allow a basis for the proper comparison of results. The randomized controlled clinical trials emerged as the right tool in the creation of medical knowledge. It became a vehicle through

which Fisher was able to elaborate the limitations of radical surgery as a medical paradigm of

practice. (See Lerner, 2001; Olson, 2002) Clinical trials came under question with AIDS

drugs as the need for treatment came into conflict with the creation of solid medical

knowledge. (See Epstein, 1996)

The challenge to radical mastectomy required a new way of doing medical research,

of comparing findings, and further emphasized the importance of the earliest possible

diagnosis. This necessity fueled the need to develop better diagnostics as well as to fully

engage women in the process, creating a partnership between patients and physicians.

Prophylaxis and Prevention

Prophylactic treatment for breast cancer is a recent phenomenon. It followed defining

high risk for the disease. The definition of high risk included the identification of Lobular

Cancer in Situ (LCIS) or pre-cancers on mammograms and biopsies. Women use

prophylactic treatment in hopes of averting the disease. (See Table 4) They include

prophylactic chemotherapy and surgery. These treatments are aggressive in treating the risk

for the disease. In most cases, prophylactic treatments are available for women at higher

'high risk' meaning having survived related cancer, having extensive breast cancer histories,

and therefore being at risk for the disease. The marker for higher high risk now is testing

positive for known genetic markers. (See Chapter 2)

However, the genetic test is not the only marker of higher high risk. Genetic

knowledge is experimental and fallible in application from families who have high rates of

breast cancer to the general population. If we see a point in the arguments over the over-treatment of early breast cancer, the treatment of women at high risk seems the most troublesome. However, decisions over the direction and content of care are individual even if the claims of averting disease by prophylactic treatments are over-stated. Some prophylactic procedures may end up allay fears more than actually eliminating the incidence of disease. (See Lerner, 2001; Lerman, 2000; Crowe, 1996; Shampo 1997)

Diagnosis and Screening

Breast Exams

Breast exams are an integral part of general medical practice. They used to be the sole diagnostic tools until mammography. They identified and diagnosed potentially cancerous lumps sooner than waiting for women to appear with larger unwieldy and painful tumors. Breast exams developed along with the surgical treatment itself. For example, Halsted's staff looked to identify cancerous lumps. They looked to symmetry between breasts (shape and size), location of potential lump, the quality of breast skin -- referring to the texture of an orange peal, nipple retraction or discharge, swollen lymph nodes under the armpit or in the clavicle. (See Halsted, 1894, 1898, 1907) Breast exams, however, did not adequately differentiate between benign and malignant growths. Biopsy as a technique filled that gap. It defined cancer on a cellular level, where the nature of atypical cells began to clarify.

Popularizing breast exams was part of a strategy to create a curable disease, to maintain and foster the success of surgery. (See Lerner, 2001) With more adequate breast examination by physicians and women, cancer as a disease could be identified sooner and its treatment could become more effective. Self Breast Examination (SBE) was the tool used for such task: both as an educational tool and as a screening tool. (See Milan, 1980) The collaborative effort between emerging cancer organizations (such as the American Society for the Control of cancer, the Women's Field Army, the National Cancer Institute) and physicians popularized SBE. (See Lerner, 2001) They sought to involve women and dispel the dread associated with the disease. (See Petterson, 1987) The surgical sword, 'the sword of hope' became the answer! (See Lerner, 2001)

Biopsy

Biopsy emerged as a technique at the interface between breast anatomy and the pathology of cancer. Bloodgood, a student of Halsted, developed this procedure to facilitate the diagnosis of cancer and its spread.[11] (See Bloodgood, 1914) Biopsy eventually allowed a temporal separation between the act of diagnosis -- the question of whether a tumor was cancerous/ benign, and the act of surgery – breast tumors or suspect tissue removal. For most of the 20th century, surgeons practiced biopsy immediately before and the operation. Biopsy was not separate from surgery. Not until the late 1960s/ early 1970s, did the two separate. This legal separation of diagnosis and treatment inserted patient choice and augmented women's role in medical decision-making. Women as activists questioned the one-step procedure of biopsy-surgery, and the implied authority of doctors to make the decision of optimal care alone. The space between biopsy and surgery allowed for women's informed consent. (See Montini and Ruzek, 1989) This separation coincided with the decline of radical mastectomy and the care environment that this paradigm structured and produced.

---

[11] In 1881, Ruge and Veit developed biopsy in dealing cervical cancer. Bloodgood adopted the procedure for breast cancer.

The temporal separation opened the space for women to make informed decisions on whether to have surgery, the extent of surgery performed, and its combination with other treatments. The challenge to the authorial style that characterized medicine grew when women refused to sign the informed consent forms that would authorize the physician to perform surgery immediately after a biopsy and before they came out of anesthesia. Women began to claim their bodies as their own. (See Batt, 1994) Biopsy became an obligatory point of passage in breast cancer diagnosis along with imaging technologies, which played a key, supporting role in screening for the earliest signs of the disease. Current, stereo-tactic, ultrasound and fine needle localization techniques coupled with mammography to grant more precision and dimensionality in biopsy diagnosis.

Imaging Technologies

Early mammograms date back to the beginning of the 20th century. However, mammography was inconsequential until radical mastectomy started to go out of favor as a cure. The ACS society supported this procedure in the 50s and 60s with the effort to develop a PAP test for breast cancer. Mammograms began to fit the need to define pre or cancerous lesions before they were palpable. Pre-cancers then became subject to prophylactic mastectomy -- a tangible option for some women. (See Lerner, 2001, 2003)

Assessments on the value of radical procedures and the perception that mammography might not be useful in breast cancer diagnosis were based on assumptions about how cancer spreads and at what point is it was necessary to intervene. Halsted argued that cancer was a localizable disease. He treated with surgery before it advanced too far. The notion of advancing too far was situational. It was pronounced in the definition of advanced inoperable cancer. Cancer as a disease spread through lymph nodes towards the end of its course, Halsted thought. (See Halsted, 1894, 1898, 1907; Chapter 1) Not until Fisher and the rise of controlled clinical trials (the beginning of evidence based medicine) were these statements challenged.

A window for the development and advancement of mammography opened. Mammography as a technique required the development of specialized films and equipment, as well as expertise in discerning cancerous from normal/ benign breast tissue. Mammography came to solidify new treatment strategies: 'surgery plus chemo or radiation' and diagnostic/ screening strategy: 'early detection can be prevention.' Mammography facilitated rolling back the number of radical and modified mastectomies performed. Mammography afforded women and physicians more time to weight options and strategies as to how to handle the disease. Recently CAD (computer aided diagnosis) and digital mammography supplement radiological perception in the reading of films and suggested that computers can improve diagnostic accuracy. (See Naas et al, 2001)

Mammography recently became digital. Digital mammography allowed for a three dimensional view of the breast. Also, mammography joined other imaging technologies (MRIs and Ultrasound the most promising of the bunch) that claim to better diagnose/ screen breast cancer extending beyond the perceptive limitations of mammograms. MRIs tend to be used to illuminate problem areas on mammograms while ultrasounds are more effective in screening the denser breasts of younger women. The addition of new imaging technologies seems to have been less contested than the addition of new treatments. This could be because the additions of treatments occurred outside the main profession in question: surgery. Radiologists are still in charge of imaging even if new technologies evolve while the status of surgeons' shifted with the introduction of adjuvant treatment. The age dependence of cancer raised the debate over the optimal time to begin mass screening from 50 years of age (1 out of 50) to 40 where the probability of cancer diagnosis is 1 out of 217. (See Naas et al, 2001) The combination of imaging techniques enables radiologists to visualize breasts and read cancer more effectively even at earlier ages.

Genetic Testing

Breast cancer causation is complex. Researchers identified a genetic component for some virulent early onset cancers. To date two genes (BRCA 1 and 2) linked with a high probability for the breast, ovarian, and colon cancers. Developing a diagnostic test would not be easy. The BRCA1 gene was a relatively long sequence located on the 17th chromosome. It is responsible for tumor suppression and DNA structure. (See Chapter 2) BRCA1 gene is the principal gene (though others exists) was responsible not only for hereditary tumors but also is found in the incidence of some sporadic cancers. (See Davies and White, 1995)

BRCA 1 and 2 testing allows women to become more aggressive in treatment and screening for the disease. If women are BRCA 1 or 2 positive, it implies that they are at 'higher high' lifetime risk for breast, ovarian or other related cancers. Men can also carriers of the BRCA genes having moderately elevated risks for prostate and colon cancers. Men can also develop breast cancer. These elevated risks lead women to consider prophylactic surgeries, more frequent screening, and/ or chemoprevention. (See Crowe, 1996; Shampo 1997)

As we look at the field of breast cancer care through time and place, we notice fluidity in the relationship between medicine and women. This relationship becomes punctuated by innovation and scientific discovery, which at times asks for a resettling of their relationship. I would like to argue that the relationships between women and medicine and women and medical discovery were essential in the paradigm shift from radical surgery to surgery plus chemotherapy and/ or radiotherapy, to the new emergent molecular and genetic definitions and treatments.

Let me pause to untangle this relationship between women and medicine as it refers to the actions of early breast cancer societies and later grounds the women's health movement.

Women and Illness

Women experience cancer with dread. For most of the 20th century, women equated breast cancer with a death sentence. After surgeons established a paradigm for its cure, the radical procedure offered hope for a significant postoperative life. The quality of life for survivors became a concern. Physicians began to challenge the perception that breast cancer equals a dreadful death and to persuade women that breast cancer is medically manageable. Before I outline the emergence of breast cancer societies that served to popularize the medical success with this disease even as the relative value of 'success' has been put to question, I will outline women's experience with breast cancer treatment.

Illness Experience

During most of the 19th century, women's experience with breast surgery was painful. (See Burney, 1995; Ferguson, 2000) Women, who detected breast lumps and had the insight to contact a surgeon, while avoiding most other treatments of the time, became subject to a brutal operation. In the early part of the 19th century, this operation entailed the excision of the breast leaving a gaping wound that would then be subject to infection. By the middle of the 19th century, breast conservation became prominent among surgeons because their more extensive operations did not have good results.

Towards the end of the 19th century modern scientific surgery came to power with better management of wounds (avoiding infection), better incisions (to manage postoperative disabilities), and even better diagnostics to differentiate benign and malignant. By this time, women were surviving the operations, which promised to be palliative in nature not necessarily curative. Anesthesia made the actual surgery tolerable. The parameters of curative operation began to be set in the last decades of the 19th century. Surgeons placed the emphasis on radical, heroic operations. Women still dreaded cancer but also recognized the positive potential of these operations. (See Leopold, 1999; See Chapter 1)

In the 20th century, radical mastectomy dominated breast cancer care. Surgeons added to the array of incisions to target advance (metastasized) cancers. Pathologists allowed better diagnosis of breast cancer and its likely spread through the body with biopsy of lump and lymph nodes. Women subjected themselves to radical operations as it was the only option available and legally they had no other choice in the course of treatment after diagnosis. (Leopold, 1999) Going in for a biopsy of a lump then could imply that a woman might come out of anesthesia minus a breast. During the later part of the 20th century, women and some doctors challenged the parameters of radical surgery. Women sought choice over treatment altering the conditions of their care. (See Montini and Ruzek, 1989; Butler and Rosenblum, 1991)

The experience with breast cancer was still traumatizing. The psychosocial aspects of the disease came to the fore with key activists. These activists use their lives as a way to educate women, medicine and society about how to better handle this disease. It was education by example. The most prominent patients in the second half of the 20th century were: Rachel Carson, Betty Ford, Rose Kushner, and Audre Lorde. Their writings have shaped current activism and experience with the disease. (See Knopf-Newman, 2004)

Breast Cancer Societies

The American Society for the Control of Cancer (ASCC) was founded in 1910. It is an earlier formation of our contemporary American Cancer Society, promoted the radical surgical cure of breast cancer. Not surprisingly, physicians dominated this society. ASCC intensified outreach efforts during the thirties, but was not as successful in generating effective publicity for the surgical breast cancer cure.

The ASCC founded the women's field army. It formed in 1936 to wage a war against cancer in the trenches. The women's field army went house to house to convince women that cancer is curable. At the same time, the national cancer institute (founded in 1937) promoted further research into the treatment and causes of cancer. This institute gave direction to the efforts made to target the disease. (Lerner, 2001) These societies supported the surgeon's place in breast care. They popularized the breast self-exam and solidified a surgical paradigm in treating the disease.

Women's Health Movement

Women had an uneasy relationship with radical surgery. The women's health movement gave voice to such uneasiness. The most vocal voices expressed forceful opposition to a particular way of conducting medicine by the late 60s early 70s. Women began to break their invisibility in dealing with breast cancer. They understood how they became implicated in the structures that decided for them (See Clarke and Montini, 1993) and were not fully active partners in their medical decisions.

Women broke the invisibility through written work such as journal articles and books. Publications, which chronicle the disease experience, generated public response. They challenged medical practice to shift as physicians became sensitized to women's experience. Surgeons who had opposed radical surgery began more openly to take risks in challenging the dominant place of mastectomy in breast cancer as well as the style of surgical authority. (See Lerner, 2001) Despite these calls from women, the numbers of radical surgeries performed did not drop in the early seventies. (Montini and Ruzek, 1989) Most physicians responded that surgery had the most effective results, that chemotherapy and radiotherapy were not yet reliable alternatives. Some doctors also headed women's concerns and offered breast-conserving interventions.

The delays in the adoption of conserving surgeries were primarily (1) professional: the structure and gender of medical authority, the surgical tradition; (2) economic: adjuvant treatments were more costly and less available; (3) legal: surgeons delayed the adoption of new techniques in fear of potential malpractice claims; (4) socio-cultural: changing the structure of medicine to allow patient choice.

Feminist concerns fueled the early health movement. These concerns did not equally cross ethnic and racial barriers. Black women were not equal participants in feminist debates at the time. Black women faced a plethora of issues not addressed by the women's health movement, where choice in treatment seemed a luxury. For black women, getting treatment was an issue: being diagnosed in time to be able to be treated to sidestep major morbidities and complications. The diversion for the white feminist health movement was a question of economics, of different priorities, of a different culture of femininity. Indeed for some women having options was a luxury not all women could afford. (See Lerner, 2001; Zones, 2000)

According to Klawiter in the 90s, three social movements address breast cancer (1) Race for the cure, (2) Cancer Walk, (3) Toxic tour. Each had its own culture of action representing different constituents and relationships with biomedical knowledge and public policy. Each activity 'racing', 'walking' and 'touring' suggested participation in collective action in physical, emotional, and cognitive ways seeking to solicit a particular attitude towards body and illness.

The 'race for the cure' promotes a 'body machismo' in the connection of female bodies and biomedical technologies. The 'cancer walk' and 'toxic tour' both articulated body victimization themes, either displaying chemically and surgically effected bodies or through props. These movements call for a different relationship of body to medicine and women to disease. The toxic tour focuses on the environmental aspects of the disease. The cancer walk highlights the unequal access to expensive medical care: the importance of being visible as a cancer patient even if not fully restored. Finally, the race for the cure is more mainstream; it supports a medical model of the disease. (See Klawiter, 1999)

Treatment Strategies

The turn in medical therapeutics modified (at times diminished, at times retained) the radical scope of surgeries even as it expedited the 'early' of earlier intervention. Even as the old surgical arrangement expedited mastectomies in the course of cancer as a disease, it did not see the value of in x-ray mammography and relied mainly on breast exams. The adoption of mammography followed the adoption of clinical trials. It happened in the 1970s with a substantial time lag from the first mammogram. This lag posits the question if radical surgeries as a practice paradigm and surgeons as a profession inhibited the development of procedures that potentially countered it/ them. Others have argued that is not the case. However, this can be an unintended consequence of a field dominated by one profession.

A challenge to radical surgery as a paradigm came before the use of any alternative treatments. In the treatment arrangement of radical surgery, the expedited early translated to education campaigns by entities such as the Women's Field Army in the 1930s later the American Cancer Society. (See Lerner, 2001) In the newer arrangement, mammography, radiology, chemotherapy joined with a more limited scope for surgery. They required re-education campaigns and public investment in screening on a larger scale than before.

The two 'early' in the breast care arrangements acquired different meanings: the early of radical and the early of adjuvant. Even as the scope of surgery diminished, the style of treatment was still aggressive. High dose chemotherapy and prophylactic treatments still ring as aggressive interventions. Defining 'women at high risk' for invasive cancer prompted different treatment strategies and suggested a different handle over cancer and women's bodies. The scope and timing of interventions has shifted between the two 'early' but the treatment strategy remained aggressive.

Through innovations in screening and diagnostic technologies, a molecular and genetic redefinition of cancer and cancer risk has become possible. (See Chapter 2) Along with it comes a third 'early.' This third 'early' handles cancer by establishing biomarkers that identify and treat the potential in advance. With this third early come new treatments like vaccines, retro viral-vectors, and pharmacogenetic drugs. All point to a time when surgery may not be needed except in 'late' or advanced cases.

Aggressive

Aggressive treatment initially implied extensive surgeries at the onset of the disease. With the establishment of a radical paradigm of treating the disease, the margin of error in handling diagnostic ambiguity became slim. Physicians tended to define marginal cases as pre-cancerous and treat them as such. Tracking marginal cases promoted aggressive intervention to reduce the chance of false negatives. The implications of targeting the disease too late in its trajectory meant death. Aggressive treatment implied extensive surgeries.

The logic of aggressive interventionism also bled into other treatment modes like radiation and chemo. High dose chemotherapy or radiation, more frequent mammography, extensive surgery: all follow the aggressive treatment logic. Aggressive treatment has lead to adopting some of these procedures as prophylactic. The over treatment of early breast cancer is a reality even as we begin to speak of prophylaxis for the disease. (See Goldberg, 1996) The fuel towards aggressive treatment follows the inadequacies of current treatment modes as well as the lack of a basic understanding of cancer and the breast.

However, the mode and style of treatment is dependent of women's preference: individual tolerance to the risk of recurrence, to the risk of the disease. For some women prophylactic surgeries allay the fear and dread of cancer even if such treatments may not actually completely eliminate such risk. Genetic testing has made such prophylactic treatments a more attractive and tenable option for women whose risk of breast cancer is estimated higher high in the data. (See Lerman, 2001)

Conservative

A more conservative treatment protocol has become available for breast cancer. The arguments between aggressive treatment and conservative treatment are not new. They date back to the 19th century.

However, in the 20th century breast conservation connected with the woman's movement, with women's choice and control over the direction of treatment and physician options in managing the disease. A more conservative treatment protocol implied watchfulness of borderline lessons and surgeries that were breast conserving. Breast conservation became a viable alternative only with the better definition of cancer as a disease and 'earlier' intervention, as well as the adoption of chemo and radiation.

In most instances, a breast conserving option implied the additive treatment of chemotherapy and radiotherapy, which for most people translated to more expense. (See Zones, 2000) Thus, the shift away from radical surgeries has implicated greater variance and range in treatment protocol. However, this variance is situational. Truly conservative options are underutilized even if the results reported are as good as radical options for the particular diagnosis. The strategy and treatment options leave us wanting. They reflect limitations in the conceptualization of the disease as well as the structure of medical institutions to effect treatments. (See Retsky, 1994)

Watchfulness has become burdensome for women at higher high risk for the disease. It might be that new treatments will eradicate the logic of conservative and aggressive, as they were arguments that centered on surgery as the main therapeutic for the disease.

Biosocial Health and Illness

Health and illness are biosocial. Their bio-sociality is clearly evident in breast cancer care. Women and medicine, medicine and society, co-produce the development of care structures and expertise. Through a study of their inter-relationship, I map the experiential terrain of this disease. I seek to find ways to facilitate the productive conjunction of women and medicine, medicine and society and open medicine to a more conscious biosocial arrangement that supports a partnering between the two.

By emphasizing the biosociality of medicine, we would define a productive partnership between patients and doctors in the choice and development of treatments and diagnostics. This approach would facilitate the production of treatments sensitized to women's concerns. Today statements physicians made in defense of radical mastectomy seem outlandish and callous. For example, 'women do not need breasts over 50' or 'a mastectomy would not impact a marriage' or general attitudes of protectionism and paternalism that physicians would not employ in treating men. A partnership could be sensitized to social inequities and differences in experience.

By emphasizing the bio-sociality in medicine, we foster mindfulness in institutional practice. If we are mindful of the productive conjunction between health and social life, we can create institutions that foster productive change. These institutions direct and sensitize care to the needs of medical knowledge and successful treatment as well as to the needs of the patients and communities impacted. AIDS is a recent example where patients challenged the gold standard of clinical trials to have access to potentially life-saving drugs. The shift in treatment protocols favored providing adequate treatment to AIDS patients whose lives were in jeopardy. Medical scientists adapted to the needs of AIDS patients and navigated the productive even forceful coupling of medicine and society. Such scientists initially lamented the undesirable modifications in knowledge protocols, where medical knowledge enters the public domain prematurely. However, let us also see the adaptability of medical institutions to the urgent needs of vulnerable patients in the face of life threatening illness as a positive sign. (See Epstein, 1998)

By emphasizing the biosociality in medicine, we would mitigate the price we pay for the construction of medical knowledge. It is clear that medical knowledge comes at a price. Each of us pays our dues when we enter the world of the ill and depart the world of the healthy. Medical institutions become the sites to share therapeutic strategies with others. These institutions can and must be responsive to our needs. They can aid us in transgressing the uncertainties we face, in managing our illness experience, and in finding our way to health. Medical institutions are in essence the site of conjunction of medical knowledge and intervention. Let that conjunction be mindful of its implications.

Breast Cancer Care Topologies

Power relations are rooted in the whole network of the social. This is not to say, however, that there is a primary and fundamental principle of power which dominates society down to the smallest detail; but, based on this possibility of action on the action of others that is coextensive with every social relationship, various kinds of individual disparity, of objectives, of the given application of power over ourselves, of more or less deliberate organization, will define different forms of power.

--- Foucault, 1994 (2000)

Introduction

Breast care practices, technologies, and expertise name, define, locate a target population 'at risk.' They also define a treatable disease. In arranging breast care, medicine wields its bio-power and the state enacts its bio-politics. (See Foucault, 1997, 1994, 1990) This chapter will concentrate on how and in what ways medical bio-power effects women's experiences with breast cancer. It will also problematize the processes that configure medical bio-power to open them up for renegotiation, pointing towards the potential of a partnership-structure in medicine. My hope, then, is to find ways to notice and enhance the agency of women and to aid physician's appreciation of that agency. Accounting for women's agency is different than think of women as subjects or objects. Agency implies a self-possession and know-how, where one's works and deeds have an effect on an outcome.

Medicine enhances state biopower as it legitimizes the projects of population health and welfare. State biopower takes form through the processes of medicalization, of structuring the conjunction between medicine as institution and the world as lived. During most of the 20th century, medicalization became structured along the lines of social control. However, medical institutions in the late 20th century allows and requires a different structuring which can empower women as patients to make decisions in their care. (See Clarke et al, 2003) What does it mean for women to affect the care they receive? How does their agency translate and travel? How can medicine facilitate its emergence? How can women as patients, activists, and bodies enter into medical interactions on an secure footing?

In this regard, women's agency in breast care is worthy of investigation. Women's agency in medicine oscillates between being and having a body and self under medical scrutiny. It slips between degrees of complying and not complying (as this movement is translated in medical discourses of control and intervention). This agency enters and is inseparable from the ways that women translate and articulate it if that agency is to be understood as an effect of intentionality, in the ways that women negotiate the terms and conditions of their care.

Medical Mediation

Interviewing women[12] about their experiences with breast cancer care facilitates an understanding of how medicine works, how it frames women, breasts, and cancer, and how

---

[12] I want to highlight the theme: subjectivity and power. I use the notion of women in the plural to highlight the problematic of the subject as an effect of force relations. Using women as a category to describe the participants in my study does not imply that I am emphasizing the import of gender issues over and above race/ ethnicity, class, disability, age, sexuality, transgender dynamics. Women -- as subjects of and to medicine -- have political resonance or force in so far as women appear to be those breasted creatures that enter into dialogue with medicine as it intersects them and their bodies. I began this project with the use of a split term: patient suffering/ user of medical technology to underline the problem with the term patient and how it obfuscates agency in medical institutions. This split term highlights the contested and negotiated nature of agency in breast care. Medicine seems to vacate fleshy people in the process of care. It also ignores the issues of gender/ gendering in the process of subject formation. Certainly, women, as a term as well as a signifier of some bodies, is medicalized and has problems of its own like erasing the face of women who do not constitute the feminine in particularly oppressive ways due to race, class, sexuality, disability, transgender dynamics. Feminist scholarship has done work to unsettle the relations of sex/ gender- race- class- sexuality- disability- aging- transgender so that women as a term cannot be easily solidified and may constitute a more open space to work with even as it has at times erased and obscured the multiplicity it contained. It is important to make clear however the term women is used in the plural consciously, and the multiplicity and heterogeneity of the 'sex which is not one.' (See Irigaray, 1985) needs to be preserved in any accounts about women. I dropped the term patient in favor of

women perceive and embody an agency. Medicine itself is not a monolith. Yet, I posit that there are 'entry requirements' that form the ways women and their bodies are disclosed and anticipated to interact within medicine. Medicine complexly situates women as subjects and objects, as beings and things, within its own terrain under the pretext of maximizing control over women's health outcomes, of enhancing judgment and predictive evaluations, and of figuring ways to stage/ incite appropriate confrontations/ confessions with both women and flesh. Medicine orients women to choose 'appropriate' –medically legit -- trajectories that will lead to better health rather than illness.[13]

Medical discourses configure women and their bodies in breast care. They coordinate diagnostic/ treatment knowledge, practice,[14] and technology that do its mediating work. These techniques have acquired a pervasive 'aura' (as one participant named it) of a 'scary ritual,' and have become 'an obligatory point of passage' (see Latour, 1987; Latour and Woolgar, 1976) as one 'comes of age.' For high-risk women, the first mammogram is a defining moment in coming to terms with the relationship between aging, health, personal - familial histories, in facilitating a sense of self-control over and responsibility about life and

---

women because patient as a term is laden with connotations of bearing suffering patiently and passively (See Zola, 1991) and fails to address the agentic character in women's experiences with health. The term 'patient' -- connoting one suffering patiently, and accepting, acquiescing under the conditions suffered -- elides how patients in this case women[12] participate in their care in ways that are normative and disruptive. If interested in how feminist scholars have dealt wit the issue try Butler's "Contingent Foundations" (See Butler, 1995).

[13] How breast care trajectories are settled in and through the work of medical mediation in ways that medical institutions recognize. This work shows the constitutive limitations of intelligibility that underlie the discursive axes of risk/security; trust/ fear; responsibility/blame; support/ place that vector or dimensionalize the lived space of women's experience within medicine to make it intelligible on discursive grounds that translate it. Strauss has underscored the importance of trajectories in medicine. (See Strauss, 1993) Lacan has made clear the connection of dimensionality and speaking in his term dit-mention (See Lacan, 1999) I feel that the verb vector might help understand the constitution of, and constitutive of the subject within medical institutions. The knotting of the subject and object does not form stable grounds for knowledge. In this regard Foucault's questioning of the constitution of human sciences is warranted. However, this questioning needs to be and has been extended to natural sciences as well. Hopefully a more productive 'vectoring' of the world will result.

[14] Breast care here is taken in the narrow sense of the practices involved in breast cancer prevention, detection and therapeutics. I will mostly deal with the early detection as prevention claim and the technologies/ practices involved.

health. Discourses -- medical, publicly held or disseminated in the media, stories of friends,

lovers, mothers, daughters, sisters – permeate the breast care experience and are central in

comprehending the ways this experience is configured and configures the articulation of

intention and agency for women in the face of doctors, insurers, and policy makers. In

thinking about action in medicine, the notions: agency, control, intervention, transformation

are key.

Types of Medical Action

Control configures actions (doings) and events (happenings). It structures them as an

effect of a delimited set of outcomes. These outcomes at times escape the purview of

predictability, visibility, and surveillance. Agency obliges acts (the doing) to be congruent

with the articulated intentions of actors (the saying) that at times exceeds or re-cedes the

unfolding of events (the happening). Intervention is a stylized kind of action that is staged to

be tested under/ within a scientific framework and furthers notions of medical or state

controllability and transformability. Transformation is an effect of deterritorialization, (See

Deleuze and Guattari, 1987) of profoundly altering the terms and conditions of intelligibility

that have operated in medicine, how its mediating work placed women (as subjects and

objects) with its field of operations and how women themselves perceive, conceptualize and

negotiate their place in medicine.

The fuzziness between these notions, their mutual diffraction (See Haraway, 1997) is

interesting: instances, where an effect seems to be delimited but does not follow from any-

one person's agency or institutional intervention, and the process of its delimitation escapes

view; instances, where acts are agentic yet the anticipated effects escape control or are too complex to be modeled for future interventions or shed light on the conditions of possibility for speech and/ or action; instances, where control and its effects are re-posited and challenged by agentic acts and/or speech; instances, where control and agency are congruent, where some intervention is possible if deemed warranted; instances, where a recognition and transformation of medical framing/ dimensionalizing takes place, where what constitutes agency, control, and intervention as conditioned by medical institutions is transformed.

Bio-power in breast care is an effect of controlling, of manipulation and re-situation of persons on domains that delimit the possibility of appropriate agency: like figuring some women as part of a 'high risk' population for breast cancer, which implies being subject to increased vigilance and further medicalization. This chapter interrogates: (1) how women enter into medical discourses and practices as users of medical technology and expertise, becoming its subjects and objects; (2) how women figure or challenge the normative thresholds of their entry and (re) inscription; (3) how breast care mediates, and (re) situates women in the context of their care under the pretext of what hazards, and in the name of what notions of health? Two themes are central: grasping the problematic of women's agency in medicine and its relations to the conditions that enable it; and describing how the work of mediation – being the effect of control, agency, intervention, transformation -- happens in medicine.[15] The questions of transforming the relations between women and medicine, of re-

---

[15] The work of mediation and the work of purification are said to be distinct and set in opposition within the modern moment for Latour. I would argue that the definitive marker of modernity are modern institutions and their practices. Within medicine for example, the work of mediation and purification or classification go hand in hand in producing subjects and objects. What is interesting are the points where managing the decision between the two is problematic. How do you treat a patient under a partial anesthetic juxtaposed to one under total anesthesia. Is the objectifying effect of the handling of bodies with medical institutions necessary for its work of mediation to occur? How do decisions about the agency of the patient get negotiated within those very practices? It is hard to say that medical institutions have never really been modern. In fact they are profoundly and at times terribly modern in the ways that they mediate and classify bodies, technologies, animas and people.

constituting the medical field, are complex and cannot be rendered as an effect of one sort of activity or agency. Thinking of agency as the property of a subject is problematic. Reworking agency as a notion strengthens the place and influence women can have in structuring breast care in particular.

Medical control delimits the domain of 'acceptable,' or normative patient-agency to constitute the grounds that situate women involved, and fashion what and who women need to be in their biomedical interactions. Medical discourses are mediators (both in the sense of go-between and that of arbitration); they situate medical interactions amid a constellation of breast care practices, technologies, and knowledges. These discourses convey a cohesive picture. They portray breast cancer as a disease, the breast as a particularly risky body part and a thing, the overall woman. Women become a being that has the quality of a thing in some medical instances sometimes the objects of medical knowledge, sometimes the mute subject in interactions. The very women as persons at times become subjects able to speak about the conditions of their care. More recently, women engage in biomedicine as decision-makers. They become agents in the direction of care. The apparatus of medical knowledges/ practices/technologies does mediating work that situates women as objects, subjects, agents. In the recent structure, medical interactions mitigate but require and reproduce an asymmetrical accent between women and providers but open the window for women as agents. How that asymmetry is negotiated and manifests itself is in question!

The question is to see how the introduction of technologies like computers alters the grounds upon which these mediations and classifications have happened. For Latour's take on mediation/ classification look at *We have Never Been Modern*. Also, I want to make clear that even if certain social enclosures have retained some of their modern character, that others have increasingly lost them.

I identified a matrix of knowledges, practices, and technologies in interviews with women, who had at least one mammogram. This matrix helps visualize the ways through which women situate/ are situated in the breast care terrain. This terrain is opened by and dimensionalized through notions of Risk-Safety, Trust- Fear, Blame-Responsibility, and Estrangement-Support. First, I will describe the matrix of practices, discourses and technologies used to constitute a breast care arena under the purview of medical institutions. Then, I will focus on how these discursive axes produce women as conscripted subjects shaped by the work of medical mediation, how this mediation can be transformed to enhance women's agency. Timing (early- late) plays an important as a fifth axis in the dynamic character of interactions as well as the ways they are structured.

Let me describe each discursive axis. (1) Breast cancer risk inscribes hazards to breasts grounding and binding women together as group under the medical gaze. Risk links the production of medicalized subjectivities with the coordination and rationing of resources that legitimate medical work. (2) Trust as a strategy masks medical control and intervention. It negotiates the entry of women as subjects in medicine by assuming that women and their bodies are particularly implicated, being inherently risky and diseased as they age. Trust is a threshold for emotion management (fears, hesitations, anger) so women can be appropriately conscripted as willing subject to/ subjects in medicine.

Medical subjection affects women. (3) Disciplining women's agency is effected through the proliferation and circulation of formal and informal 'moral tales' of blame-responsibility. These stories clarify a direction -- place and orientation, a self and its appropriate relations in biomedicine. These stories demark the psychic terrain for the articulation of women's agency in ways that befit medical objectives. Breast care stories popularize/ defuse certain types of medical and/ or social controls/ interventions. (4)

Consequently, women's actions echo in and order worlds (psychic, social, medical). Women

muster support; women become estranged. In both instances, women's place is affected by

how they are called forth, who or what they are connected with, and how and why they dwell

in medicine and a multiplicity of social worlds that women both occupy and occasion. (See

Graph 3)

Agency and Mediation

Matrix of Diagnostic Intervention

I will first show how a matrix of diagnostic knowledges, technologies, and practices

consolidates a breast care apparatus, how it solidifies a particular distinction of subject/object

in breast care. Even if some of the technologies and practices are historically contested, they

dwell in the domain of 'trusted tools.'(See Clarke and Fugimura, 1992) Table 3 describes a

matrix of medical practices, technologies, and body parts implicated in breast cancer

diagnosis. Columns relate breast-care practices with providers, technologies, and body parts.

Rows correspond with the sequencing of more or less invasive practices. The ordering of

rows can reflect the relative experience of the woman in the situation.

In terms of columns, the domain of expertise involved corresponds to 'provider'

specialty: radiology, oncology, genetics, histology, and surgery. No specialty exists to figure

the experiential knowledge of women or their lovers with their breasts. Or the clinical

experience of the feel of any woman's breast: a tacit knowledge? Invasiveness is a vector and

has to do with how women and their bodies are involved, the extent to which women are objectified/ subjectivized. The placement of rows is tentative and dependent on the sensitivities that women experience and report.[16] (See Table 3)

'Early detection is prevention' has become the prevailing strategy. It minimizes the pursuit of 'preventive'[17] breast cancer research and questions over breast cancer causation. Breast cancer causality has been increasingly become molecular genetic and as a consequence still an individual responsibility. The nature of cancer causation is still underdetermined and complex. (See Chapter 2 and Theoharis, "Genes, Germs, Sins, Toxins") Breast cancer detection and diagnosis is a multifaceted project. It requires coordinating expertise, tools, practices, body parts, and people through multiple institutional linkages. Diagnostic processes, then, are legitimately applied to breasts, to women's case histories and blood lineage, and to imagining what breast cancer is, how and which cells or tissues proliferate out of control, and what their genetic constitution might be.

This diagnostic/ detective apparatus complexly constitutes women's bodies and experiences. It informs their understanding of their breasts and it circumscribes the parameters of their participation or compliance in the production of medial expertise and the regimentation of their breast health. Consider the following interview snippet vis-à-vis breast exams.

---

[16] The technology of a table is very much limiting in so far as its 2d. It doesn't show how invasiveness as a function of (subjectification, objectification) enters into play and how it enters differently depending of the technologies and practices used. (See Table 3; and Theoharis "Hyper-Real Insight into Flesh")

[17] Drugs like Tomoxifen are now constituted as a prevention strategy. The use of Tomoxifen as prevention is a strategy outside the general rubric: early-detection is prevention. (See Fosket, 2004)

Weaving Practices Together

> *My physician does routine exams. My doctor taught me how to self-exam because my friend told me that a lot of people had found out that they had cancer through self-exam. One of the ladies her husband found it for her. It's very incredible. Oh you have a lump here. Oh... so scary.*

Strung together are formal and informal actors, actants,[18] discourses, body parts, notions of disease, lumps, emotions, and medical prescriptions. The actors, actants, actions multiply. (1) The clinician involved in standard routine practice of breast exams. (2) The doctor taught her how to do self-exams so that she would self-monitor in intervals where standard exams did not take place: the trust in her doctor's advice. (3) The friend highlights the importance of self-exams because medical technologies are fallible and because people could develop cancer between routine exams. (4) The story of one of the ladies' husband who 'found it out for her' in his encounter with his lover's breasts. The didactic tale instills further the will to self-regulate and to seek more and better medical attention. (5) The husband/ lover attends to his/her lover's breasts. (6) The lady herself telling the didactic tale repeated ad infinitum in the circulation of disciplining breast care tales. (7) Cancer, the potentiality and unpredictability, eludes expert and lay fingers needing to be monitored and not easily pined or pointed out in tissues. (8) Breasts solicit attention and incur risk, place in motion medical discourses, technologies, practices, knowledges, and strategies to maintain health and to involve experts, lovers, friends, women, and men. Breasts become both objects of desire and of health and subject women to risk, to medical and informal scrutiny. (9) The assemblage of technologies and practices used to monitor breasts in various situations. (10) The scariness

---

[18] Actant is Latour's term for things that act. He, also, shoes how larger collectives of humans and non-humans are implicated in our practices, how science orchestrates these collectives. (See Latour, 1987,1999, 1983)

surrounding cancer and the emotional turbulence that ensues from its potential discovery. (See Pickering, 1995)

Women, lovers, breasts, medical discourses, stories, doctors, fingers, technologies, techniques, expectations, emotions, tissues, blood, tears, cells are skillfully woven together through the work of medical mediation to form the fabric that constitutes breast care. A necessary question is how does this interweaving happen? Risk- security, trust- fear, blame-responsibility, estrangement- support are prominent threads in stitching together women's experiences, in aligning actants, actors, discourses, intentions, perceptions, the passage of time, anticipated and unanticipated outcomes.

These tropes are woven in stories and experiences about breast care. The implication of what is spoken exceeds the statement and the intent of the words uttered. In that sense, these tropes also weave the fabric situating women and doctors; technique, knowledge and experience in breast cancer care. These tropes transport/ transfer knowledge, understanding, between groups and ensure legitimate medical being-ness and thing-ness to women, their breasts, and the technologies/ practices involved. They are the central nodes that orient/ solidify a breast cancer care map. (See Graph 3)

Why Breast Care Topology?

By juxtaposing topology to typography, I show how we can understand medicalization differently through the two descriptive strategies. Since I am interested in the work of norms and the production of subjects that are dynamic, topology seems to be a better analytic tool. Topology allows us to delimit the psychic and discursive, where a multiplicity of experience becomes intelligible. This intelligibility is a product of looking symmetrically at what all women said. In other words, I placed no value judgments on respondent statements. Topology allows me to see how medicalization as force structures the experience of women I have interviewed.

If medicine created concrete types as profiles of patients, those types would become normative and lose the flexibility of topological thinking.[19] [20] By that I mean that we would have the creation of types rather than a multitude of patients, all subject to disease. Types are clear. That clarity may be false. It may be a bi-product of labeling adverse effects to be property of communities or individual behaviors. Clarity in type does not account for shifts in perceptions and attitudes. In other words, it is hard to temporalize types. Types may also be stigmatizing and used as instruments of oppression.

In certain instances, a topology can yield points of concentration. How force is applied to intervene in the concentration of adverse instances is key in not turn a temporal node into a transcendental type. Medicalization, then, is productive. It opens a field of experience with illness. It opens a space of intelligibility where the world of patients is ordered and oriented in their interactions with social institutions. Breast experiences as a topology become a psychic, discursive, material space co-ordered by medicine, as a social and scientific institution, and by women, who become immersed in it through the disease.

Risk- security, trust- fear, blame- responsibility, estrangement-support are dimensions I identified, which orient or turn women in breast care. I use these tropes as nodes

---

[19] For Lacan use of topological thinking emerges in the construction of the subject. (See Lacan, 1998) Topological thinking emerges in Deleuze with the notion of *the Fold* to account for the bended nature of subjectivity: as words folded around experience/ emotions/ intentions. (Deleuze, 1993) His fold is an extension of Leibniz proposition of the monad. (Leibniz, 1992)

[20] Typology/ typography tends to speak to determined shapes of subjects that do not warp in/ through time or interaction: typology being a class of subjects described from the outside. (See Weber, 1946); typograpgy is the self-writing of the subject becoming proper and determined in shape. (See Lacoue-Labarthe, 1989)

standardized by medical institutional practices but also inhabited by women. They are both formulaic and fluid in the ways they inform women's experience, in how they justify certain interventions and controls, and how they trace out a map or charter multiple trajectories that women are advised to follow. I highlight the trouble underscored by the translations between institutional and interpersonal discourse. I will flesh out each dimension through a few quotes to illustrate the range of responses I got from the interviews I conducted. Quotes used speak to each domain and show how a few women have translated these nodes in their experience. As an analytic description of their experience, my understanding is partial and partially resonates with medical, political, social discourses as well as women's embodied experiences.

High - Low Risk

In breast care, risk as a discursive technique assumes at least four strategic domains and uses. (1) Risk is a probability event, insofar as a numerical value is attributed to it. (2) Risk is an interpolative event, insofar as risk refers to a particular group of individuals who assume a new identity, 'I am high risk.' (3) Risk is an accounting event, insofar as money is made or saved through its strategic use.[21] (4) Risk is polysemic. It means different things to doctors, to women examined, to insurers, to policy makers, yet binds these groups together under a common if complex rubric. (5) Risk is multidimensional involving some elements

---

[21] Francois Ewald traces the connection between insurance and risk in "Insurance and Risk," so does Daniel Defert in "'Popular Life' and insurance technology." Robert Castel sketches how modern institutions use risk in "From Dangerousness to Risk." (See Burchell. Gordon, and Miller, 1991) If interested in the history of statistics and probability, Ian Hacking wrote a book. (See Hacking, 1975)

figured as controllable by women and/ or institutions and some not. A discrete concept of

risk operates in the interactions between health care providers and women in breast care.

Medical/ Evaluative Risk

Medical risk is a discursive technique that doctors use to determine the probability of

health and illness as well as the type of care needed. Medical risk is an instrument for

determining and negotiating treatment and diagnosis. It is an instrument for an insurance

calculus. From an insurance perspective, medical risk defines individuals or groups most

susceptible to disease, ones who require more scrutiny, and/ or potentially dumping to the

public sector programs. In terms of insurance, risk aversion equates to capital gained through

the diminishment of dollars spent on care. Predictive values ascribed to risk clearly do not

forecast outcomes of any particular women that might be deemed 'an outlier' – but are used

to evaluate potential capital health expenditures and liabilities. Genetic information might be

able to better pinpoint individual risk to disease. However, taking risk assessment seriously

in insurance and employment contexts might lead to discrimination and the implosion of

collective pooling of risk as we know them. Collective pooling of risk is the bedrock of

social insurance programs. Today, risk defines overall trends of individuals and their breasts

under medical scrutiny and makes them subject to a political and/or insurance calculus of

health, security, and value.

Defining a population under the medical gaze is an effect of risk discourse, a modern

institutional technology. Through a differential use of breast care techniques, risk wields

group identities and forms grounds for comparison between women. Medical risk, then,

evaluates the chance of breast cancer along four domains. (1) Continual risks associated with the passage of time and the aging processes; (2) chance risks evaluated through women's family history and DNA testing, (3) lifestyle risks assessed through a scrutiny of behavioral factors, and (4) circumstantial risks associated with the presence of findings, environmental, social or occupational factors.

Economy of Perception

> *It's really a strange situation where you feel that you might have a serious medical problem. And in the end you don't. And **you were low risk** to begin with. And then you end up owing this huge amount of money that has gone down the drain for something that everyone thought was probably benign anyway. So, I think philosophically: I, sometimes, wonder [laugh] why am I going through this extremely expensive medical technology [fine needle aspiration] if there was an 8 % chance that there was something. And it is important to rule things out. But I think that is the take home message for me. And yet, I feel extremely lucky that I had great practitioners throughout the process.*

> > *Yea... in fact the past few years I've been getting them [mammograms] every six months because, umm, **I'm high risk**, because of my family history. And umm they sighted these masses. And they were alarmed at the masses that I had in various different locations. So they, you know, they got on it right away when they noticed it. **I am high risk**....*

The juxtaposition between the first and second quote shows how risk is referential. It refers to the potentiality of a disease and directs women's thinking as well as provider response. In the first instance, the equation between risk and capital is clearly visible.[22] The high price associated with further investigating and utilizing diagnostic technologies such as needle aspiration becomes better justified only under conditions of 'higher risk.' Risk discourse is underlined by a problematic of uncertainty. Its deployment intends to maintain institutional control in portraying a sense of security, of comfort and routine. Exposed, however, are the myths and costs of security in an absolute sense. The key is figuring out

---

[22] Risk becomes a political economy tool: a way to rationalize uncertainty. (See Beck, Giddens, Lash, 1994; Luhmann, 1991 for a macro view; my analysis is embedded in medical interactions.)

how to balance the need to 'rule things out' (no real certainty ever) and the resources involved in the process e.g. what is acceptable risk? At which moment is a mobilization of recourses necessary?

Even though 'it is important to rule things out,' 'the take home message' becomes for the first woman the need to evaluate the medical drive towards increased use of detective/ diagnostic technologies. This evaluative process is the site where women's agency might be exercised in deciding if and when to seek what kind of care and how to get better be informed. An evaluative dimension is required to effectively acquaint patients with risks and disease trajectories. The need for evaluation underscores the unequal grounds behind requirements of competence, literacy, and access to economic, emotional, familial resources in making of breast care decisions and facing breast cancer facts.

Having 'the peace of mind' – a sense of security -- to reflect philosophically demonstrates how health under the strategy 'of early detection is prevention' becomes a commodity. Health becomes a commodity whose value is negotiated through risk, the perceptions/ assessments of risk, which then is reflected in terms of capital. Capital is gained or lost in the valuation. Risk-averse behavior may translate into better health outcomes. Risk discourse easily translates into capital: meaning for her money owed to the insurance company and the provider, capital gained in the exchange for providers and medical institutions. The discrete value associated with risk: 8%, is a dubious statement masquerading as fact, pretending to account for the slippery condition of being constituted at some level of risk for breast cancer. This valuation may or may not justify further investigation. Under the guise of objective assessment, the strategy of defining aging and women's bodies as inherently risky brings all women under the medical gaze. Perceptions of risk become matters of life and death, of capital and time.[23] Timing medical intervention becomes essential in the management of risk. Timing solidifies knowledge and uncertainty, practice and action, capital and loss.

The attribution of risk is a legitimating vehicle through which providers and women negotiate procedures. In the current breast care paradigm, increased medical surveillance tends to guarantee better health outcomes. Medical technologies become the technical preceptors able to gaze for and sight the embodied potentiality of cancer. Medical technology may also be prone to error. Risk value is not just a perception of a potential event. Risk identity is not a unique phenomenon for breast cancer. For medical institutions, risk values become predictive of and constitute the potential incarnation of cancer in the fatty breast tissues. Risk value, then, becomes a threshold for medical action. Medical surveillance precedes and follows it. Medical surveillance defines the parameters of risk, which then buffers medical action. Risk obligates[24] increased utility of practices and furthers itself in pronouncing judgment over life, conduct, and health. In this sense risk as pronounced translates into the grounds for medical interactions and subject formation, it becomes an identity.

Risk, as an institutional discourse, evaluates the likelihood of cancer in any masses found and furthers the hunt for its potential finding. It increases the encounters of breasts with probing eyes and feeling fingers to see or feel masses, lumps, to apprehend shadows in mammograms, which then raise alarm and further incite intervention and control. It sets

---

[23] Derrida conceptualizes the relation of time, death, and capital. (See Derrida, 1992)

[24] Howson in "Embodied Obligation" makes clear how the pronouncement of detection as prevention obliges women to participate in the medical surveillance apparatus. Health in the neo-liberal mode of governing oneself becomes embedded in the notion of choice whose outcome would be foreclosed by the provision of adequate education/ information. (See Howson, 1998)

women on a slippery impossible slope of health as a product of vigilance and compliance. Risk becomes an identity, a way of being in reference to cancer, uncertainty, and death.

Identity-Identification

The statement 'I am high risk' operates in women's awareness as an indication of a probable encounter with the dreadful/ dreaded mark of cancer. High risk might materialize in women's flesh as cancer. It raises alarm, solicits attention, and further fuels the will of investigation to find sites where the chase could take place. Many masses are sighted, few are suspect, and 'high risk' resonates as a fact and label, as a justification for the dubious potential encounter with the site/ sign of cancer. Risk is an institutional identification and a license to judge and probe everyday conduct, to regiment individual lifestyles, and to require further surveillance in the name of a healthy life. These actions are normative.

Medical doctors use risk (1) to pin down within a degree of certainty future outcomes and determine viable insurance ventures;[25] (2) to contextualize dangers to health within a rational scientific framework to make them tamable and manageable; (3) to establish a sense of security through surveillance, through utilization of medical technologies 'to rule things out' without noting that the fear of 'getting it' or the side-effects of medical technologies themselves. (See Douglas, 1992, 1986)

Risk is not just an institutional tool. It, also, becomes a personal identity where an individual alters both perceptions of self and actions. Where a person's subjectivity is re-organized around the task of averting a disease. The cross from external evaluation to self-

---

[25] Risk operates as a prognostic variable to determine how diagnostic regimen will be used. Predicting the future is an important element of control within the breast care terrain. On the importance of understanding how prognostic judgments are made. (See Anspach, 1993).

perception, from medical label to identity requires trust in the assessments of providers and the tools used. Combined the dimensions of risk-security, trust-fear constitute the basic parameters of how women as subjects are positioned in medical interactions and become then subject to medical interventions. Women are constituted as subject in medicine through being at risk and having trust. These are evaluations of a state of health and a state of soul (mind/ emotion). Blame-Responsibility and Shame-Support, which are the two other constitutive dimensions, become normative forces. They pull upon the subject towards trust and the acceptance of being at risk. Early-late, the time dimension, consolidates time and action in terms of the trajectory of the disease. It orders interactions/ interventions that aim to shift the position of the subject/ body from being potentially in 'ill health,' from 'lacking trust.' This shift implicates an acceptance of responsibility as well as the finding of community where support and resources exist to successfully navigate the disease or the concern for the disease. (See Graph 3)

In a setting where the risks to health are not shared, capital and knowledge play an important role. Capital and knowledge open doors to institutions that hold the tools to save life. Implicit in the commodity structure for health is a soft form of social Darwinism. Those worthy enough to be saved will have the right stuff: capital, attitude, connections and knowledge to open the gates. Let me move to the dimension of trust-fear. Without trust in expert medical judgments of breast-'facts' and institutional practices of breast gazing, risk cannot do its mediating work.

Trust–Fear

In breast care, women must learn to trust the tools used to assess their risk and the expert interpretations/ evaluations of what those risk values mean for their health. Trust as deployed in breast care is multivalent and operates on at least four levels. Trust in (1) the 'right' lifestyle choices that will ensure better outcomes (level of situating oneself in charge of one's body and its processes though a self-fiction of control, discipline, self-mastery). (2) Trust in sharing the burden of responsibility for being healthy with the 'right' kinds of experts (level of institutional and interpersonal interaction). (3) Trust in the use of appropriate medical technologies and practices that can diagnose cancer early enough to be treatable (level of institutional practice). (4) Trust in the claim that the deployment of appropriate medical knowledges and practices can predict, diagnose, and improve outcomes (level of appropriate information). The deployment of trust is interwoven with the institutional fabric of medical practice in breast care, and is masked under notions of compliance with medical regimens and assessments. Trust underpins compliance, which "is usually defined as the extent to which patients' behavior coincides with medical advice" (See Hunt, 1989: 315).

To address how and if women follow, negotiate, navigate medical advice is more complex and dependent on the situations women have encountered, how they articulate their agency, how medicine delimits and configures 'options' for them, instituting moments when volition could be more or less legitimately overridden, honored, or sidestepped. The deployment of trust is key in how medicine translates women's experience and is the site where women's agency may be undercut or enhanced. To empowered women, we need to devise strategies that open a space and a place for women to negotiate better and appropriate conditions of care. Women must also participate in shaping the direction of further breast care research and technologies to address her breast care needs while making sure that the expertise and technologies defuse and democratize.

Trust is interpersonal and institutional -- the site where notions of self, subjectivity, and identity are negotiated. Trust is a relational effect and affect. Trust, as a trope, is problematic in at least four ways. (1) Trust delimits the range of 'appropriate' emotions within breast care. (2) As a result whatever unanticipated emotions do surface in bio-medical situations are figured as disruptive. (3) Medicine requires trust in its authority as an institution employing personnel, technologies, infrastructures, and political will. (4) Trust veils the issue of power without addressing the inequities that underlie it. Let me briefly describe how trust works through a few interview snippets.

The first interview quote refers to a biopsy incident that ruptured 'the trust' the interviewee held for her breast care providers. She was angry about how she was treated, about how she felt pinned down like a 'farm animal' on the surgery table, and about how she was not addressed when she inquired into a 'joke' made in reference to the length of her breast incision. She felt that how her providers treated her reflected an absence of an intelligent being present even if she was under only a partial anesthetic. The second interview snippet shows the important work trust performs in grounding the interaction between breast care providers and women.

Vulnerable and Necessary

> *There was a level of trust there that was very precious and vulnerable that that will never be there again.*

I really, think that people are quite different in terms of their needs and it is important to trust the provider to gauge where and when information would be provided.

Women deploy trust differently in these two quotes. The first one stresses its vulnerability. The second highlights its importance. Clear is the power differential that underlies the need for trust's deployment. The deployment of trust in breast care conceals its importance in smoothing over power differentials between breast care providers and women, and in veiling the necessity for the smooth operations of institutions.

Trust becomes the psychic place to manage emotions. Emotion work done through trust mediates the interactions between women and doctors. The breast cancer care arrangements potentially enhance or hinder this process. (See Hochschild, 1979) Needing to trust becomes the label for a complex process of managing emotions. Trust-fear (re) articulates the actions compliance-non-compliance within an emotional landscape that is experienced by the woman. Trust-fear provides nuance and depth to the care interactions pointing to the need for psychological support in handling medical information and making decisions. Managing emotions is key in full participation and clear decision-making.

Women's agency becomes subject to the work of trust-fear the work. The range of emotions circumscribes and delimits it. Take for example the following section and interview quote. A negotiation between the interviewee and a provider around the uncertainties of diagnosing a lump takes place. In trying to figure out if a lump is anything more than just breast tissue: a process of watching and examining over a period of time (about two years) is set forth. Even if there is no change to the lump, alarm was raised enough that a requirement of carrying the examination to its conclusion: biopsy, partial lumpectomy, and surgery. The trust in providers is necessary. People also have different needs that must be acknowldged.

For some expedient action is key at all costs. For some costs and benefits are in the balance. For some the costs of surgery are too great.

Providers and Practices

> *But each time she said, "No I don't think it is anything." and I trusted her. Every time she examined me. She could feel it. And she said are you feeling this too and I said yea. Cause I could feel it too. And she said, "You know I really don't think it's anything." And that's when she kept saying but if you feel like you want to... and of course the mammogram showed nothing. Mammograms wouldn't show it. In fact, I even told the technician could you make absolutely sure that this spot gets it because I have a lump there. Oh sure, that is when she flattened me out. Ah! She says, "You do know, I know it's painful but the picture comes out better -- the more flatter you are I guess." And it is true! The picture does come out better. I say, "OK." I can't really stand it. I was concerned but I knew that that was the spot she was trying to get, where I had the lump. So I was fortunate.*

Trust is pivotal in negotiating an intervention and in communicating across different sites: the private office visit and the clinic where she gets her mammograms. This negotiation highlights the necessity and fallibility of mammography: the painful but necessary flattening out of breasts to get "the better picture," to capture the lump on the print. Her picture did not show anything. But she did do a biopsy that turned into a partial lumpectomy.

One technology or technique precedes the other. One became a necessary passing point without its findings being obligating. Cancer is slippery and there is room for personal preference as well as provider error. Trust in the technology and technician is necessary. When the technician had to flatten her breasts to the point where the pain concerned her, she knew and trusted the technician was trying to get a picture of the lump, to make it visible in the background of the breast tissue.

Questions of accuracy rose. These point to the limitations of current screening and diagnostic practices. Accuracy is also a source of mistrust if not fear. Questioning how medicine conceptualizes breasts, as objects, is part of its limitations. Flattening out is emblematic of how both women and their breasts are intelligible in breast care. But is this flattening of flesh and person necessary? (See Chapter 2; Theoharis, "Hyper-Real Medical Insight into Flesh;" Moi, 2002)

Breasts as Medical Objects

> *Yea. That's important. Because especially in women's health there need to be better techniques that are more accurate and comfortable. Because it [mammography] really hurts. Why should it hurt? I think its because they want to get better pictures. If they don't press enough they will not be able to get a clear picture. It needs to be flat enough to be like an axis horizontal and vertical. And they cannot use higher potency rays because they are afraid that they will hurt the tissue.*

> > *Maybe "it is true" that when breasts are really flattened "the picture does come out better." Yet, why not plan and develop technologies more sensitive to body volume, to breast shape and contour? Why not develop and plan for technologies that do not require flattening out of breasts along a determined set of axes and angles to make them visible, intelligible, readable, and open to medical gazing? Why not develop technologies that empower women to care for themselves instead of building upon the medical-institutional panoply? Most certainly there are other ways of breast seeing and examining!*

Trust is required in each case although the level of trust differs in terms of degree and kind. It depends on the perceived authority, the level of interaction and relation, the intonation of reassurance, the perceived importance. Trust endorses the technology and its pictures, the doctor's skills, the surgeon's cutting, the radiologist's reading, the histologist's reading, the geneticist reading, the technician's technique. The need for trust veils any residual doubt and fear.

Breast care realities are complex. Technologies are fallible. Providers at times are indifferent, inappropriate, and rushed. Technicians too are inconsiderate and inept. Surgeons cut the wrong place or too much and too deeply. Trust is pivotal and earned. Good provider, technology, technician, surgeon stories also about. My point is that the model of trust does not adequately translate and illuminate the social bond that women must develop with breast care providers, practices, and technologies. Trust in technologies, practices, expertise, and techniques is essential in making the work of handling women and their bodies possible, in shoring up medical authority. The social bonds in medicine are made complex by the proliferation of medical expertise, technologies, and practices that re-organize the medical field.

Let me take up the trust in technology since breast care technologies are doubly doubted especially in their side effect. (See Beck, 1992; Beck et al, 1994) I will illustrate doubt and trust with two examples: Mammography and Tomoxifen. The interviewee is conscious about the need to develop technologies to prevent, treat, and better diagnose breast cancer. She is very well aware of the dangers implicated in the side-effects of experimental and normative technologies, in-tuned to the high price women have paid in their flesh, blood, life for the development of newer and better treatments. She is a willing participant in breast care but not a naïve one.

The first interview snippet deals with the problematic of almost being a subject for a Tomoxifen study. She describes her thinking and questioning of her eligibility to participate. The second interview snipped questions the side effects that mammography as frequent ex-rays might have side effects by the cumulative exposure to radiation in modern medical practices.

Technology: Side-effects and Accuracy

> *And then I was going to be in a study for Tomoxifen. And they wanted me to be in the trials for the Tomoxifen. And they said to me, "You wont know whether you are getting the Tomoxifen or whether you are getting a placebo." And I filled out all the paper work and then I started reading about Tomoxifen and then I thought. That is a hormone! And it is. It is a hormone. And so I went to my doctor and I said you know they want me to be in a Tomoxifen study and she said, "No I don't think so!" And I*

said, "Oh OK." [Laugh] I kind of went, "Should I or shouldn't I?" And she said "No! That's a hormone." And she said that the side effects have to do with the uterus.

> *Now here is another thing that I am worried about the mammogram. Is just how many mammograms can... well they say that the radiation you are getting is very low its like going through an airport. But if you figure how much radiation you are getting really, because when I have to go get my teeth ex-rayed that is an ex ray. OK. When I go, have anything wrong with me, you have an ex-ray on top of my yearly mammogram. So when my dentist asks me to ex-ray my teeth. I ask is it really necessary. We just did it two years ago. Nothing hurts so I really don't think you should do it. And they say oh OK well.... That is the only thing that worries me.*

Well... for me the technology is really fascinating. So... the idea of a machine doing the testing... in my head is more accurate. [Laugh] so that is good. And then the tech is not a ... the doctor who is doing the exam.... You are relying on their knowledge in the exam. In the mammogram I am not relying on the tech. Hopefully the tech is positioning everything right so you get the best picture but... the actual film is going to tell the story as long as that tech can get everything to be readable.

I am less concerned about the scientific assessment of risk in these cases: if indeed she as a subject would have benefited from the Tomoxifen study or if indeed radiation from x-rays is negligible that ex-rays are negligible and not deleterious in a cumulative sense for women. I am interested in the manner of her questioning, in how she decided if the treatments are necessary, and who she consulted to make her decisions about her care. I am interested in the following questions. Who did she ask? What did she ask? How she acted with regard to that information? How does she reconstruct her memory of that acting?

I am wondering if and how that ambivalence towards technologies, techniques, and providers can be directed in the development of technologies that are sensitized to the needs of women as their users. An ambivalence is visible and directed towards treatment at hand in both instances, mostly to the work that is visible to her: the surgeon and GP, not the histologist or radiologist through in some instances that work also becomes visible. This ambivalence is qualified by the way 'experts' talk about these technologies. Still, her own reasoning is interesting in thinking about for example the cumulative effect of exposure to radiation, wondering about questions that need to be forcefully posed to the technologies: their side effects on bodies and environments.

Tomoxifen is a new addition to the breast care panoply. The risks of mammography seem known and discreet: "they say that the radiation you are getting is very low it's like going through an airport." Underlying both is ambivalence towards technology and its development that at times is tempered with fascination and even reverence. The technology is objective and godly in how it opens up the body and makes what is anything, nothing, or something readable. The film tells the story in an unequivocal fashion in contrast to people that can get their stories mixed up and confused, whose expertise is not quantifiable. Though the radiologist tells the story of the mammogram that agency gets erased. In this instance, technology is supreme and trust in it is not required. The technology tempered by a high quality technician doing the positioning will allow the picture to speak for itself. This standard for technology can only be achieved when it is accepted as a closed box, if the ways that it handles the body are acceptable, if its side effects on bodies and environments known. Yet that status is highly provisional for mammography is not the closed, well-defined box that she perceives. (See chapter 2)

To recap, trust as a construct underlies: (1) the decisions made when all the facts are not known; (2) decisions made when the facts are known but the expertise of knowing is not had; (3) when the facts and faculties of knowing are had but the practices of doing the tests are not; (4) when technologies used to make up facts are no longer 'accurate,' when the pictures or inscriptions they make are not pertinent, clarifying, or are fallible; (5) trust that even if everything is defined and routine that things will turnout as they should. Trust is necessitated in every breast care juncture for medicine to do its emotion work. Trust in

handling past risks or case histories and not being immobilized by them. Trust in making our

decisions about care. Trust as a construct structures medical descriptions, our understanding

of what is going on, and how what decisions about the kinds of care are pursued.

Trust is Not <u>The</u> Issue!

> *It wasn't that she didn't trust the doctors it was... well she just said that she was not*
> *going to be cut up like her mother and of course that surgery is awful. It looks*
> *terrible. Slash and burn. And umm... that is what they did to my mother. Of course*
> *we all saw my mother. And that is when she said no I'm not going to do this.*

Trust in the appropriate use of medical tools has a moral undertone. In the end,

women have to live with the decisions made about their care. Not participating in breast care

regiments or not moving along certain trajectories leaves women open to judgment as well as

adverse complications from the disease. How that judgment is made introduces another

juncture where inequity impacts breast care practice. Making decisions for oneself requires

skills, knowledge, and time to do research, to have the confidence to ask questions, the

ability to negotiate the conditions of your care within an increasingly complex and

fragmented system of health care. The question of how, if, when, and which women get the

best care and benefit from what kinds of care available becomes exceedingly involved and

social fraught with issues of inequality and injustice.

The deployment of both trust, on an emotive level, and risk, on a rational one, leads to

assessing and attributing differing levels of responsibility-blame to women and to caretakers.

Parables about caring for oneself and another structure and inform the experiences women

have with medicine and the status that medical providers in addressing and configuring

breast care practices. Tales are retold to mobilize women's trust in medicine and illustrate how desirable and undesirable outcomes are (re) negotiated and (re) figured to strengthen understanding and inspire confidence in breast care.

Blame-Responsibility

So far I have shown how risk-security and trust-fear dimensionalize breast care. I was interested in how these tropes made intelligible breast care experiences for women, and how they held a group of women together as subject to medicine. The breast care terrain is crystallized through judgment, through the attribution of blame and/or responsibility to women, care-providers, insurers, media, and politicians. Judgment is central to establish whose agency, control, or intervention takes place and is accountable. Judgment becomes more pertinent when an outcome is undesired. In this sense, agency is qualified mostly in terms of a negative operation. Credit that is positive judgment always is shared. When clarifying whose agency did what through judgment, agency becomes constructed as a property of a subject and not of a process or a collective effected through institutional controls or interventions. Agency then is minimized and located in the particular doctor technician, technology, practice or patient. Figuring out a positive place for women to act from is essential if their agency is to be realized within breast care. This place needs to be collective in appropriately pooling positive and negative.

Figuring how judgment is arrived at or suspended, how it mediates women's experiences is central. Through understanding judgment, we see how, when, and where women's agency has been short-circuited, sidestepped, or honored as women are silent get cut out of the network of credit and are easily blamed. Yet it also raises profound questions about the ways we account for health-events, how we think of what is justified, why and how we attribute cause/ effect to illness or health. In attributing health as an effect of women's or medical work of care, illness is also thusly attributable.

Blame-Responsibility is an effect of medical and social judgment. Key questions are whose judgment, whose standards, what criteria of health and illness are operating as norms. I will briefly underscore the kinds of questions adjudicated in breast care. Roughly, I have identified at least five domains. (1) Judgment of lifestyle: "Am I doing the 'right' things to take care of myself?" (2) Judgment at level of interactions, "Have I trusted providers and technologies/ have I complied with breast care practices?" (3) Judgment of practice, "When, where, how often do I get my mammograms/ breast exams?" (4) Judgment on information held and the making of my breast care map, "How current is the information that I use to make my decisions and where did I get it?" (5) Judgment of outcome, "Who is to blame or is responsible for my bad/ good health?" Decisions in each of these domains are contested. Answers to these questions, however, are key in situating women in breast care and in understanding how, why, what decisions are made about their care, and how agency, control, intervention is translated into the attribution of blame or responsibility.

I use the blame-responsibility to illustrate that judgment always bifurcates in order to solidify and clarify the terrain narrow and wide of right/wrong and just/ unjust. I illustrate how blame-responsibility operates in two interview snippets. The first one describes a process of re-negotiation and a judgment on information given by the providers. She questions both the practices of care and any provider judgments: the extent and quality of information that she was offered. She felt excluded from the decision making process and was not well informed about the content of her care or who had made what decision when.

Accountability

> *Who is responsible for the fact that this person was never informed that she would not be seen for a needle aspiration that in fact when she was told she would get a biopsy that did not mean that she would get a needle aspiration?*

> > *Hmm. I'm glad that I did it [follow through with breast lump findings]. And I think it is an important step in terms of the aging process. (Laugh) And also just being responsible for my body and taking advantage of the technology and the care available and how fortunate I am to live in a place where the best is available both in terms of practitioners and equipment.*

The second snippet describes the responsibility assumed by women to make informed decisions about 'the care available', about the health of 'my body', about 'taking advantage of the technology,' and about realizing 'how fortunate' she is 'to live in a place where the best is available.' Being self-directed is central in negotiating care and in being well informed about what options are on offer. Implied is a requirement of hyper-vigilance and total information that is itself a tyranny.

The question of information is central in making decisions, in being 'responsible' for one's health, and in negotiating/ navigating access to the best care available. The fact that health is presumed to be the 'normal' state of bodies while being a product of work for both women and providers is what underpins the responsibility/ blame accounting for health and illness. If health is the normative value and assumption, which medicine operates to restore, then illness is deemed to be the result of an irresponsibility, either on the part of women and providers, or the technologies and infrastructures involved. This logic sidesteps the questions of systemic and social ills. Breast care trajectories radiates from favorable or unfavorable outcomes. The outcomes negotiated and valued through judgments about content and quality of care, the decision-making that went along with it, and the process of accounting evidenced through blame-responsibility narratives.

Social inequalities crisscross the ways women are en-framed in medicine even as they obfuscate the effort to make *all* women's breast care experiences intelligible through the *same* constructs. Reading as responsible and successful the women, who have the information, the resources, the ability to negotiate the terms/ conditions of their care, and navigate the structures of care delivery, is problematic. It effaces and blames women for not seeking adequate care as a presumed effect of their negligence, ignorance or shortcomings. Apportioning responsibility has political and ethical implications. Responsibility and blame as tropes situate a self-evident locus of agency on an individual rather than an institution, and it appropriates and re-articulates women's agency on terms that negate her experience with illness.

In the following quotes, I give two examples that highlight the importance of information in making breast care decisions and the implied judgment about the ways that information was shared and/ or unearthed, what 'lessons' or consequences were drawn out, and how the stories were framed. The first instance is a retelling of a story that was probably read or heard in the news. The second is a retelling of a family story, an older sister story. Both are given weight through disciplining daughters and other family members. Women themselves discipline each other, e.g. becoming subject to medical practice/ knowledge). This is the bystander effect. That is, women by their participation and observation amplify but at times may confuse the provider message. The first interview snipped highlights the question of being haunted by what is not known about your family history, a heredity tale. "Your mother's health and illnesses can say a lot about yours." The second snipped deals with how to deal with "your mother's illnesses." Learning how to handle 'high risk' is not easy. Choosing not to follow along a path of medical intervention and control is also

difficult.

The Power of Stories

> *Because umm there was a -- I think it came out in the paper. It wasn't breast cancer*
> *it was ovarian cancer. And it was two sisters. One of them looked up to see what their*
> *mother had died of cause she died when they were little. Their mother had died at the*
> *age of 45 of ovarian cancer. So the sister [sp, sigh] she said you know I better go in*
> *and have myself checked out for cancer. So she went in and she was 45, and sure she*
> *had ovarian cancer. Yea... they had to remove everything. So the other sister was 42.*
> *I don't know I guess I better go in... she went in and ovarian cancer. So she said OK*
> *out they come both of the... she had everything taken out. One was OK the other one*
> *wasn't. She had both removed. And the other sister was already like totally....*

> *Because I remember her saying I do not want to be cut up the way mom was. She said*
> *I'm not going to go do that [silently]. So she chose not to so she could have been*
> *saved. She didn't want to be. She didn't want to go through that. And she was a*
> *different type all together from my other sister and I. We went to the doctor for*
> *everything – not for every little thing. We are very health conscious. And we go to the*
> *doctor. But she was not that type. She didn't think it was necessary. She would*
> *always... she didn't like hospitals. She didn't like doctors.*

What is not known can be dangerous and threatening. The need for knowledge

underlines the uncertainties of health and illness. This uncertainty is contained in the word

nothing. (1) Nothing is an estimation of risk-security. (2) It is a reassurance. Women can trust

the process that they embarked on in taking care of themselves because they have done x, y

or z and therefore it has to be nothing. (3) It is an effect of judgment because if it is

something, the flow of events and actions needs to be re-examined. One must be accountable

for the not nothing. Beast care trajectories become precautionary tales. These tales are taken

as psychic safeguards against the anxiety that surrounds cancer as a disease. They frame the

terms and narratives of women's experiences, and are a source for the words to name what is

or has been going on.

Anxiety proliferates over 'nothing.' Nothing is provisionally a something that may not yet be named. It exists tentatively and reassuringly against that dreaded something or is rather cautiously nothing-yet causing 'scare' and dread or eliciting reassurance. Every time a high-risk woman goes to her annual mammogram the potential 'nothing' balloons into anything and yet potentially a something to be watched, waited on, gotten at, cut out.

Attitude Is Key

> *There is so many women that that they do all of these things and they miss it. Even the ultrasound. It goes by the ultrasound. It gets by the mammogram. It gets by everything. And then there are doctors who say lets wait and see... and there it is. And then women are saying well wait a minute. OK yea lets wait and see... they don't want to have surgery. "Oh yea let's wait and see." And there are women who are really aggressive. Get it. Cut it. And that is like me. I'll say I don't care. Cut it. Cause she gave me the choice. Well, I don't know we've been watching this thing and it has not changed and it has not gotten bigger. She said but um, "How do you feel about it?" And she asks me and I said: "Cut it out." I don't want to watch. I don't want to wait. I said no cut it out. See and so she did.*

Options are outlined. (1) Be aggressive about getting treatment even for the 'nothing.' (2) Be watchful to see, to examine and to actively do nothing yet. (3) Be lax not bothering at all because nothing is not a thing to worry about. Responses to breast care are highly moralized and anxiously coded on a scale of appropriateness to account for illness. It is not hard to see how that accounting would lay responsibility and blame for not being vigilant enough to follow through. It also shows the anxiety surrounding the inefficiencies with detecting breast cancer. "It," that is cancer "gets by everything."

How can we give weight to women's experience without taking away from scientific expertise about cancer? How can we open-up a range of acceptable attitudes and self-help practices? Ho can we be more accommodating about different ways of doing heath and illness? How can we open-up ways of being in and with medicine? How can we retain the sense of agency and compassion?

Estrangement-Support

Which women dwell comfortably in medicine? Which are ill at ease and why? How are women and their bodies called forth and connected with providers and practices, within a complex institutional array of technology and expertise? How are women connected with the socio-political and interpersonal process of making decisions about their health? I want to make clear how discourses used by medical institutions, by political structures and by our communities open up word-spaces (topologies), where actions and situations gain their coherence. Word-spaces constructed by providers, politicians, and the media, by lovers, family and friends, by women themselves inflect situations and actions. That is, these words act on both micro and macro levels. They are not simply words spoken or written. They act they have material effects. Their actions take place through our understandings. Our understanding becomes grounds for comparison and order, for connection and disjunction, for community and society. Not all words carry the same weight, nor all become the axis through which we constitute experience. (See Butler, 1997a; 1997b; Foucault, 1973; Bowker and Leigh-Star, 1999)

These notions are specific to a particular care setting and to each woman's experience. They also cut through our experiences. (1) They are polysemic tropes shared across diverse actors and settings. (2) They are axes orienting and evaluating actions, actors, situations towards and away from health/ illness. (3) They are psychic residences and strategies for opening up possibilities and for dwelling in words and in events. (4) They are factual or obligatory statements that call forth rousing alarm anxiety, and spring forth in the emergence of collectives. (5) They are provisional utterances that are silenced, re-framed, shamed, de-legitimated, or honored and highlighted as exceptional and exemplary. (6) They are lines, threads, networks, or interactions connecting and interweaving to make medical knowledge/ practice/ technology, to ground women's experiences/ agencies, and to inform social processes. These words need to be intelligible, negotiable, and navigable.

The place that women, medical practices and technologies, political institutions, and public will and sentiment produce and co-habit is dependent upon at least five conditions. (1) How can we build breast care infrastructures in ways that facilitate access and address issues such as transportation and communication? (2) How can we mobilize political processes and popular will or sentiment to address breast health issues? (3) How can we establish of guidelines of appropriate rationalities as markers of proper practice so that both standards of appropriate care and accommodating templates to negotiate and circumnavigate interactions between women, provider, infrastructures, social worlds is possible? (4) How can we grant coverage for breast care services and treatments? (5) How can we mobilize resources to develop and improve technologies, practices, and provider-expertise in ways that honor and strengthen women's place in their breast care. Let me briefly illustrate how the tropes risk-security, trust-fear, blame-responsibility call forth, connect to, and dwell with women and medical/ political institutions.

First, risk-security names, calls forth women and institutions, to negotiate in public what to do in what contexts. Risk-security defines what doings are appropriate for providers and women as well as cancer is and means in what situations. There are at least three issues. (1) The risks associated with the development and use of an array of technologies (See

Tables 3 and 4) (2) When to mobilize what technologies? What is an acceptable level of risk? How are risks evaluated and by whom? What role do different players have in the process? (3) How risks are distributed environmentally, occupationally, and socially? How do they affect illness and health? The relation between health and justice impacts infrastructures, attitudes, resources, and the participation of women in breast care as well as its politics.

Risk discourse defines women. It is the logic that rationalizes the care that is delivered. Risk discourse in the hands of insurance reproduces particular relationships between capital and health. It then becomes a side effect of factory-style medicine. This can lead to estrangement for the most vulnerable. Estrangement is an effect of coming to terms with risk and what risk values mean for oneself and for loved ones. Estrangement is a process and an outcome. Estrangement is an effect of how health care is delivered – being on a treadmill, the drive through. It is an effect of the psychic space opened-up by risk as it is used by medicine. Let me briefly illustrate how estrangement emerged in an interview. She became estranged as her mother had died of the complications relating to breast cancer. Her mom is the main link, main support. After the mother's death, the process of caring for herself became routinized. She required distance from her family, as it was difficult and painful to be around.

Emotion

> *I took distance. My family was a very painful family. And cancer didn't help. But I was not directly involved in my mom's care. It was painful just hearing about other people's pain around it.*

> *For the longest time, I felt vulnerable. And umm I don't know now that my mom has died not directly of it but.... Yea. Umm. Since my mom died I've become more estranged. I don't feel as dependent on any ties to this world as I was. I guess I really don't care that much right now. I mean I just go through the motions of getting checkups and stuff but I don't think too much about it. I don't feel directly influenced.*

The potentiality of cancer is alienating and alarming. In facing cancer, a woman must face her mortality. The threshold of acceptable risk is subject to our tolerance of uncertainty and the availability of resources to handle our concerns. Risk perception then is different from risk assessment. Risk assessment guides provider recommendations. Risk perceptions grounds women's responses to illness. Women at risk might be estranged from or may not have a support system. Women may not be able to put the effort in creating new connections and community and learning better copying skills.

Simply grounding communities through an assessment of risk is not sufficient to create support for women at risk. This is a first step. Being part of the community is being able to share with the world at large the experience. An absence of community can be as deadly as the absence of appropriate information and/ or medical technologies and practices. Addressing the adverse effects of being at risk upon our community -- ones personal life support, needs to be at the center of the study of new technologies, such as genetic testing, whose effects on women and their families is still perplexing. (See Chapter 5) If constructive supports exist like family members, friends, or partners, then the process of and prospects for participating in care are enhanced.

Support has to do with developing life-bonds. Trust-fear as an axis delimits the range of emotions and becomes the ground for developing supports not only across the patient-medical divide, but also among everyday interactions. Trust-fear is limited in this regard. Trust may be an effect of support, clarity, community, but a sense of being supported is not simply produced by trust. Feeling support is the result of tangible trustworthy actions like actively listening, facilitating decision making, simply being present. Requiring trust to safeguard against fear and immobility and to shore up medical authority makes the issue of support, which may precede and follow trust, invisible. It, also, fails to appreciate the complexity of medical decision-making and the emotion work required in handling a breast cancer diagnosis. It limits with who and what women feel connected. A medical model of situating women and providing care presumes that strong supports exist, where information is shared, where women connect, are empowered, and motivated, that spaces exist for coming together, and that they are equally available and welcoming for women from different backgrounds and situations. The forces of support estrangement illustrate much a more complex social situation than trust-fear alone.

Let me briefly show how an extended family that is high risk for breast cancer could be a place of strength and support without suggesting that this is the case for all women or that it is emblematic of all extremely high-risk families of women. What is highlighted is the process of sharing information, of following through with appointments, of efforts to update and look out for appropriate services and tools. Breast cancer care becomes a place of coming together, of sharing: a gathering.

Gathering

> *Every time an article comes out I'm looking or magazines. It is all kinds of information: word of mouth also within the women in my family. We always are telling each other. Oh did you hear this did you hear that did you hear the latest that sort of thing. We relay all the time all the information. All the time! And especially when one of us is going to come up for a biopsy or a mammogram. We all ask each other well how was the mammogram. You know, "Are you going?" We remind each other. And like I say the race for the cure we all work at it. Yea so... we are pretty well... it's a major family effort. It really is!*

Care in this context becomes 'a major family effort' of sharing information, of reminding, of grounding and supporting each other, of bonding. Building up the social ties that hold one in place is a conscious effort. One of these efforts of gathering is the race for the cure. Other such communities of action exist. (See Klawiter, 1999) The race for the cure supports the medical research into care and cure. Gathering then is first the familial gathering. Secondly, gathering is movement to raise funds or to seek justice through social/ political action.

Not all women find support in the same ways. Some have more contentious relationships with medicine and medical practice. Some do not have the familial support, nor the resources/ energy to keep active, be engaged, and informed. Medicine, as it acts, needs to take such questions into consideration. Medical outcomes depend on it.

In opening breast care to women's agency, women need to develop the terms to talk about their own experience. Women, who speak for themselves, are key in finding ways to name what is going on with their bodies and to articulate how to transform their interpersonal relations to support their breast care needs. Not having the terms to name what has gone on with your body can be stifling. Developing strategies to solicit support is also needed.

Place

> *I had an aunt who died of breast cancer on my dad's side. To me I wasn't really sure if that would have meant anything cause it was on my father's side but it was someone who had died in the last... the year before that. So, It was in my head. But at the same time this was happening and it is better to know as early as possible. It was nothing. The results came back. It was something like a tissue. I don't even know what they call it. It wasn't anything to be worried about. I don't even know to tell you what it was. Hopefully it is in the charts somewhere.*

The provisional nothing appears again. She disavowed the family history present for it to be nothing. The results show 'it was something' but not *that* something, but rather a something that does quite have a name and does not need to be worried about. A something lingers still in her head and hopefully somewhere in the charts cause if it does turn out to be something more someday, then that whole process of accounting will need to take hold. This experience is troubling. Women need to have terms for speaking about their experiences. The nothing here is also something that can be forgotten for the time being.

Language allows for the creation of a place, a record for the something forgotten. This experience of placing allows for a sense of being with, a sense of relationship and communion with what is unpleasant but also keeping it at a distance to maintain a sense of poise and self-control. There is comfort in the idea that even if she needed to review what happened to her a record exists where the nothing is classified and held. The work of articulating that nothing into a something not to worry at present empowers a sense of being in control and a way to talk about it. In this regard, women live by and through the languages they share and use, the languages that cross provider-patient interactions, the language that institutions also set into play. Even as in this case the specific language is forgotten. In this regard, discourse is both local to a setting and trans-local in how it is translated in another communication. The use of a particular discourse defines a community, a society, and an individual. Discourse travels or is the bridge across different scaling of events; it allows for the construction of specific kinds of perspectives. (See Theoharis, "Hyper-real Medical Insight into Flesh")

So far I have shown how estrangement-support is a dimension where women open up a place within medical language and institutional interactions from which to speak, engage, and act. The term 'nothing' seems rather interesting in how it is used. Women and breast care providers, practices, and technologies are called forth and connected through this process. The question of inhabiting and opening up a space in ways that honor how women do health and illness is key in unfolding a place where women have agency in breast care. This doing of medicine calls for a new kind of ontology, a different sense of timing and effect. (See Mol,

2002) The next chapter deals with the challenge of genetic testing. This chapter sketches the range of current practice with an emphasis on women's actions, thoughts, and language. I hope to facilitate the creation of institutional structures that empower women and are sensitized to the multiplicity women's concerns.

Timing and Sense

With their participation in breast care, women embody discourses of risk-security, trust-fear, blame-responsibility, estrangement-support, and thus are embedded in a medicalized ordering of their bodies, actions and minds. This medicalization takes place through strategies that rest upon trajectories of achieving health and evading illness. The breast care apparatus diligently bifurcates not only between a medically informed self set in control over an unruly cancerous body, but also between self and ideo-typical others situated in breast care. This process is a biosocial. (Rabinow, 1992; Foucault, 2003) I picture it as a topology. Medicine figures 'correct' or 'reasonable' ways of calling forth women, providers, social and political resources. It connects and re-interprets the links between and amongst women and their care and how women dwell within the routine practices and interventions.

Timing medical actions early in the trajectory of the disease is crucial. Timing affects each axis. In terms of risk, delaying is risky. In terms of trust, delaying might imply that women are distrusting their providers or the technologies involved. In terms of blame, delayed action can result in being blamed for potentially poor outcomes. In terms of support, delayed action might mean lack of support and/or access. However, delay might also be the result of lack of information or know how which would be again risky. The timing of medical action is a result of a complex arrangement between providers and communal supports, women and their bodies. The simple declarative sentence: breast cancer prevention is early detection might then have more weight and meaning in the lives of women at risk for this disease if the full complexity of their situation is better understood.

Overall, this chapter illustrates the relation of women and their breast health, the ways that women's agency is both articulated and hindered, and the work of medical mediation. This work produces an asymmetry between providers and women placing more validity in the hands of the former. Can we discern the dawn of a post-sick-role-medicine, the possibility of a medicine more symmetrical and accountable in decision-making? Would an honoring of different ways of doing health and illness require a restructuring of medicine, its relations to the communities it serves, its production of new kinds of techno-scientific products that may no longer be called cures? Would the models of cure and care be still relevant? To be caring for humanizes medical structures but is translated to certain settled inter-dependencies. Curing implies that one party is able to direct the process of becoming healthy for another. What if care and cure resides in empowering, in instructing situations specific to each woman's needs, sensitized to her body to avert and overcome disease.

Timing Intervention

I just lived with it. It was always in the back of my mind, but I never really did anything to allay my fears or wondering really. I was kind of in a state of, I can't say denial, but I didn't want to know. So yes, the information was there. (Anonymous Interviewee)

Introduction

With increased interest in genetic testing, understanding women's use of genetic information can assure a smoother introduction of the test from medical trials to clinical practice. Proponents of the test suggest that genetic information facilitates women's decisions about their care because it opens a window of opportunity for high-risk women to participate in more frequent surveillance, chemoprevention, or prophylactic surgeries. In this regard, BRCA 1 and 2 testing allows women, who are at higher high risk for hereditary breast-ovarian cancer to shift the emphasis from early detection (reliance on frequent screenings) to prophylactic surgery and chemoprevention. The test targets women who suffer from early onset or invasive cancers as well as women who are difficult to screen or diagnose with current methods. Women, then, are called to act in the face of potential genetic risk for the disease. They must assess, consider, decide and act once they find that they might be subject to the test and test positive. The question behind this study is to illustrate women's decision-making in the face of a new and untested medical tool and to see how their consideration of BRCA 1 and 2 testing affects their subsequent treatment choices.

Some caveats about genetic testing and information. (1) Genetic testing is not calibrated for the application to moderate or low risk populations where the presence of BRCA 1 or 2 mutations may not imply an elevated risk for breast cancer. (2) Genetic information is probabilistic and not diagnostic. This means that having the mutation does not imply that one has breast cancer, but that one is more likely to have it in the course of a lifetime if positive. (3) Genetic information elevates the use of prophylactic treatments, whose long-term value remains unclear. (4) Genetic risk also seeks to demarcate discrete values for higher high risk of breast cancer or its recurrence. These values are questionable and may provide false comfort. (5) Breast cancer, as we understand it is multi-causal and the relative role of environment, genetics, viruses/bacteria, and lifestyle is not yet fully understood. Numbers linked to a genetic mutation still pose questions about the ways genes link to cancer as an outcome, as well as how genes interact in sequences of other events. (6) Finally, BRCA genes create a family or ethnic legacy in handling the disease, which may be stigmatizing. (See chapter 2)

Understanding, then, how women assess breast cancer risk and how that vulnerability reflects on them and their families, is central to showing how women act and what the implications are for genes as actants. Assessing breast cancer risk is a multi-event process that includes providers, women, and information gathering. Understanding assessment as a process illuminates the role that genetic testing can play in women's health care decisions including the decision to test and what to do with all the information gathered. As women consider testing, they also consider prophylactic surgeries and the effects of a positive or negative result on themselves and their family.

Assessing Breast Cancer Risk

Findings

✓ *Most women rely on an informal process of risk assessment. This informal process is event driven: e.g. mother's cancer, sister's cancer, aunt's cancer or information driven: new study or significant piece of information that elevates perceived risk.*

✓ *Medical assessment of BRCA 1 or 2 risk seems to be more prevalent for women who do not necessarily have cancer themselves or who were concerned about risk for family members. Providers also play a role in shaping risk perception. They mirror (validate or check) women's perceptions.*

✓ *Women learn how to manage their cancer risk through the experiences of close family members and friends. Support groups and psychological counseling are starting to play a role as well. Their role increases as emphasis is placed upon psychological wellbeing as a factor for recovery and survival. Both counseling and support groups can be a great place to process information gathered, to think through how to act, to experience others processing.*

✓ *Women's knowledge resources include a combination of information from family members, doctors, and personal research into family history, media, e.g. sources like the web, newspapers, and ads.*

✓ *Most women consider genetic testing when they are diagnosed or personally affected with breast cancer. This is in part due to a test requirement that a person affected with cancer is a better candidate for BRCA 1 or 2 testing.*

As genetic testing is integrated into standard clinical practice, questions like why women test, how they perceive the usefulness of the test, and what they do with the test results come to the fore. We have found that women's perceptions of breast cancer risk play an important role in assessing the probability of a cancer diagnosis or recurrence, the adequacy of current and considered medical interventions, as well as the utility of the test itself. These perceptions are dynamic and event or information driven. Understanding the events/ information that shift women's perceptions of vulnerability helps clarify how women come to consider genetic testing in the first place, and then what they choose to do with the information gathered whether they decide to test or not.

Vulnerability

Heightened vulnerability to cancer follows from three types of relations: relation with a close associate who suffered from the disease, a relation with vulnerable body parts, a relation with vulnerable moments in a life-course. By understanding how women experience vulnerability, I can illuminate the situations that propel women to consider genetic testing. These situations relate to events that raise the level of perceived risk beyond a threshold that calls women into direct action. Sometimes these events are traumatic and have debilitating effects on women's ability to cope with the disease or its possibility. Sometimes they awaken women to risks that they had not fully considered for example research into family history 'that lit up like a Christmas tree'. A positive effect of feeling vulnerable to breast cancer is the start a 'fact finding' mission that would lead to more deliberate action. However, not all women experience medical care in the same way. Some women are confused by more information. Some women prefer not to take on the full burden of their health care decisions and wish to share them with a spouse or doctor. So the question is to enable women to identify how much they need to know to come to terms with the complexities of medical care for breast cancer, for women to set the parameters for caring.

- Women become vulnerable to cancer through relations with family members or persons in their immediate environment who have been diagnosed with the disease. Resemblance can play a role in connecting or distancing from a family member. This role can be psychological since an association with a person that had the disease impacts women's self-perception of risk for the disease. Resemblance can become a self-fulfilling prophecy if a cancer diagnosis follows. For those who think of breast cancer in terms of family history without a direct knowledge of genetics, resemblance becomes a rough equivalent for a notion of heredity even if that notion is faulty. For example, an interviewee knew that half her genes came from her dad the other half from her mom, still felt that she looked like her dad and therefore would not be susceptible to mom's cancer if it was hereditary, which turned out to be false. Caring for a family members or close associates also increases women's sense of vulnerability especially if that family member had a difficult time copying with the cancer diagnosis and treatment or if that family member died. The death of family members links palpably a cancer diagnosis with death. If this is a frequent phenomenon, it links notions of cancer and death with a family legacy.

- When women feel vulnerable, they at times identify beasts, ovaries and/ or genes to be at fault. These 'parts' becomes 'time bombs.' Thus, vulnerability to cancer becomes localized in this particular body part. This part can be identified as inherently risky and removed. 'Female' parts (breasts, uterus, ovaries) in particular are perceived as at high risk. Locating cancer risk to a vulnerable part might facilitate the willingness to consider surgeries. At the same time, this bodily location of risk can alleviate anxiety when the part is removed through mastectomy, oopherectomy, or hysterectomy. The logic of locating cancer risk to a body part comes under question with the notion of a BRCA gene. Even as prophylactic surgeries are proposed as the initial treatment response for women at higher high risk, the notion of genetic causation shifts the therapeutic ground for the disease from a tissue or extra-cellular process to an intra-cellular/ genetic one. (See Chapter 2)

- Vulnerable moments in a life course relate to the perceived age dependence of cancer onset. The timing of events in ones life or the life of mother, sister, and aunt takes on meaning. At times, it could be connected to hormonal events such as pregnancy or onset of menopause. Descriptions of body parts as 'time bombs' establish the vulnerability of the part, but also the question of finite time to disease. A family legacy of breast cancer compounds some women's sense of vulnerability to dread and futility. The timing question extends to the onset of the disease. Early onset cancers tend to be more deadly and not as much subject to routine screening. Early cancers are more prone to create a sense of association with a vulnerable moment in life course, e.g. turning thirty. In general though, cancer is age dependent as cells are more likely to become malignant as we age. Women over 50 are frequently perceived at significant risk for the disease independent of their family histories. So nearing menopause can also create a sense of being at risk and feeling vulnerable.

I described three kinds of vulnerability to cancer: (1) through an association with a person who has had cancer; (2) through an identification of a vulnerable body part; (3) the identification of a vulnerable moment in the life course. (See Table 5) Being vulnerable to cancer leads to questions of managing emotions and then assessing risks before considering actions and making decisions.

Cancer and Emotions

Managing emotions is an important task when facing cancer or its risk because feelings of vulnerability can impact wellbeing, which in turn can cloud decisions. This management deals with feelings that emerge from past, future, present events. (See Graph 5) Managing emotional knots is important for establishing a pathway to clarity and action.

Managing emotions at times has to do with 'face work.' Positive attitude at times is an 'emotional state' at times it is the act of putting on a 'face' that allows women to move forward even if the emotional issues are not fully resolved.

Having a positive attitude allows women to participate in breast cancer care and to face the risks at hand. The underside of a positive attitude is a feeling of futility. These feelings may inhibit timely action, as no action may seem appropriate or appear to have a positive effect. Though some women feel futile about their prospects of recovery, but still follow through with treatments. If positive attitude leads to feelings of being immune to risk, than no action might be taken to pursue care that would be warranted. Positive attitude is a buffer between unproductive debilitating stress or worry and a willingness to live life and manage actual risk or the care of a difficult illness. Positive attitude is not a substitute for proper consideration and action -- whatever is necessary for each woman -- since there are different styles of handling risk and managing emotion. Positive attitude can become a burden for some women as a way of putting on a happy face on unhappy circumstances. It must not be requisite in medical interactions. The structural relationship between vulnerability, knowledge, and action, then, hinges on the ability to identify and cope with actual risks, to seek available recourses to manage it, and have faith in the selected course of action as well as the providers involved. Emotions are not static. It is oriented towards events past, current and present. These events may be real or imagined. Graph five is a sketch of how emotions are temporalized in reference to potential situations and actions.

Clearly, experiences of cancer risk sensitize women to information that seeks to establish it. The experience of vulnerability may lead to a sense of faith or inevitability. The translation from experiencing vulnerability to establishing targeted risks that can be managed requires identifying situations, effects, or behaviors that impact the likelihood of cancer. Thus, a sense of vulnerability can translate into knowledge seeking to manage the uncertainties of living with the risk of breast cancer or its recurrence. The determination of actual risks as opposed to the feelings of being at risk is a complex and under-determined process that requires further study. Physicians play a role in defining and targeting actual risks to women's health. In the interactions between medicine and women clarity over proper course of action emerges. Conflicting information can exasperate women's confusion and sense of futility. (See Table 5 the column for vulnerability).

Establishing Risks

In moments of vulnerability, women seek to evaluate actual risks for the disease. Women establish their risk through personal experiences and through information gathered. Events such as an experience with cancer, e.g. a cancer diagnosis of self, a close relative (mother, sister) or a close friend effect a woman's perception of being at risk and are moments for some when "knowledge seeking" begins. If directly involved, these events are primary experiences in instructing how women will handle the disease. Primary experiences -- not a personal experience but that of a close relative -- can open a window for personal risk assessment even if that assessment follows that event. Primary experiences sensitize to the potential of such event in a woman's lifetime: the sense of being at risk spikes. A primary event, then, is a direct experience with the disease that affects the learning curve with diagnosis and treatment.

The number and quality of primary experiences lead some to conclusions of cancer being deadly, difficult, linked to self and children. Subsequently, interest in genetic testing will peak or trough depending on the evaluation and perception of risks. The relationship between primary experiences and ones own cancer risk is not necessarily a direct relationship. Some women feel invulnerable to cancer only when several family members have experienced the disease. Some women feel vulnerable when immediate family members are affected. Some women feel vulnerable because several persons in their neighborhood or job were affected. Some women feel vulnerable because they learn about added risks associated with procedures like HRT or fertility drugs in combination with some family history. The turning points are secondary events. These events associate a perception of being at risk with actual pieces of information to make risk appear high or specifically genetic.

Secondary events shift the sense of vulnerability as the result of information gathered through physician interactions, personal research, or the media. These shifts can be in either direction: corrective or reinforcing in positive or negative direction. These events affect a woman's sense of vulnerability and open a range of actions to manage these perceptions and actual risks. Secondary events can be powerful and trigger specific interest in genetic testing by reinforcing the perception of hereditary causation. The sequence between primary and secondary events varies leading up to consideration. Sometimes a genetic risk may not become clear until the two are joined to raise the threshold of hereditary risk to the point where the test is useful. The pathway is deferent depending on the woman. Some women may be ineligible to test because no members who had cancer are available to test.

Primary and secondary events then accumulate and trigger changes in risk perception. The change heightens a sense of urgency because these events mutually reinforce or amplify each other. Risk perception becomes actionable when it leads to seeking ways to manage feelings of vulnerability and actual risks. This management points internally through emotion work and outwardly though face work, what women describe as 'positive attitude.' Feelings of futility sometimes take over when the sense of being at risk is too high and the inevitability of death seems near. A negative accumulation of events could lead to diminished risk perception or a redefinition of actual risk (primary and secondary). This negative accumulation follows research into family history that yields negative results because the types of cancer are not related e.g. that there might be a preponderance of some kind of cancer, but not the ones thought to be linked to the gene: ovarian, breast, colon and maybe prostate. Two, the incidence of cancer doesn't suggest a genetic link. Whatever the outcome, an evaluation of medical procedures along with genetic testing takes place, so that women know more about what to do in planning of surgeries, chemoprevention, increased vigilance and surveillance, telling relatives.

The distinction between primary and secondary events is really an effect of a visible shift in risk perception, an urgent sense of vulnerability, and the potential for learning to cope. Personal experiences with the disease tend to have more of an impact. However, the accumulation of many events diminishes their direct impact. In some cases, women become fatalistic or think they are immune until affected. Some define themselves at higher high risk or at low risk without actual evidence. How women perceive their cancer risk is pivotal in deciding to test and in making decisions about their health regimen. A woman's risk perception may be congruent or in conflict with how physicians involved define actual risks. In this regard, a woman's perception is a product of the interaction with the situation, with the information she gathers about her family and her life decisions, with her experiences of other person's struggles with the disease and with her own. The negotiations with physicians happen along the lines of defining risk in terms of utility for treatment. Women's interest is in defining risk for her self, for her kin and for society at large. A conflict does at times present itself.

This conflict plays itself out as disconnect between providers and women, between actual and perceived risk. The disjunction of actual risk and perceived risk is important. Actual risk is usually associated with physician definitions in reference to women's sense of vulnerability. Two cases I found in the data are interesting. One is a reference to a woman who underplayed her breast cancer risk because her mother was not diagnosed, but she had three aunts who were diagnosed. The other is a reference to a woman, who felt she was at exceptional risk because her mother was diagnosed and yet looking at her family pedigree such sense was not borne out. Some women have little sense of their family history and what are genetically relevant cancers until they consider genetic testing.

Overall, women rely on an informal process of establishing risk. These perceptions are event or information driven. Primary and secondary events alter women's sense of vulnerability to cancer. Some times, they are personal, familial experiences with cancer. Other times, they are information driven: information given by providers, the media; information gathered through personal research, or during the consideration of testing itself. In this regard, *perceived risk* is not a linear or unidirectional a variable. (See Methods and Definitions) Conflicting information about the nature of cancer risks causes women to feel more confused and vulnerable. *Usefulness* seeks to resolve the distinction of actual and perceived risk. (See Methods and Definitions) It revolves issues of test characteristics, which physicians use to ascertain who is a good candidate for the test and what is the appropriate course of treatment. Some women experience barriers to testing as a result. These follow references to costs, potential insurance discrimination, and test availability.

Women are more likely to consider genetic testing if there is a preponderance of cancer in the family. Some participants initiated seeking genetic testing to clarify their personal risk. Some have strong family histories and are concerned about family genetics, about the strong links between cancer and death, and about the legacy they leave their children. Some have received conflicting evidence from their doctors about their genetic risk and seek to clarify it. Some were diagnosed with cancer, but are not sure why, so genetic testing will in their mind clarify at least one source of causation. The translation of feelings of vulnerability to actual risks to genetic risk and ways to manage them happens through knowledge seeking and interactions with providers, with other women who have cancer, or with family members. (See Table 5 column *perceived risk*)

Genetic Risk

> *I see it as two separate things – one having cancer, the other carrying the gene, you know. I mean I understand one sets you up for the other, but I don't understand that one means you have cancer and that therefore you had a mastectomy, you know. But then I have not dealt with death, you know, I have not had family members die over breast cancer. And you know, maybe if my mother had died of breast cancer, I'd be more likely to think that way. (Anonymous interviewee)*

Women come to understand their genetic risk through their interactions with providers, other women, life events, and their own knowledge seeking efforts. Attitudes towards breast cancer causation inform the relative the place genetic testing in treatment. Combined they link up with how women handle cancer and death and reflect upon their sense of vulnerability. Vulnerability links up with knowledge seeking which impacts the testing decision. In this regard, four points seem worthy of further investigation as they establish a relationship between women's vulnerability and the perception of genetic risk for the disease. Vulnerability is reflected through the connection of cancer and death and of cancer and self.[26] The perceived strength of genetic causation reflects the perceived link between genetic markers and cancer as outcome.

- A perceived/ established strong link between heredity, cancer, self, and death. This link suggests women do not feel that they need to know the result of this particular genetic test, or that they need to know to make sure that they take measures to diminish their actual risk or share the concrete knowledge of that risk with their family members.

- A perceived/ established weak link between heredity and cancer for her self, but strong link between cancer and death. These women tend to feel that genetics plays a minor role in cancer for them but have had experiences with cancer morbidity in their close environment.

- A perceived/ established strong link between heredity and cancer for her self, but a weak link between cancer and death. These are women do not believe that cancer is necessarily a death sentence because that has not been their experience. They are women who have had faith in medicine and have found success there, and/or have seen women in their family handle this disease, and/or have faith in their ability to overcome this disease.

- The perception that cancer is multi-factorial. In this regard, heredity has no special role in her healthcare decisions as of yet. These women are not clear about the role of genetics, and genetic testing in their risk assessment. So genetic info doesn't impact their sense of vulnerability, or they feel uncertain about its value. They might choose to test, however.

---

[26] I had proposed a formula to establish the quantitative effect of (exposure to cancer as a disease) in relation to the qualitative effect of a sense of vulnerability or even assessed risk. Such numerical value may not be very useful but it does speak to the process of accumulation of experience and sense of vulnerability. {Exposure to cancer=Sum of the degree of relatedness or affiliation * degree of involvement}

These points have not been explicitly asked for in the interviews so cannot be fully traced. The intersection with women knowledge seeking behaviors begins to shift in women's intent to test. Besides establishing the intent to investigate genetic risk and seek testing, we have to concern ourselves with what counts as measures of genetic risk. Women describe genetic risk in these ways: a family tree or pedigree, a connection to an ethnic group at risk, the possibility of a 'fluke chance' mutation, or a concern for future generations. Concern for future generations can be problematic if women begin to make reproductive decisions over the possibility of passing along 'faulty genes.' Connecting a 'faulty gene' to an ethnic group is equally troubling.

In the best case, the implications of BRCA testing will effect medical management decisions of breast cancer or its risk. BRCA testing, then, seeks to establish relationships between existing genetic markers and any heredity causation for breast cancer. How women associate cancer, death, and BRCA genes speaks to their sense of vulnerability and/or sense of control over breast cancer as a risk or disease. The loose or tight linkages indicate potential interest and intent to test. BRCA knowledge is not neutral information. Some women use it to establish actual risks and negotiate procedures, some to warn family members, some to advance medical knowledge. (See Table 5 attitudes towards genetics)

Considering Testing

Findings

✓ *Women who consider the test have five distinct attitudes.* **I need to know** *my genetic risk for x or y procedure, for my peace of mind, for my family, for the good of science.* **I already know** *that I am at higher high risk because I have an extensive family history or had several bouts of cancer.* **I am not affected** *because the genetic test* *will not impact my decisions one way or another either because it is a new test or because I have already done most of the surgeries I need to manage my risk. **I am uncertain** if the test is valuable for myself or for my family. **I do not need to know** my genetic risk because I have a difficulty with the idea, because my family has difficulties, or because it is not valuable information.*

✓ *Women consider testing to better define their cancer risk and modify existing medical decisions, to define the cancer risk of family members (sisters, children), to advance medical knowledge, and to better understand if they need to have prophylactic procedures such as surgery or chemotherapy or not participate in risky procedures such as HRT.*

✓ *Most women time their testing decision prior to informed consent. The main purpose of informed consent is a buffer: to ensure that women have considered the implications of their decision to test before testing. The geneticists or genetic counselors settle whether women are test worthy.*

✓ *Most women decide what they would do with a positive test prior to informed consent. This tends to occur in interactions with providers: oncologist, surgeon, geneticists, or other women. Some providers require genetic testing before suggesting a particular high risk or prophylactic procedure.*

✓ *At this juncture providers play three roles. They are informants about the test or study at hand. Advisers in influencing the direction of a decision to test or not. Finally, they also are gatekeepers enabling or disabling women's access to the test or to particular treatments.*

BRCA 1 and 2 refer to genetic markers for 'female' cancers: breast and ovarian cancer though colon cancer are also correlated. Women consider genetic testing to define cancer risk, to allay vulnerability to cancer and its recurrence, to be more vigilant in screening or prophylactic medical procedures such as hormonal therapy and surgeries, to define heritability for their blood kin (family members and children), to prepare emotionally for what is to come, and to advance science for future generations. The process of considering testing is not as clear as Graph 4 depicts.

The graph is meant to be illustrative and schematic. Women consideration of genetic testing oscillates between three poles: *Vulnerability, Usefulness,* and *Knowledge Seeking.* (See Methods and Definitions) When vulnerability to cancer is understood by women and physicians to be potentially genetic, then the notion of test usefulness comes into play and fuels knowledge seeking behaviors which include research, contact with providers and women who have decided to test. Physician interactions establish usefulness of knowing whether or not one is BRCA 1 or 2 positive. Women need to be mindful of how much information they require to decide either way. Genetic counseling sessions have served as thresholds or buffers to make sure women have understood the implications of testing and have access to adequate information.

Usefulness

Test usefulness does not necessarily translate into genetic knowledge seeking. The translation from *usefulness* to test decision occurs in the process of consideration. Medical *usefulness* plays an important role. It results from an evaluation of medical tools available to manage actual risk. The physician is the structural/ institutional arbitrator of *usefulness.* Insurance at times structures medical judgment based on cost and demand. Barriers to access to test occur through coverage or availability. An economic accounting of risk establishes insurability that is the willingness for insurer to pay for what kinds of procedures. This accounting does not follow medical necessity or the need to develop new tools. In other words, insurance may limit the hand of the physician in seeking genetic information before establishing the utility of other procedures and may not be looking into long-term usefulness over short-term gain.

Negotiating usefulness happens in (1) physician interactions, (2) in insurance company interactions, (3) in university protocols that fill the gap of insurance coverage, (4) attitudes of family members. In physician interactions, the issues surround the usefulness of test for treatments such as prophylactic interventions or for the evaluation of risks for family members. Some physicians also question at times the efficacy of the test as a measure of actual risk or whether there is adequate evidence for the test to be included in clinical practice and for what cases. Some physicians also warn of the potential for insurance and employment discrimination on the basis of genetic information. For insurance companies, it seems that there is no universal coverage for the test and that some women face issues of cost. An actual instance of insurance discrimination was not reported, but the fear of that instance and fear over being dropped after a cancer diagnosis prevents some women form testing. Universities have research protocols where a lot of women where able to participate. In these studies, women get anonymous testing. They, also, cover some of the costs of the test. Being in a study implies stricter guidelines and protocols.

Finally, family members also came into the dialogue of *usefulness*. Questioning if they would like to have access to that type of information at a particular time. Some initiated the quest into genetic testing. A lot of women considered genetic testing because of family member sister or daughter had been interested in it and they were the living family member, who has had a cancer experience and who was able to test to help locate the gene. Testing family members that had breast or ovarian cancer was at times a requirement. This requirement gives contextualizes to the number of women who have or had cancer and were considering genetic testing in our study. Sometimes not having a family member with cancer was a barrier. The venues, through which women sought genetic information, were relevant in terms of the test requirements/ characteristics and the style of genetic counseling they received. These venues varied in our interview sample from university studies to private genetic clinics, as did the means through which women paid. Some women chose to pay out of pocket to avoid insurance discrimination or because the insurance would not cover it. In this regard, our sample is skewed to women who have means, education, and access to test.

Minority women were underrepresented in our study. This was due in part to the way interviewees were selected. Some doctors recommended women who considered genetic testing to contact us. Some women found out about our study and wanted to participate. No specific efforts were made to solicit/ select underprivileged women. There might be structural impediments or boundaries for minority women to access information about genetic studies. The barriers might be economic, might refer to particular style of medical management or a willingness to participate in research studies. This issue requires further study because the participation of minority women helps in designing future institutions where all have access. The test had also acquired an ethic label. It was frequently referred to as the 'Ashkenazi test' referring to women of Easter European Jewish descent who are at high risk for breast cancer. This association can be problematic if it becomes stigmatizing. However, there is no evidence in the interview to suggest that that had occurred.

Knowledge Seeking

Vulnerability affects *knowledge seeking*, which in turn is limited by *usefulness* (both test requirements and characteristics). This completes the triangulation of considering BRCA testing. (See Graph 4) Genetic testing may not always be perceived as useful in deciding a particular course of treatment, but the process of considering genetic testing is informative and has an effect on women's knowledge and subsequent treatment. *Usefulness* and *vulnerability* effect *knowledge seeking* as a behavior: usefulness as external limit or reinforcement and *vulnerability* or more general perceptions of risk as an internal propeller.

Knowledge seeking is a posture that shifts along five nodes: *Need to know* whether they have the gene whether they end up testing or not; *Already know* that they have the gene whether they test or not; *Not affected* by knowing if they have the gene whether they test or not; *Uncertain* whether knowing that they have the gene is beneficial choosing for the moment not to test; *Do not need to know* whether they have the gene whether they choose to test or not. *Knowledge seeking* connects to the state of mind of the interviewee at the time they considered genetic testing. (See Methods and Definitions)

A person may swing from one category to the next in the length of an interview or even in a sentence as they are sorting through the testing decision. The moment after the precipitating event (the event that initiates or terminates consideration) is the moment chosen to assign a particular stance to an interviewee. This posture might change when some choose to reconsider testing.

- *Need to knows* tend to be on a fact-finding mission, whether they decide to test or not. 'Need to know' numbered 22 out of 68 interviewees (32.4%). There were more likely to test. [17/22 or 77.3 % Acceptors / 5/22 or 22.7% Decliners] All the decliners faced barriers to testing. These barriers referred to questions of access: financing, availability, and eligibility. Most had college [C: 27.3%] or some college [SC: 36.4 %] education. Some had a high school diploma. [HD: 31.8%] Few completed grades10-12. [10-12: 4.55%] They had slightly higher than average knowledge scores. [Mean score 9/12; Average 8.3/12]. Their age clustered in the 40s: 36.4 % and 50s: 22.7 %. [30s: 22.7%;

60s: 4.55 %; 70s: 9.09 %]. They were more likely to have cancer. [68.2 %; 31.8%] Most

had at least one kid. [16/22 or 72.7%; 6/22 or 27.3%] They felt vulnerable at times to

cancer, the gene and/or death but were rarely fatalistic. Almost all had some family

history. Almost all had at least one parent who had cancer. [At least one parent 77.3%;

other family 13.6; no family history 4.5%]

- *Already knows* tend to have a sense that they probably already have the gene. They

  numbered 11 out of 68 interviews (16.2%). They were most likely to test. [5/11 45.5 %

  Acceptors; 6/11 54.5% Decliners] Most decliners chose not to test [4/6 or 66.6%]. Some

  faced barriers. Most had college or some college education. [C 36.4%; SC 46.4%; HD

  9.09%; 10-12 18.2 %] They had average knowledge scores. [Mean score 8/12; Average

  8.3/12]. Their age clustered in the 30s: 81.8% and 40s: 18.2%. They were somewhat

  likely to have cancer. [54.5% to 45.5%]. About half had at least one kid. [5/11; 5/11 one

  not applicable] They expressed fear to cancer and death but not to the presence of the

  gene. Sometimes being fatalistic. Sometimes being surprised that they tested positive. All

  had family history. Almost all had at least one parent who suffered from cancer. [At least

  one parent 72.7; other family 27.3]

- *Not Affecteds* do not report vulnerability to the gene. They numbered 20 out of 68

  interviews (30.4 %). They were also less likely to test. [75.0% Decliners; 25.0%

  Acceptors] Some decliners faced external and financial barriers. [60.0%] Some chose not

  to test or faced other self-imposed barriers. [40.0%] Most did not have a college

  education. [7-9 5.0%, 10-12 5.0%, HD 40.0%, SC 30.0%. C 20.0%] Knowledge scores

  were near average. [7.9/12 to 8.3/12] In terms of age they clustered in the 40s: 50.0% and

  50s: 20.0%. [30s: 15.0%; 60s: 5.0%; 70s 10.0%] Some had cancer. [65.0%] Some had at least one kid. [50.0 %] No one felt particularly vulnerable to the new gene markers. One acceptor felt vulnerable to family history. Most had a parent with cancer [70.0%]; one decliner reported other family cancer [5.0 %]; five decliners reported no family history. [25.0 %]

- *Uncertains* were not clear about the value of the test. They numbered 10 out of 68 interviews (14.7 %). All declined to test. Most decliners chose not to test. [Choice 50.0%; Other self imposed 20%] Few faced external [20.0%] or financial barriers [10.0%]. Most had some college or college education. [C 20.0%; SC 60.0%; HD 10.0%; 10-12 10.0%] Knowledge scores were average. [8/12 to 8.3/12] Their age clustered in the 30s: 30.0 % and 40s: 50%. [50s 10.0%; 60s 10.0%] Most had cancer. [80.0%] Most had at least one kid. [70.0 %] Most felt vulnerable to cancer. Few included the gene or death in the list of vulnerability. Most had at least one parent with cancer. [80.0%] Some had only other family members with cancers. [20.0%]

- *Do not Need to Knows felt uneasy about the test.* They numbered 5 out of 68 (7.4 %). Most declined to test. One chose to test but declined the result. None faced barriers. Most had some college or college education. [C: 20.0%; SC 40.0%; HD: 20.0%; 10-12: 20.0%] Knowledge scores were average. [8/12 to 8.3/12] Their age clustered in the 60s: 40.0% and 50s: 20.0%. Some were in their 40s: 20.0%. They were more likely to have cancer. [60.0%] All had at least one kids. Most felt vulnerable to death. One to cancer. One felt vulnerable to the knowledge of the gene! Most had at least one parent with cancer. [60.0%] Some had only other family members with cancer. [40.0%]

Overall then, *need to knows* want to gather genetic information for their personal use, for their family members, or to help advance medical knowledge. Some found that the knowledge to be useful for their medical management decisions. *Already knows* tend to feel that they already have the gene because of their family histories. Some will test to confirm how they feel. Some decline because they feel they do not particularly need the information. Some face barriers. One acceptor in particular was surprised to test positive even though her aunt had tested positive. Her parents did not have cancer but otherwise she had extensive family history. *Not Affecteds* are not impacted by the information either because they face barriers to testing, or if they are accepters, they feel like they have already done what they could in terms of treatments. In other word, they test because it is one more thing they can do. *Uncertains* are doubtful about the relevance of genetic information to their management decisions. However, they are prone to want to change their minds down the road. *Do not Need to Knows* feel vulnerable to genetic information itself or find the test not very useful! One chose to test, but did not want to know the result because she would feel guilty if she knew and passed the gene to her daughter. *Knowledge seeking* modified though *vulnerability* and *usefulness* as part of the process of considering testing leads to the *testing decision*. (See Graph 4) I have graphically represented the path from knowledge seeking to the testing decision. (See Graph 6)

Testing Decision

The testing decision can be reduced to yes- no- maybe at another point in the testing trajectory the question: accept - decline - reconsider or retest. As such, the testing decision appears as a choice of direction, as a crossroads. That view, however, underplays the consideration and circumstances leading to that decision, which then bear upon how the information was gathered, and which point these decisions and events will lead. That reduction is clarifying. It also forgoes the complexity and underdetermined nature of action.

In other words, it does not look at the stage or setting for action and how it structures results, or the quality of negotiations taking place. This in turn under plays the process of consideration.

The testing decision as an act follows a series of events that shaped the field through which it becomes. Testing as a decision is a singularity. It might shift with time. It consolidates the events that lead up to it, the manner and style of negotiations that have been taking place, as well as prospective assessment of actions depending on the testing outcome. One way or another, testing as an act brings forward a new set of circumstances that reevaluate current strategies for managing cancer risk or cancer as a disease. Testing impacts the interviewee and, by the nature of genetic relatedness, one's kin: siblings or children (own/ next generation). The complexity of the testing decision is interesting as it intersects with knowledge seeking. (See Graph 6/ Table 6)

So the question then becomes who are the acceptors and decliners and how do they act after the process of consideration? Does who they appear to be before testing matter in how they act with that information? Clearly speaking of types of actors is misleading: as a person cannot be fully illumined through their statements or actions. We can focus on the type of action and the qualities of statements. We need to look at the potential continuity discontinuity between prior events, current considerations, and forward-looking actions? Is such a tread of continuity present for those involved? Can that thread connect to the stance they take in reference to testing consideration and testing decision? Then, we need to see what bearing does the testing decision have on the person, their kin, and their future actions.

For the first question, the answer is yes for some and no for others. Not all are deliberate about the possible impact of the test to bring that to bear upon the present and future because some do not feel vulnerable to the test information enough to reflect upon it. Some are reactive to a set of circumstances. Some decisions are over-determined by prior events so present considerations have no real weight on the course taken. Some act on the presumption that they know the outcome even as they test. Some women choose to test to gather the knowledge for the next generation, to answer why they have been subject to this disease, or to help advance medical knowledge. Some women choose to test to gather evidence for particular prophylactic procedures. Some test because it is another tool to use. In terms of timing, some women decide that they would do with the test near the moment they consider testing. Some decide somewhere along a series of encounters with physicians, family members and personal research.

Weighing the decision is key. To simply, *need to knows* have a stake in testing; *already knows* seek confirmation; *not affecteds* deal with over-determined situations either by their choices or by the environment; *uncertains* ponder the value of the test; *do not need to knows* have a stake in not knowing. The weight of the decision to test then impacts the future directions most for those who have a stake. Some re-evaluate their stance after testing positive or negative and some when they confront the question of informing kin.

Medical Intervention

Findings

✓ *Physicians perform procedures after consideration of breast cancer risk or cancer recurrence risk. Genetic testing at times plays a role to define risk at others it does not. In this regard, physicians structure medical interactions.*

✓ *Most women over the childbearing age tend to handle ovarian cancer risk aggressively because they perceive current screening methods for such risk are ineffective. Some women choose to have hysterectomies not just oopherectomies.*

✓ *Some women choose to handle breast cancer risk aggressively because they feel exceptionally vulnerable to cancer. They feel like they cannot live with the cancer risk or cancer recurrence so surgery best fits their needs.*

✓ *Some women choose to know their genetic risk before deciding their treatment. Some re-consider treatments after testing where the value of the test information might change. Some reconsider their decision to test or question the test result.*

✓ *Some women choose not to consider prophylactic procedures in dealing with breast cancer risk or recurrence like preventative mastectomy. After being diagnosed with breast cancer, they are more likely to consider prophylactic mastectomy on the other breast.*

I established how considering testing leads to the testing decision. What are the effects of the testing decision on medical management? I look at the coordination of two sets of results reflected in Tables 7 and 8. One refers to medical management decisions in reference to both knowledge seeking and test results. The other gathers medical management decisions in reference to both knowledge seeking but along the testing trajectory. The data in these tables is numerical. The focus will be placed on procedures likely to be affected by considering genetic testing as to capture any effects. In this regard, prophylactic surgeries will be highlighted. Timing does affect other medical management questions like surveillance and chemoprevention. Women, who do not use the genetic test to answer the risk question or the timing of treatment question, will act differently.

In this regard, the knowledge seeking categories reflect that differential value of the genetic test and its capacity to clarify the hereditary risks for developing breast and ovarian cancer. Genes might also lead to new types of treatments: gene therapy or pharmacogenetics because they begin to shift the logic that underlines the surgical cure: that breast cancer is a local disease that can be halted by better surgical procedures. (See Chapter 2) This logic has lead to the use of prophylactic procedures as a means of reducing risk instead of clearly developing alternative efficacious treatments that actually cure the disease.

- *Need to know acceptor*

From the 17 acceptors 7 tested positive (4 with cancer/ 3 no cancer), seven tested negative (5 with cancer/ 2 no cancer), three were inconclusive (2 with cancer/ one no cancer). (See Table 6)

In terms of therapeutic breast surgery, four out of seven positives required therapeutic breast surgery: one chose a lumpectomy during consideration, two were mastectomies one was during, two were bilateral: both were during. In terms of prophylactic surgery, one BRCA positive person, who also had breast cancer, considers prophylactic breast surgery in the future. One chose to rule prophylactic breast surgery out altogether. One had a second mastectomy during test consideration. In terms of prophylactic oopherectomy/ hysterectomy, however, the story is different. Three positives persons, who had breast cancer, also planed hysterectomies (these included the ovaries) after being tested. (See Table 7 and 8)

From the three positive persons, who needed to know and were cancer free, two had double prophylactic mastectomies. One had the procedure performed prior to considering testing. One chose bilateral surgery after the result. In terms of ovarian cancer risk, one had hysterectomy during. Two had a hysterectomy after learning of a positive result. One had an oopherectomy after retesting because she initially did not want to have the procedure. (See Table 7 and 8)

In terms of seven acceptors, who tested negative, five had cancer and two did not. From the five that had cancer 3 were breast one was ovarian, one skin cancer. (See Table 6)

From the three who had breast cancer one had a mastectomy, one had a bilateral, and one was planning on a lumpectomy, which she decided because she tested negative otherwise would have chosen a bilateral. The one who had a mastectomy also had a prophylactic hysterectomy during her consideration of genetic testing. The one who had skin cancer was undecided on whether to go on HRT, which might be a risk factor for breast cancer. The one who had ovarian did not really contemplate her breast cancer risk. The two acceptors who tested negative and didn't have cancer were both considering prophylactic procedures. One had already a prophylactic oopherectomy and was considering a bilateral. She decided against it after the negative result. Her sister had tested positive. The other considered both prophylactic oopherectomy and bilateral but was relieved when she did not have to make those decisions. (See Table 7 and 8) One acceptor, who did not have cancer, had an inconclusive result. (See Table 6) She has chosen not to do any surgeries. (See Table 7 and 8)

In terms of breast screening, five acceptors have reported no change: two positives, two negatives, and one inconclusive. Three have reported including more surveillance such as sonograms or more frequent mammograms: two positives, one inconclusive. One negative has reported that she believed mammography was inaccurate. Two believed it was no longer needed because they had bilateral surgeries. In terms of ovarian screening, two reported no change and they were both negative, three reported change in including screening and they were positive, one had reported that it was not accurate and she was negative. One reported no need to worry cause of the hysterectomy. (See Table 7 and 8)

- *Need to know decliner*

All the five *Need to Knows* declines are decliners with barriers. Three had cancer and two do not. (See Table 6) From the three who have cancer, one had a bilateral prior to considering testing, one had a lumpectomy followed by a mastectomy during, and one had a lumpectomy. None of these decliners had ovarian prophylactic surgery. From the two that did not have cancer, one considered prophylactic mastectomies; the other opted for no surgeries. (See Table 7 and 8)

In terms of breast screening, two decliners reported no change. Two decliners reported surveillance after consideration and one had no report. In terms of ovarian, two reported including the screening test post consideration. (See Table 7 and 8)

- *Already know acceptor*

Five acceptors are in the already know category: three positives, two negatives. No inconclusive results reported. (See Table 6)

For the three already know acceptors who tested positive: one had breast cancer; one ovarian cancer; one no cancer. (See Table 6) The one with breast cancer had a therapeutic lumpectomy during. The one with ovarian had a therapeutic oopherectomy during and a prophylactic double mastectomy post. The one, who did not have cancer, had a prophylactic oopherectomy during and bilateral breast surgeries post. Two tested negative; both had cancer. One had ovarian. She had a hysterectomy prior to testing. Testing linked her ovarian with mother' breast cancer. One had breast cancer: she had a lumpectomy and was considering prophylactic oopherectomy. (See Table 7 and 8)

In terms of breast cancer screening, two positives were interested after consideration. Two negatives reported no change. For ovarian screening, one positive reported interest; one negative would consider it; and one positive thought it was a bad test. (See Table 7 and 8)

- *Already know decliner*

Four already know declines were without barriers. Two decliners faced barriers. (See Table 6)

From those without barriers, one had cancer. (See Table 6) She was treated by a lumpectomy followed by a mastectomy during her consideration of genetic testing. She is considering prophylactic surgery for ovarian cancer. The other three had no surgeries. One thought that testing related to consideration of prophylactic surgeries. (See Table 7 and 8) The decliners with barriers both were cancer free. (See Table 6) One had no surgeries. The other had prophylactic oopherectomy following the consideration of testing. (See Table 7 and 8)

In terms of breast screening, one decline with barriers reported more frequent mammograms; four decliners reported no change. For ovarian, two reported no change. (See Table 7 and 8)

- *Not affected acceptor*

Four out of seven not affected acceptors tested positive. Three out of seven not affected acceptors tested negative. No inconclusive results were reported. (See Table 6)

Of the positives, three had cancer. (See Table 6) One had a therapeutic lumpectomy followed by a mastectomy and a prophylactic post result mastectomy. She also had a prophylactic hysterectomy. One had a therapeutic mastectomy during and prophylactic mastectomy/ oopherectomy post. The last one had a mastectomy prior, a prophylactic oopherectomy post, but was considering a prophylactic mastectomy on the other breast. The one that tested positive but had no cancer was considering a double prophylactic mastectomy but had neither surgeries. Of the negatives, two had cancer. (See Table 6) One had a therapeutic lumpectomy during. The other had a therapeutic mastectomy and a prophylactic hysterectomy prior. The one that tested negative and was cancer free had a prophylactic hysterectomy post. (See Table 7 and 8)

In terms of breast screening, three acceptors who were positive chose to increase or add mammograms. Two acceptors who were negative chose not to change. In terms of ovarian, two acceptors positive chose to one add screening and one screen more frequent. One acceptor negative chose more frequent screenings. All were post result. (See Table 7 and 8)

- *Not affected decliner*

Five out of thirteen declines had no barriers. Eight out of thirteen decliners had barriers. (See Table 6)

From those with no barriers, three had cancer; two did not. (See Table 6) Of the three who had cancer, one had a lumpectomy prior but planned a hysterectomy after. Another had a lumpectomy followed by a mastectomy before and an oopherectomy during. The last one had a therapeutic lumpectomy during and no further surgeries considered. The two that did not have cancer: one was considering a bilateral but did not have any surgeries. The other had no surgeries as well. (See Table 7 and 8) Of the eight who had barriers, four had cancer and four did not. (See Table 6) From the four that had cancer one was not clear what her treatments were. One had a therapeutic and a prophylactic mastectomy prior. One had a double therapeutic mastectomy prior and therapeutic oopherectomy during. The last one had a therapeutic mastectomy prior and an oopherectomy during. From the four that did not have cancer, one had prophylactic bilateral mastectomies and oopherectomy during. The other three have chosen not to do any prophylactic surgeries. (See Table 7 and 8)

For breast screening, one chose more frequent exams post consideration. Two decliners with barriers and seven without chose no change. For ovarian screening, one decliner with barriers initiated after. One decliner thought screening was ineffective and opted for surgery. Two decliners did not change. (See Table 7 and 8)

- *Uncertain decliners*

Seven out of ten uncertain decliners had no barriers. Three out of ten uncertain decliners faced barriers. (See Table 6)

Of the decliners with no barriers, five had cancer. (See Table 6) One had a therapeutic mastectomy before. One had a therapeutic mastectomy and a prophylactic mastectomy/ hysterectomy before. One had a therapeutic lumpectomy during and a prophylactic oopherectomy prior. One had a therapeutic mastectomy prior and a prophylactic oopherectomy during because there was no good screening for it. One, lastly, had cervical cancer and had a hysterectomy. She would not consider a prophylactic mastectomy. (See Table 7 and 8) Two did not have cancer. (See Table 6) Neither opted for surgeries. One cited she was too young for them. (See Table 7 and 8) Of the decliners with barriers, two had cancer. (See Table 6) One had a therapeutic lumpectomy during. The other had a therapeutic mastectomy during. She also considered a prophylactic mastectomy on the other breast if she reconsidered the test and if she were positive. One had no cancer. She had a prophylactic oopherectomy during. (See Table 7 and 8)

In terms of breast screening, one decliner shifter to more frequent exams and sonograms. Three chose to add screening. Three decliners with barriers reported no change. Two decliners reported no change. For ovarian, on decliner with barriers and one with no barriers started screening after consideration of the genetic test. One decliner with barrier and one decliner reported no change. One decliner reported no pay by insurance during. (See Table 7 and 8)

- *Do not need to know (acceptor and decliners)*

One out of five do not need to know was an acceptor who declined the results. (See Table 6) She had a therapeutic mastectomy prior and considered a prophylactic oopherectomy deciding ultimately against it. (See Table 7 and 8) Three out of five had breast cancer. (See Table 6) Two had therapeutic mastectomies. One of them stated that she would not consider a prophylactic mastectomy for the other breast but would consider an oopherectomy. One was in the process of choosing between a lumpectomy and a mastectomy but had not yet scheduled the procedure. (See Table 7 and 8) Lastly one had skin cancer. (See Table 6) She stated she would not do a prophylactic mastectomy. (See Table 7 and 8)

In terms of breast screening, four do not need to knows (one acceptor/ no result and three decliners) reported no change. For ovarian screening, two (one acceptor/ no result and one decliner) reported including ovarian screening after their consideration. One reported no change. (See Table 7 and 8)

Timing Question

Timing comes into play in deciding which procedures to do when and when to talk to family members about risk concerns. The most time depended procedure in reference to genetic testing is prophylactic surgery: mastectomy, oopherectomy, or hysterectomy. The results show that considering testing affects women's attitudes towards breast cancer risk and towards prophylactic procedures. In some cases, it solidifies a sense of urgency to act on plans set in motion and the need to act immediately. It, also, raises questions that need to be further addressed like how/ when to speak to family members about their genetic risk.

Need to knows had prophylactic surgery 10/22 (45.5%) and half after consideration of testing. Four were for breast cancer with two after a positive result. Three were ovarian all prior or during consideration. Five were hysterectomy with four post and one during. Two were combo breast and ovarian or hysterectomy. *Already knows* choose prophylactic surgery 3/ 11 (or 27.3%): two bilateral post, one ovarian during, one hysterectomy post, one combo post. *Not affecteds* had prophylactic surgery 12/20 (or 60.0%): 4 breast (1 double/ 3 other) with two post one during and one prior; five ova with three during and two post; four hysterectomy with three post one prior; and three combo with two post one during. *Uncertains* had prophylactic surgery 4/10 (or 40.0%): one other breast prior; two ova during; two hysterectomy prior; one combo prior. *Do not need to knows* had no prophylactic procedures.

Not affecteds had the most prophylactic procedures. So it makes sense that they were least affected by considering genetic testing. *Need to knows* most planed their procedures after consideration. For them, the timing question was most affected by genetic information. *Already knows* had procedures post result if they tested positive and were cancer free. So in that regard they were depended on the confirmation of the test. *Uncertains* show that the consideration of the test had no barring. In fact it might be that their attitudes towards prophylactic surgery that impacted their consideration of the test. *Do not need to knows* simply are not interested in prophylactic procedures.

Genetic testing in particular, then, raises the issue of timing medical procedures irrespective of their efficacy. Genetic testing, also, alters the definition of women at higher high risk. The test seeks to reduce the complexity of cancer risk for some women to a genetic question. Women at higher high risk are ones who are BRCA one or two positive. Some women do not take up the genetic definition of their risk as central at this point. Some fear the implications of a genetic definition of their disease. Some welcome genetic testing as a chance to do something before cancer has occurred which in their eyes is already too late. Some see it as a new test that is potentially beneficial and might lead to new therapeutics. Some see it as untested: too risky to base medical decisions.

In this regard, any barriers women faced have differential meaning for women who could not test depending on whether they *need to know*, an *already know* or are *not affected* since attitudes towards prophylactic surgery and surveillance varies. In terms of chemoprevention, *not affecteds* were also more involved but the numbers are minor and may not be significant enough to report for all groups. So the question, then, is how much information does a woman require to decide and to act? Some are not as deliberate in their decisions. Others are. Each woman asks and answers that question differently. That answer also reflects her attitude towards risk and uncertainty, as well as her innate sense of timing in the face of cancer as a disease. Telling family and relatives also depends on whether women are a need to know, an already know, a not affected. Generally need to knows have an ease in articulating their reasoning.

Women as Actors, Genes as Actants

Genetic testing is a new screening technology. It promises to be a more 'scientific' assessment of genetic risk for breast, ovarian and related cancers. Whether genetic testing offers better information, than standard risk assessment based on family history is in question. It must be evaluated on those grounds to justify the present move from the experimental to clinical settings. At best, genetic testing supplements existing processes of assessing cancer risk (both professional and informal). Strengthening current methods of risk assessment and breast cancer risk evaluation prior to allowing genetic tests is important, as we do not know the implications of testing for the general population.

In considering genetic testing, women must decide whether it is appropriate for them to test and what to do with the test results once they are gathered. Women as actors need to establish how much information and of what quality they require to make the best decisions for their care and then to act. Some women require the best up to date experimental info others do not. Some want to play a central role in their medical decisions; others do not. Some feel like they would like to try a new procedure after it is fully understood and tested and others do not. Some are weary of new tests and procedures. Irrespective of how women act in medicine, the best care must be afforded that is congruent with women's style of making decisions and with new procedures available. Physicians in this regard can be responsive to different styles of medical decision-making and to recommend another physicians if there are incompatibilities.

Genetic testing is not the only means to gather information about risk. If women are averse to it, no pressure need apply. On the other hand, if they feel they need to know, that is also a different question. Requiring a test for a prophylactic procedure may put unnecessary strain on women who do not feel comfortable yet with genetic information. However, prophylactic procedures seem to be on the rise. Questions about if they are warranted need to be front and center. Prophylactic procedures manage not only the risk for the disease but alleviate anxiety about cancer. To what extent prophylactic surgeries reduce risk and those feelings are accurate remains to be known.

Genetic testing, at the moment, sits well with the existing medical paradigm, which crudely put has become: cut first and ask questions later! The extent to which such strategy is efficacious remains to be known. Genes have the power to redefine us: that is how they act upon us. They act upon our present, our ancestry and lineage, and our potential future. When we are talking about managing the onset of future disease, we run into problems of contingency and probability. Both are very difficult to settle. Facts matter. The ways we construct them matters. Accuracy matters.

In this regard, we are talking about the creation of medical scripts for each contingency: the construction of medical hyper-actions where all seems to be known in advance based on a genetic script. Such knowledge claims seem dubious. It depends upon a metaphor: that genes are scripts of past, present, and future, that they might then be the language of life creation. Genes are locations or better a subset set of base pairs on a large twisted molecule (DNA) in the nucleus of each cell. To compare the permutations of genes to an alphabet, and DNA to a language is to simplify the biological processes of translation, encoding, gene dominance, and gene expression. In this regard writing and editing the genome would appear to be a simple job: the job of enhancement medicine in pursuit of a healthy bodied world with the additions of cosmetics and fitness.

In so far as it would be really difficult to prove the future manifestations of those diseases, and the validity of such scripts in delimiting a future event, taking action before more definite knowledge and understanding of potential event or error is questionable. In this regard, medicine is best served to develop strategies that deal with actual instances of disease and to fully delimit scripts of cause/ effect rather than acting on probable events. In the case of cancer, it means looking at the specific macro/micro molecular dimensions of the disease more carefully including genetics with an eye to develop better therapeutics. In the end, it means identifying and moving beyond the limitations of the surgical paradigm for the disease.

Conclusions

We build institutions to manage the world we inhabit. Illnesses such as cancer shake our institutions and our lives. Cancer is now a chronic condition or concern. It is also a condition that has yet to be cured. Even as we have measured success in treating some types of cancer, we still are riddled with questions: what roles do our inherited genes play? Or are genetic changes that lead to a cancerous cell due to intra/ extra environmental factors? (See chapter 2) This discussion really leads to a question of arranging actors, actants, and knowledge in experimental sites and translating that knowledge into therapeutic action then clinical practice through the clinical trial. The question for medical institutions is: How can they successfully open up avenues for research into such new treatment arrangements while ensuring that when appropriate old structures are retained?

Three areas are worthy of note. First, the question of arrangement: how should medical knowledge link up with the care apparatus (the juncture between experimental or clinical) to produce knowledge that has positive effects. Second, the question of magnitude: how can the shifting of scale from small experiment to large population be effective and respectful? Managing a trial sample is different from managing the care and care delivery of a population. Lastly, the question of institutional growth: How do structured collectives like institutions learn and grow in connection with individuals or social groups to avoid stifling aspects of orthodoxies or conflict?

I have examined these questions through a detailed study of breast cancer care paradigms. First, I looked at the construction of breast cancer knowledge/ practice with regard to treatments and women's experiences, than I looked at how that knowledge became a powerful social force through the grounding of experience in the definition of situations and the formation of subjects, in the timing of intervention and the structuring of interactions.

Medical Actors, Actants, and Knowledge

Medical Actors, Actants

To answer these questions specifically for breast cancer, I began with a study of the therapeutic paradigm, how it formed, joined and competed with other domains of expertise in handling the disease. I looked at how the main tenets of this paradigm became institutional in structuring the juncture between women and medicine: first in terms of the emergence of a paradigm of care; second in the modern redefinition of disease; third in the constitution of screening and therapeutic technologies that interface with the disease; fourth in the development of a language to structure and guide the experience; and lastly in the question of timing treatment for successful outcome.

I assessed the argument that breast cancer treatment paradigms shift from a solely therapeutic: early radical surgery, to the rise of screening technologies combined with various degrees of surgery and chemotherapy or radiation. In the process, surgery has retained a central role. In fact, the surgical paradigm for the disease still holds. Early radical surgery, in the form of prophylactic mastectomy, staged a comeback for women at hereditary risk or higher high risk for the disease. The two organizational tenets of the disease: early and radical structure the configuration of medical knowledge and practice. Women are asked to time their decisions and practice in ways that will support this model of action. (See chapter 1)

At best, the adjuvant treatment model for breast cancer treatment is a tissue-conserving alternative to major surgeries. Some of the tenets of Halsted's paradigm were challenged, e.g., at which point is breast cancer a local disease or a systemic one. Mastectomy as a centerpiece for breast cancer cure declined in practice but was not replaced. Chemotherapy, which targets new cells even cancer cells and indiscriminately poisons them, also doesn't seem to be effective as a molecular technique. Radiation reduces cancerous tissues by burning down large tumors to make them subject to surgery for advanced cases. Each of these had arisen as a modifier or substitute for surgery. Surgeons still eliminate damaged or suspect tissues. (See Chapter 3)

What has happened more recently is a re-definition of breast cancer. Breast cancer has become intra-cellular and molecular: fueled by estrogens and therefore requiring the prophylactic use of Tomoxifen -- a hormone that blocks estrogen receptors, or the result of dioxins or other toxins, which may act as estrogens. It also became genetic. BRCA 1 and 2 as genetic markers seem to be most prevalent for women with extensive family histories. No virus has yet been identified to cause breast cancer. The direction of pharmacogenetics is promising with the development of specific drugs for specific micro-causes. Herceptine, in particular, reduces incidence for the disease among high-risk groups and early onset women. In this regard, breast cancer as a disease is now handled bit by bit, not in toto for each case (where each instance was presumed equally deadly and treated equally radically) with new technologies that seem to affect the molecular and cellular dimensions of the disease. A cancer vaccine might also be promising for certain kinds of breast cancer. Such vaccine was developed for the Human Papiloma Virus that is the said to cause cervical cancer. We are not sure to what extent what kinds of viruses or bacteria or fungi might be cancer or breast cancer causing. (See chapter 2)

Genes, viruses, toxins, and hormones are actants involved in describing cancer causation. With them come new sets of actors: geneticists, molecular and viral biologics, toxicologists, geneticists, immunologists and endocrinologists. These actors employ them to propose solutions on how breast cancer works in the body, how to screen for it, and how to treat it. They jockey to convince each other and the public of their efficacy. Lines of continuity and contradiction emerge as each attempts to explain the same phenomenon. We understand this phenomenon as boundary work between professions and boundary object construction. The two go hand in hand. Are cancer genes inherent? Are they viral or retroviral? What triggers them? When will a cell become malignant? It seems like a multi-step processes takes place, where several events eventually lead to a malignant cell that then duplicates at a faster rate and is undetected or overwhelms the immune system. These scientific actors arrange the experimental setting where they can record actants and where knowledge gleams forward and where new therapeutics emerge that can be tested and better understood in their effect on the body.

Making Medical Knowledge

Knowledge of self, body and situation is partial and interested. By interested I mean that it is vested in a course of action and has a specific orientation. By partial I mean that it has a perspective and it cannot be absolute. The application of knowledge is future directed. That futurity is depended on the process of envisioning the now and the tomorrow and re-evaluating the past. That reevaluation must be on the terms of the past so as to avoid an ideological and selective mining of the past for present needs to justify a preset course of action.

Facts must be respected and established as such. Facts are not simply emergent points of convergence or justification between competing discourses. Facts emerge within the boundaries of apparatuses that hold our reality together and in that regard are apparatus specific and constructed. Thus, they are not relativistic. From the perspective of the apparatus: a singular event and outcome is sought. From the perspective of the scientist, the apparatus is made to fit the event that is taking place. At times the same event may yield different results depending on the apparatus. This is intra-action. (See Barad, 1992) Some constructs are better than others. Some apparatuses are better than others. Some scientists are better than others. Scientists jockey to construct adequate apparatuses, adequate scripts, and procedures that will define the constitution for the emergence of indisputable fact.

Scientific facts and social facts differ. Scientific facts are structured through explicit material semiotic configurations of laboratories under conditions that can be controlled and duplicated. Social facts cannot be thus condensed or controlled. Some social psychological experiments have attempted to introduce that kind of level of detailed configuration. However, how general these results are is questionable. Most often, social-psychological solutions are multiple not singular in their constitution leading to the constructions of several types of outcomes and situations. They are not relative. They are polymorphic. Most social phenomena cannot be reduced to such scale of controlled simplicity. Social phenomena are observed through work in the live complexity of unfolding events. Complexity does not mean that social facts are unknowable. It also does not imply divine intelligence. In fact, dive agency leads to bad social policy as it veils the issues and needs at hand. Social and psychological facts have been clouded by an attribution to divine process. Social facts are grounded in the study of discourse and action as it is lived, constituting the rules and interventions of large or small actors or collectives.

Medical facts are biosocial. Thus, they are easily subject to two types of error: one that of attribution to divine intelligent or agency or two that of being singularly determined, not fully taking into account the sociality of the body/ psyche at hand. Medical facts then rest between tools/ knowledges that study and configure nature and society. Medical facts habituate in institutions that create specific cultures and norms to facilitate its specificity. For example, radical mastectomy become habit: practiced even as some justifications for the procedure eroded. Radical mastectomy still garners credit because of its legacy and tradition based on the particularities of individuals embedded in hospitals as collective structures even as Halsted style operations are no longer in use.

Evaluating knowledge and experience can be objective if by that we mean clearly adjudicating tactics used and having in mind the goal at hand. Knowledge itself as we experience it becomes interested in the structures of our lives. It cannot be objective. It is interested in the course that it furthers what or whom it strengthens or weakens. It can take a neural stance or facilitate movement in a particular direction. It can be aimed at improvement. It can be symmetrical in evaluating possibilities and alternatives. It also can suspend final or absolute judgment, as fact is apparatus contingent or judgment partial to the act of witnessing. A neutral stance implies an open mindedness, the possibility of re-evaluation, the acknowledgement of process and outcome and error. Objectivity as a stance may be less tenable. It implies a full and final accounting of fact. It places that requirement as possible and necessary for forward motion towards a particular objective. It is an error to assume any application of knowledge to be objective or disinterested. The application of knowledge is goal directed and partial. Those goals need to be evaluated, regulated, and be ethical in both means and ends. They must be mindful of their partiality and how they are experienced.

Experiencing Medical Knowledge

Any movement stemming from such experiences shake the structures of care, which structure our experience. Collective experiences can redefine the discursive foundation of intelligibility, the structure of care, and/ or the pathways that conjunct experience and institution for the purposes of intervention. The juncture of experience, knowledge, and institution needs to be the site of careful investigation. We live in a world of complications. A world where the effects and side-effects of our actions loom larger than we anticipate, where memory, community, and accountability are essential to cope with complexity, to distil an ethic of being with, to inhabit institutions, knowledge, and authority. Our knowledge is the weave of practical understanding. An understanding structured by both limitations and possibilities, where our collective experience matters and must be honored and preserved as memory.

Sociology as a body of knowledge has an institutional structure. Sociological knowledge results from a process of gathering information, distilling evidence, constructing practice and protocol just as medical knowledge. However sociological knowledge seems to be less determined than natural science. It is multi-layered. This is because human activity, human beings are not readily reduced to operational scripts and definable components. In my analysis, I sought to define the range and quality of human experience in breast cancer I sought to define human experience through concepts that cut across institutions, individuals and situations.

I utilized axial analysis of such constructs to identify the range, pulls, and orientations of human thoughts, actions and what structures them. The parameters of analysis emerged in and through the institutional, social, interpersonal settings of the experience with illness. In this regard they become foundational. They are essential to the intelligibility of illness experience within our medicine. Thus, experiencing medical care becomes intelligible though these specific constructs. They are the grounds for paradigms of intelligibility that hold and grant coherence to diverse medical practices, knowledges and interactions. Social knowledge is fuzzy. We experience it in the constitution of medical institutions, in the definitions of social policy, in the definition of social problems and ways to target them.

Medical Paradigms, Norms, and Power

Medical Paradigming

Paradigms are a constellation of concepts and rules that hold together a knowledge-practice apparatus where facts are produces and actions justified. This apparatus gathers knowledge or produces particular effects of knowledge in practice. In this regard, paradigms are material-semiotic-praxis arrangements. Medical paradigms in particular involve the coordination of human and technological action to facilitate the effect of healing. Medical paradigms have punctuated trajectories or cycles: (re) settlement; credibility and institutional growth; trial, readjustment, or redirection.

For breast cancer, the period of settlement occurred at the turn of the 20th century. The hegemony of certain constructs that followed is clear. These constructs allowed for a credibility campaign to enroll publics, the government and other members of the medical community to the task at hand and behind the professions involved. Mid 20th century brought a time of question with regard to the scope and style of medical operations for the disease. At the time we saw the rise in credibility of radiotherapy and chemotherapy, which lead to the adoption of the clinical trial as a standard for medical practice and a new configuration of patient/ doctor. A new strategy of care emerged which used surgery more conservatively in addition to chemo, radiation and by the 70s mammography. Late 20th century saw the rise in credibility of mammography. Mammography allowed the time for less extensive operations and more deliberate decision-making. Chemoprevention and genetic testing have began to sketch out the parameters of a prevention strategy. This strategy seems so far to retain certain parameters of breast surgery as therapeutic suggesting however that breast tissues are inherently prone to cancer. Molecular and genetic definitions of cancer also hold the promise in shifting cancer away surgery as its main therapeutic.

In terms of institutional growth and credibility campaigns, the American Cancer Society and its predecessor had served the role of an advocate of a certain treatment paradigm that would offer hope. Women's health movements challenged medical practices and questioned their authority. They sought an expanded role for women to make their health care decision and for physicians to provide medical options. However, such a role was contingent upon the ability of women to play it. Women who were educated and had the means were best suited to negotiate better care. This raises issues of unequal access to quality care.

Medical Norms and Normals

Medical treatment paradigms, then, are the grounds upon which social forces gather to construct norms of behavior and normal individuals in medical interactions. Norms and normals are not inherently good or bad. The question is in the application of what kinds of force and to what ends. In breast care then, an ideal patient is one who is vigilant, knowledgeable, positive, responsive to medical advice, and a survivor. The construction of a singular ideal, however, is problematic. It requires that a normal become normalizing and always suggests a narrowed path to arrive at it. Medicine, then, must be multi-normal. It must be flexible and responsive enough to facilitate a range of decisions styles, actions, and situations by both accounting for actions and their effects and producing best outcomes.

How can we construct normals without having them be normalizing? That is, social forces must not be unidirectional nor grounded in one ideal mode, style or being with disease. How can that be achieved? Three points seem clear. One is to suspend final judgment on certain styles of seeking-care or self-care. However, medical facts must be judged judiciously. Two is to place the emphasis on learning (managing stress and complex emotions, learning scientific facts about the disease and treatment options) versus being an ideal type. Three is to ensure that communication occurs in a language and manner compatible within the situation at hand. In this regard, the question is not the construction of a norm or a normal but defining multiple strategies for successfully engaging in medical care to achieve the desired objectives.

What resides behind normalization or socialization as processes in breast care? Can medical power be multi-local and not oppressive? In breast care, the construction of norms and normals occurs through the constructs of risk-safety, trust-fear, responsibility-blame, estrangement-support, and early-late. These tropes are directional. They do allow for the kind of multiplicity I mention but they also can come down on the side of placing judgment.

The accountability for medical outcomes, errors, and decisions is collective. Health and wellbeing are both collective and personal goods. Collectivities are responsible for the creation of durable equitable structures, maintaining and directing knowledge, and informing of what is possible and available. Individuals and collectives bear a responsibility in learning to navigate the institutions. Individuals must bear more the responsibility and have the freedom to make the decisions and choose the directions of care.

Medical Power

Power is not necessarily the effect of knowledge. Knowledge can be impotent, indecisive, and ineffective. It is only knowledge that is deemed credible, that is applied in a mindful, learned, and experienced fashion that can have a positive healing effect. Knowledge becomes operational, then, and powerful through the actors that employ it: institutions and movements, leaders and led. In this regard, power can be a conduit of knowledge. Medicine is a clear example of an interested institution whose role is to produce and translate knowledge into practice and habit, to adapt to new demands, structures, and situations and to produce healing.

The structure of medical judgment also shifts with the structure of medical institutions, and the structure of medical paradigms. The nexus of power/ knowledge in breast care is illuminated at the point at which action is taken. Timing is really a settlement of the judgment to act. The question of timing a particular action then speaks to the power of the knowledge that propels forward a course of treatment that decides an action. What if that knowledge is fallacious or misleading? The consequences are that the action is not efficacious. In the case of breast cancer, inadequate timing may lead to unnecessary or invasive procedures or a lack of appropriate action.

The concepts of early-late consolidate timing in breast care. Timing procedures early with the best therapeutics at hand is the model for cure or success. The positive effect of adequate timing is to be healed. This takes as givens knowledge, time, and capital. Medical timing is knowledge dependent and it is a good as the institutions and knowledge/practice structures we create.

Medical Institutions

Durable Structures

Paradigms ground durable structures. They bring together an array of actors and actants. These structures need to invest in people and new technologies as well as provide adequate care for many in need. Durable structures house professionals. These professionals become responsible for the direction of future research. These professionals can inhibit research that doesn't fit their interest. In breast cancer care, the curve with regard to radical surgery poses questions of habit in medical structures, but also of professional interest among surgeons.

The surgical profession established itself through radical techniques that would treat conditions that had not been treated before. Breast cancer is one such disease that became subject to the surgeons knife. It granted credibility to the surgical profession. Surgeons constructed narratives of hope in a 'cure' grounded on the prompt radical surgical treatment of a dreadful disease. The apparent success boosted modern scientific medicine. With credibility came professional power and influence in a social sense. The question is how to facilitate the growth of durable structures without creating a professional hegemony that will stifle new directions.

I did not explicitly study the growth on institutions over time to handle this disease. How breast care institutions shifted with new treatments paradigms is interesting for future study. I did study the shifts in knowledge/ practice and its application, how women experienced these shifts. I tried to see continuities with the way women experience breast care today and how their experiences interfaced with medicine as it is practiced.

In our current institutions, health has become a commodity. This commodity structure is problematic. It reinforces inequalities between haves and have nots. The questions of inequality are important as well as how institutions can change to facilitate new directions and new arrangements to successfully engage all publics.

Institutional Learning

Medical institutions are collectives of humans, animals, technologies, and discourse. As collectives they are subject to re organization and learning. That reorganization must be slow and mindful. No process however is singularly directed or always correct. The question is to minimize error but allow learning and growth. With genetic testing we see how institutions learn to adapt to new givens about a disease, how expectations shift for women at risk, how new definitions emerge, how new actions seem rational. Before genetic testing to surgically remove breast prior to being diagnosed would have had must less validity.

Clearly, genetic testing and screening technologies refigure the parameters of breast cancer in such a way as to allow for further questions and investigation into the surgical treatment paradigm. Pharmacogenetics seems promising as a way to define treatments sensitive to the types of cancer at a cellular or genetic level. In that way, treatments may become specific to types of breast cancer as a disease and more particular to a sub group or individuals than the general population at risk. (See chapter 2)

In exploring new and in assessing the old, medical structures really should act with care. Acting with care requires acknowledging and accounting for the partiality knowledge, the possibility of misinformation, and error. Intention matters. An act, any act cannot be fully considered. It is social in its effects and side effects independent of our consideration and blindness. Acts are always embedded, dressed up in habits of contemporary communication and activity. Knowledge as experience informs our action. That knowledge becomes oriented and useful in the structures that apply it. It establishes certain developments that can follow. In this regard, knowledge and consequently mindful action are political in their consideration and in their effects. Those effects must have equity and access in mind.

Equity and Access

The questions of access and equity are really important to ask. In my study, it became clear that the way care is structured enables certain kinds of success stories for women who have the means and the know-how to navigate complex medical institutions. Making breast cancer care more easy to navigate even at the experimental setting will go a long way to ensuring that we learn about differences in our bodies, and that those differences translate into treatment protocols. The assumption so far is that all humans share enough of the genome to make the differences between us meaningless or secondary in terms of treatment. It is dangerous to ignore or heighten such differences and to imbue them with special meanings that simply cannot be supported by fact.

Access and equity go hand in hand. The issue of access is not simply a question of location. It becomes a question of being able to navigate medical care, to negotiate treatment, to stand up for procedures that may not be covered by insurance as medicine is structured and purchased as a commodity. It is to be able to seek equitable care. In this regard, we have come to trust the blind forces of capital in decisions of life and death. By letting capital decide who has health care, the issues of value seem to be a veiled. Yet when one cannot afford care one has to ask who decides who deserves to live and prosper and who does not.

As we travel between the world of the healthy and the ill, let us hope that our stay with illness will be short and temporary. Let us hope that we will develop strategies for full recovery that the institutions we produce will be mindful in the application of the knowledge gained through our experience with disease. Let us hope that we all share in the burden of creating medical knowledge as we purchase it with our lives and that we also share its fruits.

__Appendix__

Methods and Definitions

Participants in our study have considered testing for BRCA 1 and 2. We conducted detailed open-ended interviews about the participants' history with and attitudes towards cancer. We collected demographics as well as questions about their medical decision making in considering testing including descriptions of relevant physician encounters and future health plans. All interviews were transcribed and then coded by a research team using multivariate consensus coding methods. In this way, we captured not only direct responses to questions, but also general perceptions and attitudes. We entered coded interviews into the Q5 Nud*ist Qualitative Analysis Software program for data analysis and wrote brief narratives referring to each participants' personal history with cancer and their decision making trajectory.

Relevant nodes were selected for re-coding and analysis using grounded theory. I answer why participants considered genetic testing. Operational definitions of nodes discussed are as follows.

Perceived Risk

Nodes: Attitudes towards genetics and vulnerability

Perceived risk captures attitudes towards genetics and vulnerability to cancer, heredity, and death. The node on attitudes (13,1) towards genetics was included to ensure that vulnerability to cancer genetics and heritage would be analyzed as part of *Perceived Risk* as it related to the testing consideration. See *Table 5*.

Emotion management

> *Nodes: Attitudes towards cancer and emotions*

How do women manage their feelings of vulnerability and turn them into action? Feelings are reactions to events prospective, retrospective and current. Emotion management is central to action in terms of seeking adequate information, deciding how much one chooses to know or not know and then what to do about it. See Graph 5.

Usefulness

> *Nodes: Test Requirements and Characteristics as factors in decision making*

Usefulness captures how the interviewee understands medical assessments of their risk for cancer in reference to their fitness for BRCA testing (both limitations and requirements of the test). Usefulness impacts Perceived Risk nodes when there is conflicting or contradictory assessments by physicians. (See graph 4)

Knowledge Seeking

> *Nodes: Vulnerability and emotions as a Factor in Testing Decision*

Knowledge-seeking captures the interviewees' interest in pursuing knowledge about their genetic risk at the moment they begin to consider genetic testing but prior to the informed consent section. Node 23, vulnerability as a factor in the testing decision, and nodes 26s, psychological factors, combined helped outline if women wanted to know whether they carry the gene. To see how different interviews align with testing decisions and results refer to Table 6 and Graph 6.

Testing Decision

Decliners are interviewees who did not follow through with genetic testing. Some decliners act as acceptors because they seem to say they would test if barriers were removed. However, these statements are hypothetical. For the sake of clarity these interviews are still marked as decliners but with an asterix (D*).

Acceptors are interviewees who did follow through with genetic testing. Some tested positive (A+) others negative (A-) others were inconclusive (A´). One interviewee who did test but chose not receive her results is marked with an asterix (A*). See Table 6.

Testing Trajectory

Nodes Precipitating event, Consent, Reconsidering Testing/ Retesting

Testing trajectory begins at the moment of considering testing through the moment of decision that is captured in reference to the informed consent node through reconsidering testing and re-testing node. (See Table 8)

Medical Management

Nodes: Attitudes towards preventions/ detection-medical management as a factor-medical management history

Health regimen attempts to capture how interviewee's manage cancer risk. This node is complex in that it attempts to align attitudes towards prevention and detection (13,3) with medical management decisions both as a factor (20) in as well as independent of the consideration of genetic testing (50s). For a summary of issues in these nodes consult Tables 7 and 8.

Tables and Graphs

Table 1. "Early" and "Radical"

Early as opposed to advanced or late	Radical as opposed to conservative
Defines Operable/ inoperable cancers	Extent of surgery
Defines Local/ Metastatic growth	Style of surgery
Times cancer onset for intervention	A paradigm of intervention
Grounds social definition of success	Criterion for successful operations
Grounds medical policy	Grounds surgical authority
Orders diagnosis/ detection	Orders sequence/ style of treatments
Mobilizes women	"Debilitates" or "saves" women

Table 2. Publications by Country

Country	Surgeons/ Institution	Society, Journal, Date	Paper/ Book Title
England			
	Lorenz Heister,		
	Benjamin Bell Edinburgh Royal Infirmary	1739	Surgery.
	John Butler Medical chyrurgical society; royal college of surgeons	Edinburgh Medical Journal, 1818	"Practical observations on the compression breasts"
	Sir James Paget	1853.	
	Charles Moore Vice president of the Society Surgeon to the Middlesex and to St. Luke's hospital.	Chyrugical Society of London, I:245, 1867	"The influence of inadequate operations on the theory of cancer"
	Mitchel Banks Liverpool Royal Infirmary Professor in Anatomy University College Liverpool	Liverpool and Manchester chirurgical reports, 1877.	"On the free removal of mammary cancer with extirpation of the mammary glands as a necessary accompaniment"
		British medical journal, December 1882.	"Contributions to the surgical anatomy of the breast"
	Harold Stiles University of Edinburgh	Edinburgh medical journal, 1892	
Germany			
	Von Volkmann	Archival materials.	

	Küster, E.	German society of surgeons, 1883	"The treatment of the breast"
		Archiv fur kinische Chirurgie 29: 723.	"Concerning the cause of local recurrence of cancer after amputatio mammae"
	Lothar Heidenhain Küster surgical clinic in Berlin	Archiv fur Klinische Chirurgie, 1889	
	Dr. J. Rotter St. Hedwig's Hospital in Berlin	Archive fur klinische Chirurgiue, 1899	"Concerning the topography of mammary carcinoma"
France			
	Jean Louis Petite (1674-1750) Director of French academy of surgery.		
	Velpeau, A.	Trans. M. Henry. Sydenham Society London, 1856.	Treatise on the diseases of the breast and mammary region
USA			
	Joseph Pencoast	Carey and Hart, Philadelphia, p 262, 1844	"Treatise on Operative Surgery"
	Gross	Surgical papers.	
	Willy Meyer New York Post-graduate Medical School and Hospital	New York academy of Medicine; Medical Record, 1894	"An improved operation for the carcinoma of the breast"

William Halsted		
Professor, Johns Hopkins University Medical School and Hospital	John Hopkins Hospital Bulletin, 1894.	"The results of operations for the cure of cancer of the breast performed at the johns Hopkins hospital from June, 1889 to January 1894"
Joseph Colt Bloodgood		
Baltimore Maryland	American surgical association, 1913. Also, in Surgery, Gynecology, Obstetrics, 1914	"Diagnosis and treatment of border-line pathological lesions"

Table 3. Diagnostic or Screening Intervention

	Detection practice	Providers	Technology	Body-Part
1.	Self exam	Self or Lover	Hands Touch	Breast
2.	Clinical and Family History	Clinicians: Expert Nurses, General Practitioners	Discourse Pedigree	Self Breast Lineage
3.	Clinical Breast exam	Clinicians: Expert Nurses, General Practitioners	Expert hands Palpation	Breast
4.	Mammography Ultrasound MRIs	Radiologists Imaging technicians	Mammograms Ultrasound MRI	Breast
5.	Genetic testing	Genetic counselors, Geneticists, and lab technicians	Gene assay Discourse	Blood
6.	Biopsy Needle aspiration Lumpectomy	Surgeons Pathologists	Needles, dyes, microscopy, minor surgery	Tissue

Table 4. Therapeutic Intervention

Treatments	Definition	Cancer or Recurrence Risk	Cancer Diagnosis
Chemo/hormonal prevention	Use of estrogen like substances: e.g. tomoxifen	Moderate to High	prophylactic
Partial/ Segmented Mastectomy or Lumpectomy	Removal of breast lump and surrounding tissue	Low	benign or borderline
Lumpectomy and chemo or radiation	Combination therapy proposed as breast conserving	Moderate to high	Early: lymph node negative, small tumor.
Quadrentectomy	Removal of a breast quadrant	Moderate	Early
Simple or total Mastectomy	Removal of affected breast	Moderate	Early to advanced
Modified Mastectomy	Removal of the whole breast, underarm lymph nodes, might remove pectoral major.	High	Advanced cancer: e.g. lymph node positive sizeable tumor.
Radical Mastectomy	Removal of breast, underarm lymph nodes, may include clavicle nodes, and both pectoral muscles	Higher high	Advanced to Metastatic: cancer has spread to many lymph nodes probably other parts.
Supper Radical Mastectomy	Removal of breast, underarm , clavicle and/ or underlying lymph nodes, both pectorals, portion of rib cage, abdominal muscle and ample amount of skin	Higher high	Advanced to metastatic
High Dose Chemotherapy	Procedure used for metastatic cancer accompanied with bone marrow transplant or removal	Higher high	Advanced to metastatic
Simple/ Modified Mastectomy and chemotherapy or radiation	Removal of breast and chemo or radiation therapy	Higher high	Advanced to Metastatic
Bilateral Mastectomy	Removal of both breasts	Higher high	Prophylactic or advanced

Table 5. Vulnerability, Perceived Risk, and Genetic Risk

Attitudes Towards Genetics	Attitudes Towards Vulnerability	Shifts In *Perceived Cancer Risk*
<u>*Causation issues*</u> *BRCA genetic test is not predictive of cancer.* Multi-factoral causation including the environment and lifestyle. *BRCA can be genetic but there are environmental or lifestyle triggers* weak link between gene and cancer but a) strong link between cancer and death or b) week link between cancer and death *BRCA is predictive of cancer.* tight link between a) gene, cancer or b) gene, cancer, death <u>*Heritability Issues*</u> Ethnic Family history Fluke chance Future Generations	*Resemblance/ identification with family member who is CA+* *Temporality or "time bomb'* 1. Vulnerable faulty body part: breast, gene... 2. Vulnerable moment in course of life 3. Vulnerable emotional state *Positive Attitude* *Conflicting information about risk*	*Increased or anticipated increase due to information or a life event* *Decrease or anticipated decrease due to information or medical procedures* *Multidirectional Sequential change* *Ambiguous* *No change* *Not stated or coded*

Table 6. Knowledge Seeking and Testing Decisions with Results

Knowledge seeking Testing Decisions w/ results	Need to know	Already know	Not Affected	Uncertain	Do not Need to know
Acceptors positive	7/22	3/11	4/20	0	0
With cancer	4/7	2/3	3/4		
No cancer	3/7	1/3	1/4		
Acceptors negative	7/22	2/11	3/20	0	0
With cancer	5/7	2/2	2/3		
No cancer	2/7	0	1/3		
Acceptors inconclusive	3/22	0	0	0	0
With cancer	2/3				
No cancer	1/3				
Acceptors no result With cancer	0	0	0	0	1/5
Decliners	0	4/11	5/20	7/10	4/5
With cancer		1/4	3/5	5/7	4/5
No cancer		3/4	2/5	2/7	0
Decliners with barriers	5/22	2/11	8/20	3/10	0
With cancer	3/5	0	4/8	2/3	
No cancer	2/5	2/2	4/8	1/3	

Table 7: Medical Management by Knowledge Seeking and Test Result

Knowledge Seeking Type of Medical Management Test result and Decision: (A+,A-,A`,D*,D)	Need to know	Already Know	No Factor	Uncertain	Do Not Need To Know
Breast Surgery	12 /22 (4, 3, 2, 3, 0)	3/11 (1,1,0,0,1)	11/20 (3,2,0,3,3)	6/10 (0,0,0,2,4)	3/5[27] (0,0,0,0,2)
Lumpectomy	3/12 (1,1,0,1,0)	3/3 (1, 1, 0, 0, 1)	5/11 (1,1,0,0,3)	2/6 (0,0,0,1,1)	0
Mastectomy	6/12 (2,1,2,1,0)	1/3 (0, 0, 0, 0, 1)	7/20	4/6 (0,0,0,1,3)	3/3 (0,0,0,02)
Bilateral	4/12, (2, 1, 0, 1, 0)	0/11	1/11	0/6	0/3
Lumpectomy followed by mastectomy	1/12 (0,0,0,1,0)	1/3 (0,0,0,0,1)	2/11 (1,0,0,01)	0/6	0/3
Ovarian and Uterus surgery	1/22 (0,1,0,0,0)	2/11 (1,1,0,0,0)	1/20 (0,0,0,0,1)	1/10 (0,0,0,0,1)	0/3
Oopherectomy	1/1 (0,1,0,0,0)	1/2 (1,0,0,0,0)	1/20 (0,0,0,0,1)	0	0
Hysterectomy	0	1/2 (0,1,0,0,0)	0	1/1 (0,0,0,0,1)	0
Prophylactic	10/22 (5, 4, 1, 0, 0)	3/11 (2,0,0,0,1)	12/20 (5,2,0,3,2)	4/10 (0,0,0,0,4)	0
Breast Other Breast Double	4/12 (3,1,0,0,0) 1/4 (0,1,0,0,0) 3/4 (3,0,0,0,0)	2/11 (2,0,0,0,0) 0/2 2/2 (2,0,0,0,0)	4/12 (2,0,0,2,0) 3/4 (2,0,0,1,0) 1/4 (0,0,0,1.0)	1/4 (0,0,0,0,1) 1/1 (0,0,0,0,1) 0	0

---

[27] The result doesn't reflect one acceptor who chose to test but not get the result. She chose to have a therapeutic mastectomy. One more interviewee is considering a therapeutic surgery but has not decided between lumpectomy and mastectomy. Finally, one has skin cancer and no therapeutic breast surgeries.

Ova	3/12 (0,2,1,0,0)	1/11 (1,0,0,0,0)	5/12 (2,0,0,1,2)	2/4 (0,0,0,0,2)	0
Hysterectomy	5/12 (5,0,0,0,0)	1/11 (0,0,0,0,1)	4/12 (2,2,0,0,0)	2/4 (0,0,0,0,2)	0
Combo (breast/ova/utero)	2/12 (2,0,0,0,0)	1/11 (1,0,0,0,0)	3/12 (2,0,0,1,0)	1/4 (0,0,0,0,1)	0
Considered	7/22 (1,4,1,1)	4/11 (0,1,0,0,3)	5/20	1/10 (0,0,0,0,1)	1/5
Breast	6/7 (1,3,1,1,0)	2/4 (0,0,0,0,2)	3/5 (2,0,0,0,1)	1/1 (0,0,0,0,1)	0/1
Other breast	2/6 (1,0,1,0,0)	0	1/3 (1,0,0,0,0)	0	
Double	4/6 (0,3,0,1,0)	2/2 (0,0,0,0,2(	2/3 (1,0,0,0,1)	0	
Ova	1/7 (0,1,0,0,0)	2/4 (0,1,0,0,1)	2/5 (0,0,0,0,2)	0	1/1 (0,0,0,0,1)
Hysterectomy	1/7 (0,1,0,0,0)	0	0	0	0
Combo	1/7[28] (0,1,0,0,0)	0	0	0	0
No prophylactic	1/22 (1,0,0,0,0)	0	1/20 (0,0,0,0,1)	2/10	3/5
Breast	1/1 (1,0,0,0,0)	0	1/1 (0,0,0,0,1)	2/2 (0,0,0,0,2)	2/5 (0,0,0,0,2)
Ova	0	0	0	0	1/5 (0,0,0,0,1)
No surgeries					
Breast	3/22 (0,3,0,0,0)	2/11 (0,1,0,1,0)	1/20 (0,1,0,0,0)	2/10 (0,0,0,1,1)	1/5 (0,0,0,0,1)
Ova	8/22 (2,2,1,3,0)	3/11 (1,1,0,0,1)	3/20 (0,1,0,1,1)	3/10 (0,0,0,2,1)	5/5 (0,0,0,0,5)
Neither	4/22 (0,1,1,2,0)	4/11 (0,0,0,1,3)	6/20 (1,0,0,3,2)	2/10 (0,0,0,0,2)	2/5 (0,0,0,0,2)
Breast Screening	16/22 (6,5,2,4,0)	9/11 (2,2,0,1,4)	16/20 (3,2,0,2,9)	9/10 (0,0,0,0,9)	4/5[29] (0,0,0,0,3)
More or post screening	8/16 (3,2,1,2,0	3/9 (2,0,0,1,0)	5/16 (3,0,0,0,2)	4/8 (0,0,0,0,4)	0

---

[28] The oopherectomy is planned not just considered but since it has not occurred it is placed in the considered column.

[29] One is the acceptor who chose not to receive the results.

+ Other	3/16 (2,0,1,0,0)	0	0	1/8 (0,0,0,0,1)	0
					0
ineffective/ or no screening	2/16 (1,1,0,0,0)	0	0	0	
No change	8/16 (2,3,1,2,0)	6/9 (0,2,0,0,4)	11/16 (0,2,0,2,7)	5/8 (0,0,0,0,5)	3/4 (0,0,0,0,3)
					1 Acceptor no result
Ovarian Screening	9/22 (3,4,0,2,0)	5/11 (2,1,0,0,2)	7/20 (2,2,0,1,2)	4/10 (0,0,0,0,4)	3/5[30] (0,0,0,0,2)
More freq or post or possible	5/9 (3,0,0,2,0)	2/5 (1,1,0,0,0)	4/7 (2,1,0,1,0)	2/4 (0,0,0,0,2)	2/3 (0,0,0,0,1) 1 acceptor no result.
No change	2/9 (0,2,0,0,0)	2/5 (0,0,0,0,2)	3/7 (0,1,0,0,2)	2/4 (0,0,0,0,2)	1/3 (0,0,0,0,1)
Ineffective/ no screening	2/22 (0,2,0,0,0)	1/11 (1,0,0,0,0)	1/20 (0,0,0,0,1)	1/10 Not covered by insurance	0
Chemoprevention	1/22 (0,0,0,1,0)	1/11 (1,0,0,0,0)	4/20 (1,0,0,2,1)	0	1/5 (0,0,0,0,1)

---

[30] Ibid.

Table 8. Medical Management by Knowledge Seeking and Test Trajectory

Knowledge Seeking Type of Medical Management Test Trajectory: [prior, during, post, no change]	Need to know	Already Know	No Factor	Uncertain	Do Not Need To Know[*]
Breast Surgery	12 /22 [6,8,0,0]	3/11 [0,4,0,0]	11/20 [7,4,0,0]	6/10 [3,3,0,0]	3/5 [3,0,0,0]
Lumpectomy	5/12 [1,4,0,0]	3/3 [0,3,0,0]	5/11 [2,3,0,0]	2/6 [0,2,0,0]	0
Mastectomy	5/12 [2,3,0,0]	1/3 [0,1,0,0]	7/20 [4,3,0,0]	4/6 [3,1,0,0]	3/3 [3,0,0,0]
Bilateral	4/12, [3,1,0,0]	0/11	1/11 [1,0,0,0]	0/6	0/3
Lumpectomy followed by mastectomy	1/12 [0,1,0,0]	1/3 [0,1,0,0]	2/11 [1,1,0,0]	0/6	0/3
Followed by bilateral	1/12 [0,1,0,0]	0/3	0/11	0/6	0/3
Ovarian and Uterus surgery	1/22 [0,1.0.0]	2/11 [1,1,0,0]	1/20 [0,1,0,0]	1/10 [1,0,0,0]	0/3
Oopherectomy	1/1 [0,1,0,0]	1/2 [1,0,0,0]	1/20 [0,1,0,0]	0	0
Hysterectomy	0	1/2 [0,1,0,0]	0	1/1 [1,0,0,0]	0
Prophylactic	10/22 [3,3,5,1]	3/11 [0,1,3,0]	12/20 [2,4,6,1]	3/10 [3,1,0,2]	0

[*] The results do not reflect one acceptor who chose to test but not get the result. She chose to have a therapeutic mastectomy. One more interviewee is considering a therapeutic surgery but has not decided between lumpectomy and mastectomy. Finally, one has skin cancer and no therapeutic breast surgeries.

Breast	4/10 [2,0,2,1]	2/3 [0,0,2,0]	4/12 [1,1,2,1]	1/3 [1,0,0,0]	0
Other Breast	1/4 [1,0,0,0]	0/2	3/4 [1,0,2,0]	1/1 [1,0,0,0]	
Double	3/4 [1,0,2,0]	2/2 [0,0,2,0]	1/4 [0,1,0,0]	0	
Ova	3/10 [1,2,0,0]	1/3 [0,1,0,0]	5/12 [0,3,2,0]	2/4 [0,2,0,0]	0
Hysterectomy	5/10 [0,1,4,0]	1/3 [0,0,1,0]	4/12 [1,0,3,0]	2/4 [0,0,2,0]	0
Combo (breast/ ova/utero)	2/10 [1,0,1,0] [0,1,1,0]	1/11 [0,0,0,1] [0,0,1,0]	3/12 [0,1,2,0] [0,1,2,0]	1/4 [1,0,0,0] [1,0,0,0]	0
Breast Screening	16/22 [1,0,8,9]	10/11 [0,0,3,7]	16/20 [0,0,5,11]	8/10 [0,0,3,5]	4/5 [0,0,0,4]
More freq.	0	2/10 [0,0,2,0]	2 [0,0,2,0]	1/8 [0,0,1,0]	0
+ Other	3/16 [0,0,3,0]	0	0	1/8 [0,0,1,0]	0
ineffective/ or no screening	2/16 [1,0,1,0]	0	0	0	0
Ovarian Screening	9/22 [1,0,6,2]	4/22 [0,0,1,2] one possible	7/20 [0,0,4,3]	4/10 [0,0,2,2]	3/5 [0,0,2,1]
More freq.	0	0	2/7 [0,0,2,0]	0	0
Ineffective/ no screening	2/9 [1,0,1,0]	1/4 [0,1,0,0]	1/7 [0,0,1,0]	1/4 [0,1,0,0] Not covered by insurance	0
Chemoprevention	1/22 [0,0,1,0]	1/11 [0,0,1,0]	4/20 [1,2,1,0]	0	1/5 [0,0,1,0]

Graph 1 Current Juncture between Medicine and Home

Diagnostic and experimental medicine

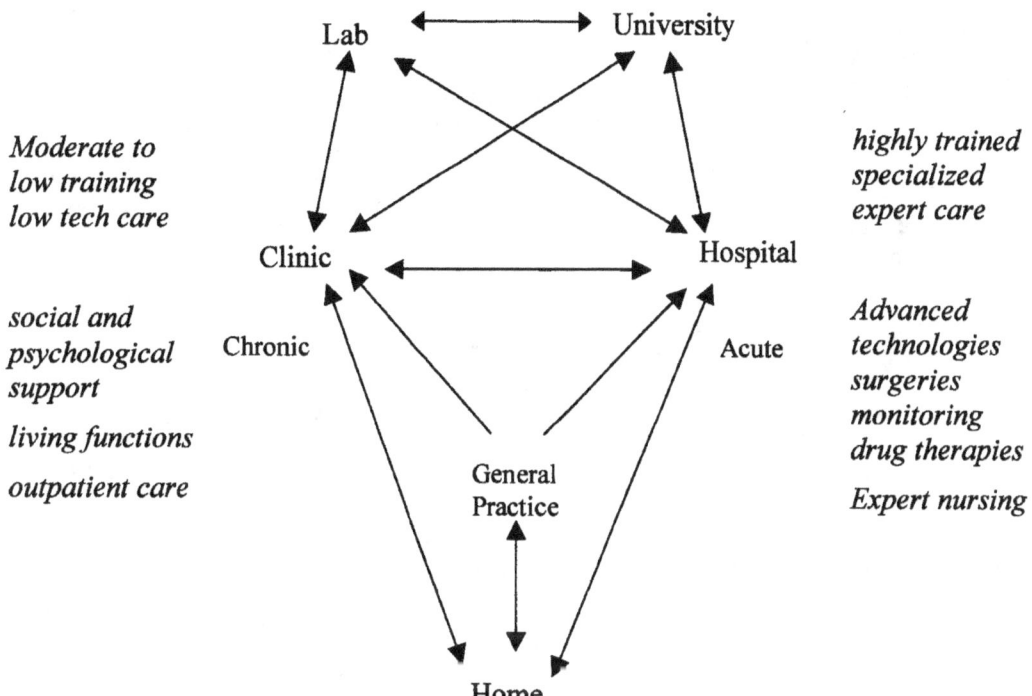

*Moderate to
low training
low tech care*

*social and
psychological
support*

living functions

outpatient care

*highly trained
specialized
expert care*

*Advanced
technologies
surgeries
monitoring
drug therapies*

Expert nursing

Self and family care
Practices of daily living

Graph 2. Breast Care Map

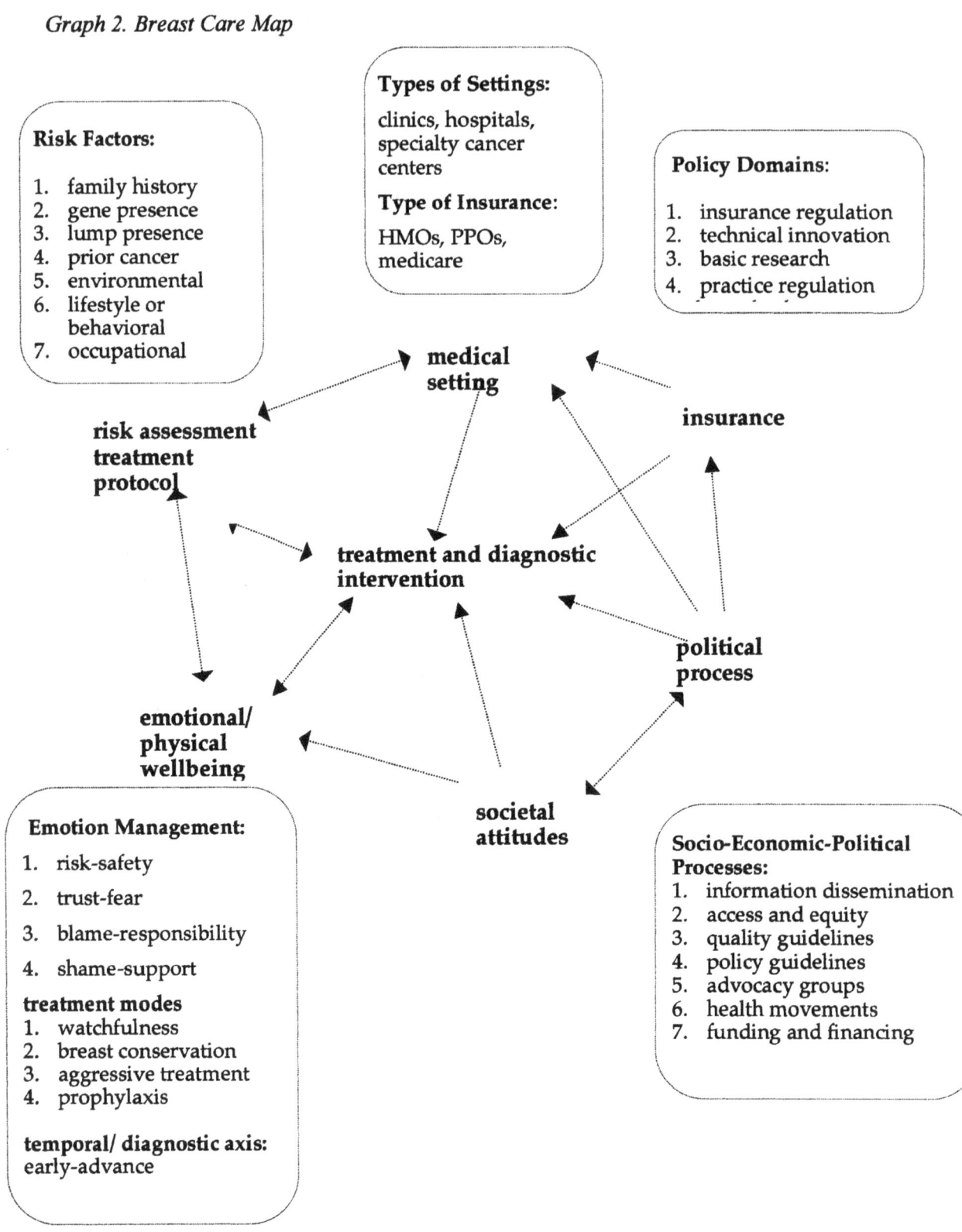

Risk Factors:

1. family history
2. gene presence
3. lump presence
4. prior cancer
5. environmental
6. lifestyle or behavioral
7. occupational

Types of Settings:
clinics, hospitals, specialty cancer centers

Type of Insurance:
HMOs, PPOs, medicare

Policy Domains:

1. insurance regulation
2. technical innovation
3. basic research
4. practice regulation

medical setting

insurance

risk assessment treatment protocol

treatment and diagnostic intervention

political process

emotional/ physical wellbeing

societal attitudes

Emotion Management:

1. risk-safety
2. trust-fear
3. blame-responsibility
4. shame-support

treatment modes
1. watchfulness
2. breast conservation
3. aggressive treatment
4. prophylaxis

temporal/ diagnostic axis:
early-advance

Socio-Economic-Political Processes:
1. information dissemination
2. access and equity
3. quality guidelines
4. policy guidelines
5. advocacy groups
6. health movements
7. funding and financing

Graph 3: Breast Care Topology

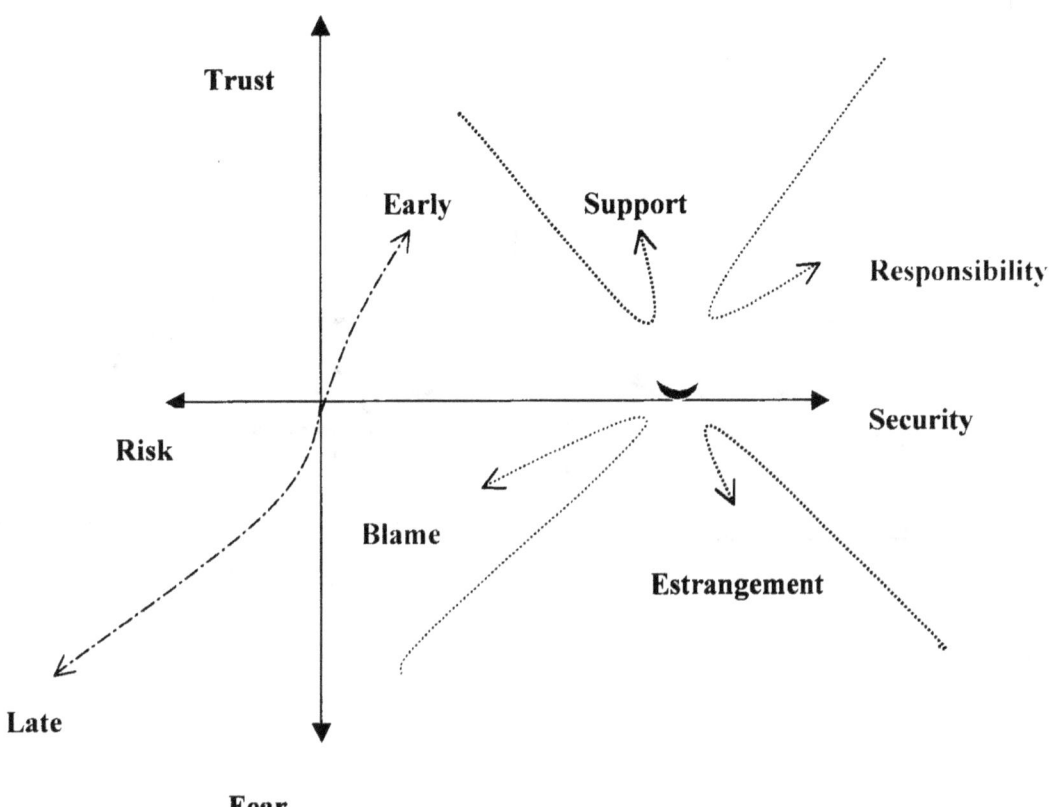

Graph 4: Considering BRCA Testing

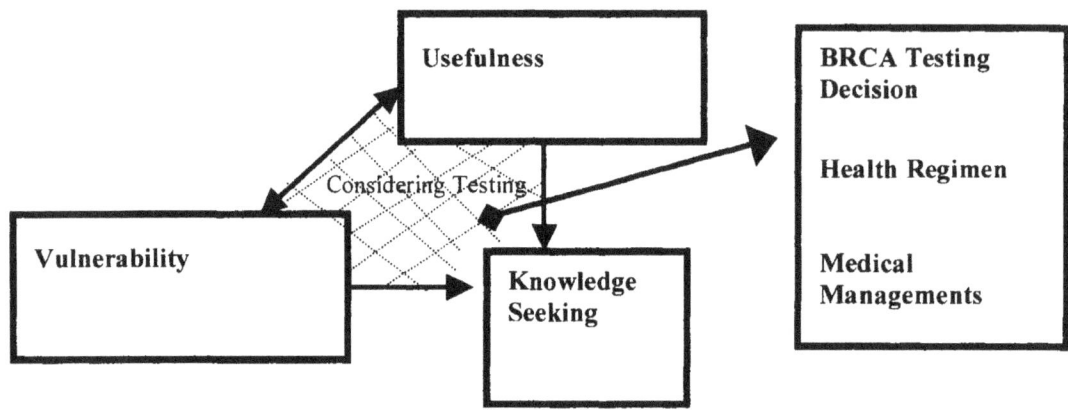

Graph 5: Emotions and Action

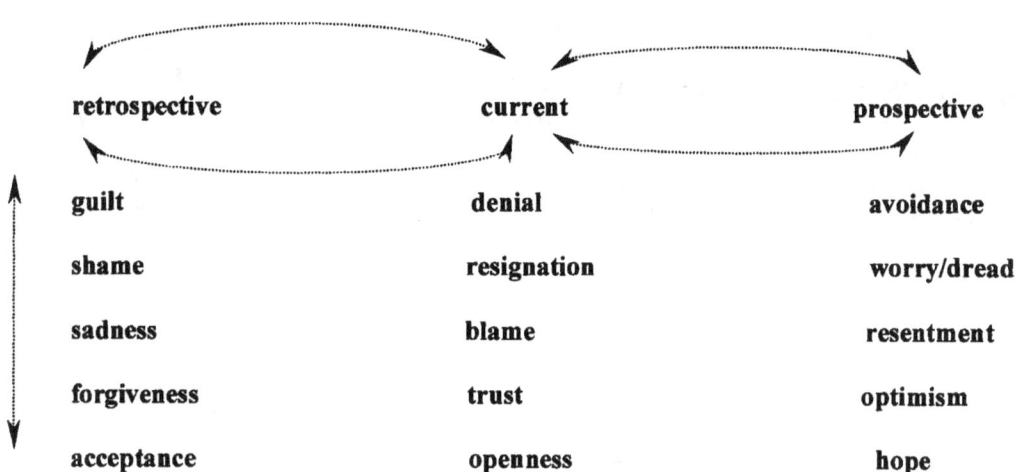

	retrospective	current	prospective
	guilt	denial	avoidance
	shame	resignation	worry/dread
	sadness	blame	resentment
	forgiveness	trust	optimism
	acceptance	openness	hope

Graph 6. Knowledge seeking and testing decision

Need to knows are acceptors (arrow blue) and decliners, who would like to know but faced barriers (arrow red) they had not yet overcame. They are most likely to (re) consider their decision in different circumstances. Already knows were acceptors (arrow blue) and decliners. Some decliners faced barriers. Some did not (arrow plum). Not Affected similarly represented as already know but with more decliners than acceptors and other differences fleshed out in the knowledge seeking section. Uncertains were all declines. Few faced barriers (plum). Do not need to know: decliners no barriers; (blue) one acceptor, who declined the result (red).

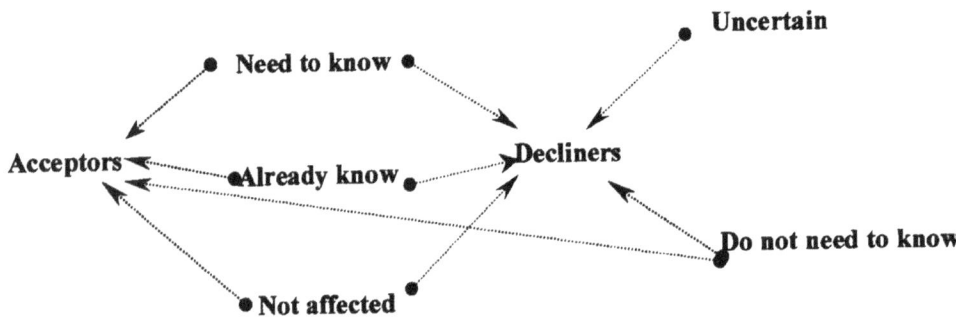

Bibliography

Works Cited

Anspach, Renee R. 1993. *Deciding who Lives: Fateful Choices in the Intensive-Care Nursery.* University of California Press: Berkeley.

Banks, Mitchell. 1882. "On the free removal of mammary cancer with extirpation of mammary glands as a necessary accompaniment." *British Medical Journal.* **2:** 1138. Reprinted in *Silvergirl's Surgery-The Breast.*

____. 1883. "The results of the operative treatment of cancer of the breast." *Liverpool Medical Chirurgical Journal.* **3:**91. Reprinted in *Silvergirl's Surgery-The Breast.*

Barad, Karen. 1998. "Getting Real: Technoscientific Practices and the Materialization of Reality." *Differences.* **10(2):** 89-126.

Barber, B. 1983. *The Logic and Limits of Trust.* Rutgers University Press: New Bunswick, N.J.

Batt, Sharon. 1994. *Patient No More: The Politics of Breast Cancer.* Gynergy Books: Charlottetown, Canada.

Bechtel, William. 1993. *Discovering Complexity: Decomposition and Localization as Strategies in Scientific Research.* Princeton Univ. Press: Princeton, N.J.

Becker, Gaylene. 1997. *Disrupted Lives: How People Create Meaning in a Chaotic World.* University of California Press: Berkeley.

Becker, Gaylene; Sharon Kaufman. 1995. "Managing an Uncertain Illness Trajectory in Old Age: Patients' and Physicians' Views of Stroke." *Medical Anthropology Quarterly* **9(2):** 165-187

Beck, U. 1992. *Risk Society: Towards a New Modernity.* Sage Publications: London; Newbury Park, CA.

Beck, U; Giddens, A.; Lash, S. 1994. *Reflexive Modernization.* Stanford University Press: Stanford.

Berger, Peter L.; Thomas Luckmann. 1966. *The Social Construction of Reality: A Treatise in the Sociology of Knowledge.* Doubleday and Co.: New York.

Benner, Patricia. 1994. (ed) *Interpretive Phenomenology: Embodiment, Caring, and Ethics in Health and Illness.* Sage: Thousand Oaks, London, New Delhi.

Bingren Liu, Yue Wang, Stella M. Melana, Isabelle Pelisson, Vesna Najfeld, James F. Holland, and Beatriz G-T. Pogo. 2001. "Identification of a Proviral Structure in Human Breast Cancer." *Cancer Research.* *61:* 1754–1759.

Brose MS, Rebbeck TR, Calzone KA, Stopfer JE, Nathanson KL, Weber BL. 2002. Cancer risk estimates for BRCA1 mutation carriers identified in a risk evaluation program. *J Natl Cancer Inst.* 94:1365-72.

Bijker, Wiebe E. and John Law. 1992. *Shaping Technology/ Building Society: Studies in Sociotechnical Change.* MIT Press: Cambridge MA; London, UK.

Bloodgood, Joseph Colt. 1914. "Diagnosis and treatment of borderline pathological lesions." *Surgery, Gynecology, Obstetrics.* Reprinted in *Silvergirl's Surgery-The Breast.*

Bogard, W. 1996. *The Simulation of Surveillance.* Cambidge.

Bourdieu, Pierre. 1998. *Practical Reason: On the Theory of Action.* Stanford University Press: Stanford.

_____. 1999. (1977). *Outline of A Theory of Practice.* Cambridge University Press: Cambridge.

Bourdieu, Pierre and Loic Wacquant. 1992. *An Invitation to Reflexive Sociology.* University of Chicago Press: Chicago.

Baumans, V. 2004. "Use of animals in experimental research: an ethical dilemma?" *Gene therapy.* **11(1):** 64-66.

Brieger, Gert. 1995. "From Conservative to Radical Surgery in Late Nineteenth-Century America." In Medical Theory, Surgical Practice.

Brown, Wendy. 1995. *States of Injury: Power and freedom in Late Modernity.* Princeton University Press: Princeton, NJ.

Burbank, F. 1996. "Stereotactic breast biopsy : its history, its present, and its future / F. Burbank." *American surgeon.* **6(2):** 128-150.

Burchell, Graham; Colin Gordon; Peter Miller. 1991. *The Foucault Effect: Studies in Governmentality.* Harvester Wheatsheaf: London.

Burney, Frances. 1995 (1811). "A Mastectomy." In David J. Rothman, Steven Marcus, and Stephanie A. Kiceluk. *Medicine and Western Civilization.* Rutgers University Press: New Brunswick, NJ.

Butler, John. 1818. "Practical observations on the compression of cancerous breasts." Edinburgh Medical Journal. **14:498.** Reprinted in Silvergirl's Surgery-The Breast

Butler, Judith. 2000. *Antigone's Claim: Kinship between Life and Death.* Columbia University Press: New York.

_____. 1997a *The Psychic Life of Power: Theories of Subjection.* Stanford University Press: Stanford.

_____. 1997b. *Excitable Speech: A Politics of the Performative.* Routledge: New York and London.

_____. 1995. "Contingent Foundations: Feminism and the Question of 'Postmodernism.'" In *Feminist Contentions: A Philosophical Exchange.* Routledge: New York, London.

_____. 1993. *Bodies that Matter: on The Discursive Limits of 'Sex'*. Routledge: New York, London.

Butler, Sandra and Barbara Rosenblum. 1991. *Cancer in Two Voices*. Spinsters: San Francisco.

Bynum, W. F. 1994. *Science and the Practice of Medicine in the nineteenth Century*. Cambridge University Press.

Castels, Robert. 1991. "From Dangerousness to Risk." in *The Foucault Effect*.

Chlebowski RT, Chen Z, Anderson GL, Rohan T, Aragaki A, Lane D, Dolan NC, Paskett ED, McTiernan A, Hubbell FA, Adams-Campbell LL, Prentice R. 2005. "Ethnicity and breast cancer: factors influencing differences in incidence and outcome." *J Natl Cancer Inst.* **97(21):** 1619.

Chide, Charles. P. 1907. *The Control of a Scourge*. E. P. Dunton: New York.

Clarke, Adele. 1998. *Disciplining Reproduction: Modernity, American Life Sciences, and the 'Problems of Sex.'* University of California Press: Berkley, Los Angeles, London.

_____. 1995. "Research Materials and Reproductive Science in the United States, 1910-1940. In *Ecologies of Knowledge: Work and Politics in Science and Technology*.

Clarke, Adele and Joan Fuijimura. 1992. "What Tools? Which Jobs? Why Right?" in *The Right Tools for the Job: At Work in Twentieth-Century Life Sciences*. eds. Adele Clarke and Joan Fuijimura. Princeton University Press: Princeton.

Clarke, Adele; Montini, Teresa. 1993. "The Many Faces of RU486: Tales of Situated Knowedges and Technological Contenstations." *Science and Technology and Human Values*. Winter. **18:** 42-78.

Clarke, Adele; Janet Shim; Laura Mamo; Jennifer Fosket; Jennifer Fishman. 2003. "Biomedicalization: Technoscientific Transformations of Health, Illness, and U.S. Biomedicine." *American Sociological Review* **68:** 161-194.

Cohen J. 2005. "High Hopes and Dilemmas for a Cervical Cancer Vaccine." *Science*. **308 (5722):** 618 621.

Cohen, S; S. L. Syme. Eds. 1985 *Social Support and Health*. Academic Press: Orlando.

Collins, Patricia Hill. 1998. *Fighting Words: Black Women and The Search For Justice*. University of Minnesota Press: Minneapolis, London.

Cooper, Sir Astley. 1845. *The Anatomy and Diseases of the Breast: With Numerous Plates*. Lea & Blanchard: Philadelphia.

Crowe, J. P., Jr. 1996. "An Update on Breast Cancer: Evolving Treatments and Persistent Questions." *Cleveland Clinic Journal of Medicine* **63(1):** 48-56.

Davies, Kevin; Michael White. 1995. *Breakthrough: the Race to Find the Breast Cancer Gene*. John Wiley and Sons, Inc.: New York.

Defert, Daniel. 1991. "'Popular Life' and Insurance Technology." in *The Foucault Effect*.

Deleuze, Gilles. 1993. *Fold: Leibniz and the Baroque*. trans. Tom Conley. University of Minnesota Press: Minneapolis and London.

_____. 1991. *Bergsonism*. trans. Hugh Tomlinson and Barbara Habberjam. Zone Books, New York.

_____. 1990. *The Logic of Sense*. trans. Mark Lester ed. By Constantin V. Boundas. Columbia University Press: New York.

Deleuze, Giles and Felix Guattari. 1987. *A Thousand Plateaus: Capitalism and Schizophrenia*. trans. Brian Massumi. University of Minnesota Press: Minneapolis.

Derrida, Jacques. 1992. *Given Time: I. Counterfeit Money*. trans. Peggy Kamuf. University of Chicago Press: Chicago and London.

Domchek SM, Eisen A, Calzone K, Stopfer J, Blackwood A, Weber BL. 2003. "Application of breast cancer risk prediction models in clinical practice." *J Clin Oncol.* **21(4):** 593-601.

Douglas, Mary. 1992. *Risk and Blame: Essays in Cultural Theory*. Routledge: London and New York.

_____. 1986. *How Institutions Think*. Syracuse University Press: Syracuse, New York.

Douglas, Mary and David L. Hull. Eds. 1992. *How Classification Works: Nelson Goodman among the Social Sciences*. Edinburgh University Press: Edinburgh

Dowd, Charles. 1898. "A Study of Twenty-Nine Cases of Cancer of the Breast Submitted to Operation." *Annals of Surgery*. **27**: 285-302.

Dreyfus, Hurbert; Paul Rabinow. 1983. *Michel Foucault: Beyond Structuralism and Hermineutics*. 2nd ed. University Of Chicago Press: Chicago.

Duesberg, P. H. (1988). "HIV is not the cause of AIDS". Science 241 (4865): 514

Elsberg, Charles. 1915. "The abdominal skin-flap in radical amputation of the breast." *Annals Of Surgery* **62**: 678.

Earle, T. C. and G. T. Cvetkovich. 1995. *Social Trust: Towards a Cosmopolitan society*. Praeger: Westport.

Ewald, Francois. 1991. "Insurance and Risk" in *The Foucault Effect: Studies in Governmentality*. eds. Graham Burchell, Colin Gordon, and Peter Miller. University of Chicago Press: Chicago.

Epstein, Steve. 1996. *Impure Science: AIDS Activism and the politics of knowledge*. University of California Press: Berkeley, Los Angeles, London.

Estes, Carroll and Associates. 2001. *Social Policy and Aging: A Critical Perspective*. Sage: Thousan Oaks, London, New Delhi.

Ferguson, Susan. J. 2000. "Deformities and Disease: The Medicalization of Women's Breasts." In Anne Kasper and Susan Ferguson. eds. *Breast Cancer Society Shapes an Epidemic*. Palgrave: New York.

Fisher, Edwin. 1985. "The Revolution in Breast Cancer Surgery: Science or Anecdotalism." *World Journal of Surgery*. **9**: 655-666.

Fleck, Ludwig. 1979. *Genesis and Development of a Scientific Fact*. Chicago: University of Chicago Press.

Fosket, Jennifer. 2004. "Constructing 'High risk' Women: The Development and Standardization of a Breast Cancer Risk Assessment Tool." *Science, Technology and Human Values.* **29 (3):** 291-313

Foucault, Michael. 2003. *Michel Foucault: 'Society Must Be Defended' Lectures at The College de France 1976-1976.* Trans. David Macey. Picador: New York.

_____. 1997. "The Birth of Biopolitics." In *Ethics, Subjectivity and Truth: Essential Works of Foucault 1954-1984.* Volume 1. Ed Paul Rabinow. trans Robert Hurley and others. The New York Press: New York.

_____. 1994. *The Birth of the Clinic: An Archeology of Medical Perception.* Vintage Books: New York.

_____. 1990 (1977). *The History of Sexuality: an Introduction.* Vintage Books: New York.

_____. 1980. *Power/Knowledge: Selected Interviews & Other Writings (1972-1977).* Pantheon Books: New York.

_____. 1979. *Discipline and Punish: The Birth of the Prison.* Vintage Books: New York, February.

_____. 1973. *The Order of Things: an Archaeology of the Human Sciences.* Vintage Books: New York.

_____. 1972. *The Archeology of Knowledge and the Discource on Language.* Pantheon Books: New York.

Freidson, E. 1970. *Profession of Medicine: A Study of the Sociology of Applied Knowledge.* Dodd Mead: New York

Fujimura, Joan. 1996. *Crafting Science: a Sociohistory of the Quest for the Genetics of Cancer.* Harvard University Press: Cambridge Mass, London, UK.Hann, Alison. 1996. *The Politics of Breast Cancer Screening.* Avebury: Brookfield.

Fuller, Steve. 1991. *Social Epistemology.* Indiana University Press: Bloomington and Indianapolis.

Gail M. H., Brinton LA, Byar DP, et al. 1989. "Projecting individualized probabilities of developing breast cancer for white females who are being examined annually." *J Natl Cancer Inst* **81**:1879–86

Garry, R.F. 2004. "Involvement of a Human Endogenous Retrovirus in Breast Cancer." Govt Reports Announcements & Index (GRA&I), Issue 18.

Gaudilliere, Jean-Paul. 1999. "Circulating mice and viruses: The Jackson Memorial Laboratory, the National Cancer Institute, and the genetics of breast cancer, 1930-1965." In Michael Fortun, Everett Mendelsohn (eds.). *Practices of Human Genetics.* Dordrecht : Kluwer

Goldberg, George. 1996. *Enough Already: The Over-treatment of Early Breast Cancer.* Paracelus Press: Tuscon Arizona.

Goldberg, Marshall. 1989. *Cell Wars: The Immune Systems Newest Weapons Against Cancer.* Fromm International Publishing Corporation: New York.

Grosz, Elizabeth. 1995. *Space, Time, and Perversion.* Routledge: New York, London.

_____. 1994. *Volatile Bodies: Towards a Corporeal Feminism.* Indiana University Press: Bloomington and Indianapolis.

Gruber F.P., Hartung T. 2004. "Alternatives to animal experimentation in basic research." *ALTEX.* **21(1):** 3-31.

Hacking, Ian, 1975. *The Emergence of Probability: a Philosophical Study of Early Ideas about Probability, Induction and Statistical Inference.* Cambridge University Press: London ; New York.

Haraway, Donna. .

Halsted, William. 1891. "The treatment of wounds with especial reference to the value of the blood clot in the management of dead space." *Johns Hopkins Hospital Report.* 2: 255.

_____. 1894. "The results of operations for the cure of cancer of the breast performed at the Johns Hopkins hospital from June 1889 to January 1894." *Annals Of Surgery* 20: 497-555.

_____. 1898. "A clinical and histological study of certain adenocarcinomata of the breast: and a brief consideration of the supraclavicular operations for cancer of the breast from 1889 to 1898 at the Johns Hopkins hospital." *Annals Of Surgery* **28**: 557-576.

_____. 1907. "The results of radical operations for the cure of carcinoma of the breast." *Annals of Surgery* **46 (1):** 1-9

Handley, Sampson W. 1927. "Parasternal invasion of the thorax in breast cancer and its suppression by the use of radium tubes as an operative precaution." *Surgery, Gynecology, Obstetrics.* **45**:721.

Handwerker, Lisa. 1994. "Medical Risk: Implicating Poor Pregnant Women." *Soc Sci Med.* 38:665-675.

Hann, Alison. 1996. *The Politics of Breast Cancer Screening.* Avebury: Brookfield.

Hann, Alison. 1996. *The Politics of Breast Cancer Screening.* Avebury: Brookfield.

Haraway, Donna. 2003. *The Companion Species Manifesto: Dogs, People, and Significant Otherness.* Prickly Paradigm: Chicago, Ill.

_____. 1997. *Modest_Witness@Second_Millennium.FemaleMan©_Meets_ OncoMouse ™ Feminism and Technoscience.* Routledge: New York, London.

Harley, David. 1994. "Political Post-Mortems and Morbid Anatomy in Seventeenth-Century England." *Social History of Medicine.* 7: 1-28

Heidegger, Martin. 1996. *Being And Time.* Trans. Joan Stabaugh. State University Of New York Press: New York.

Heidenhain, Lothar. 1889. "Concerning the Cause of the Local Recurrence of Cancer after Amputatio Mammae." *Archiv Fur Chirurgie* **39**: 97. Translated and reprinted in Robbins (ed) *Silvergirl's Surgery—The Breast.* 95-111.

Hochrchild, 1979. "Emotion work, Feeling Rules, and Social Structure." *American Journal of Sociology.* **85.** 551-575.

Holland James F. and Beatriz G. T. Pogo. 2004. "The Biology Behind Mouse Mammary Tumor Virus-Like Viral Infection and Human Breast Cancer." *Clinical Cancer Research.* **10:**5647-5649

Howson, Alexandra. 1998. "Embodied Obligation: The Female Body and Health surveillance" in Sarah Nettleton and Jonathan Watson (eds). *The body in Everyday Life.* Routledge: New York.

Hunt, Linda M., Brigitte Jordan, Susan Irwin, and C. H. Browner.(1989) "Compliance And The Patient's Perspective: Controlling Symptoms In Everyday Life." *Culture, Medicine, and Psychiatry.* **13**: 315-334.

ILAR: Institute of Laboratory Animal Resources. 1996. *Rodents.* Committee on Rodents, Commission on Life Sciences. National Academy Press: Washington, D.C.

Inglis, Brian. 1981. *The Disease of Civilization.* Hoddler and Stoughton: London.

Irigaray, Luce. 1991. *The Sex Which Is Not One.*

Jasanoff, Sheila. 1986. *Risk Management and Political Culture: A comparative Study of science in the policy context.* Sage: New York.

Jackson, Jabez. 1920. "The Requirements of technique in operations for cancer of the breast." *Annals of Surgery* **72(1):**181-187.

Jacquez, Geoffrey M., Greiling, Dunrie A. 2003. "Local clustering in breast, lung and colorectal cancer in Long Island, New York." *Int J Health Geogr.* **2**: 3.

Jacyna, L.S. 1988. "The Laboratory and the Clinic: The Impact of Pathology on Surgical Diagnosis in the Glasgow Western Infirmary, 1875-1910." *Bulletin of the History of Medicine.* **62**: 384-406

Jasen, Patricia. 2002. "Breast Cancer and the Language of Risk. 1750-1950." *The Society for the Social History of Medicine.* **15(1)**: 17-43.

Jatoi, Ismail. ed. 1997. *Breast Cancer Screening.* Chapman and Hall: New York.

Kahla, Peter. M.D.; Sebastiano Cassaro, M.D.; Felix Vladimir, M.D.; Michael Wayne, D. O.; Andangelo Cammarata, M.D. 2005. "Bilateral Synchronous Breast Cancer in a Male." *Mount Sina Journal of Medicine.* **72 (2):** 120-123.

Khalili P, Arakelian A, Chen G, Singh G, Rabbani SA. 2006. Effect of Herceptin on the development and progression of skeletal metastases in a xenograft model of human breast cancer." *Oncogene.* **25(3)**: 492.

Kasper, Anne; Susan Ferguson. Eds. 2000. *Breast Cancer: Society Shapes an Epidemic.* Palgrave: New York.

Katz, Pearl, 1999. *The Scalpel's Edge: the Culture of Surgeons.* Allyn and Bacon, Boston.

Kelly, Patricia. 1991. *Understanding Breast Cancer Risk.* Temple University Press: Philadelphia.

Kim, Jong B., O'Hare, Michael J., Stein, Robert. 2004. "Models of breast cancer: is merging human and animal models the future?" *Breast Cancer Res.* **6(1):** 22–30.

Klawiter, Maren. 1999. "Racing for the Cure, Walking Women, and Toxic Touring: Mapping Cultures of Action within the Bay Area Terrain of Breast Cancer." Social *Problems.* **46:** 104-25.

Koenig and Alan Stockdale. 2000. "The Promise of Molecular Medicine in Preventing Disease Examining the Burden of Genetic Risk" in Daniel Calahan, ed. *Health Promotion and Disease Prevention: Ethical and Social Dilemmas.* Georgetown University Press: Washington, D.C.

Kondo, Dorinne K. 1990. *Crafting Selves: Power, Gender, And Discourses Of Identity In a Japanese Workplace.* University of Chicago Press: Chicago, London.

Kung, Thomas. 1970 (1962). *The Structure of Scientific Revolutions.* University of Chicago Press, Chicago.

Lacan, Jacques. 1999. *On Feminine Sexuality, The limits of Love and Knowledge, 1972-1973: Encore, The Seminar of Jacques Lacan Book XX.* Ed Jacques-Alain Miller. trans. Bruce Fink. W. W. Norton & Company: New York, London.

Lacoue-Labarthe, Philippe. 1989. *Typography: Mimesis, Philosophy, Politics.* Stanford University Press: Stanford.

Lash, S. B. Szersynski, B. Wynne. eds. 1996. *Risk, Environment and modernity.* Sage.

Latour, Bruno. 1999. *Pandora's Hope: Essays on the Reality of Science Studies.* Harvard University Press: Cambridge, MA; London, UK.

_____. 1993. *We Have Never Been Modern.* Harvard University Press: Cambridge, MA; London, UK.

_____. 1988a. "Visualization and Social Reproduction: Opening one eye while closing the other...a note on some religious paintings." Pp. 15-38 in Gordon Fyfe and John Law (eds.) *Picturing Power: Visual Depictions and Social Relations.* New York: Routledge.

_____. 1988b. *The Pasteurization of France.* Harvard University Press: Cambridge, MA; London, UK.

_____. 1987. *Science in Action: how to follow scientists and engineers through society.* Harvard University Press: Cambridge Mass.

_____. 1983. "Give me a Laboratory and I will Raise the World" In *Science Observed.* Ed K. Knorr and M. Muklay. Sage: Los Angeles.

Latour, Bruno and Steve Woolgar. 1986 (1976). *Laboratory Life: the Construction of Scientific Facts.* Princeton University Press: Princeton, NJ.

Lawrence, Christopher. 1992. ed. *Medical Theory, Surgical Practice: Studies In The History Of Surgery.* Routledge: London and New York.

_____. 1992a. "Democratic, Divine and Heroic: the History and Historiography of Surgery." In *Medical Theory, Surgical Practice.*

_____. 1992b. "Practicing on Principle: Joseph Lister and The Germ Theory of Disease" in *Medical Theory, Surgical Practice*

Leibniz, Gottfried Wilhelm. 1992. *Discourse on Metaphysics and the Monadology*. Trans. George R. Montgomery. Prometheus Books: Buffalo, NY.

Leopold, Ellen. 1999. *A Darker Ribbon: Breast Cancer, Women, and their Doctors in the Twentieth Century*. Beacon Press: Boston.

Lerman, Caryn, et al. 2000. "Prophylactic Surgery Decisions and Surveillance Practices One Year Following BRCA 1/2 testing." *Preventive Medicine*. **31**: 75-80.

Lerner, Barron. 2003. "'To See Today with the Eyes of Tomorrow': A History of Screening Mammography." *Canadian bulletin of medical history*. 20(2): 299-321.

_____. 2001. *The Breast Cancer Wars: hope fear, and the pursuit of a cure in Twentieth Century America*. Oxford University press.

_____. 2000. "Inventing a Curable Disease: Historical Perspectives in Breast Cancer." In *Breast Cancer: Society Shapes an Epidemic*. Palgrave: New York.

Levi-Stauss. 1963. *Structural Anthropology*. Basic Books: New York.

Lister, Joseph. 1995 (1867). "On the Antiseptic Principle in the Practice of Surgery." In David J. Rothman, Steven Marcus, and Stephanie A. Kiceluk. *Medicine and Western Civilization*. Rutgers University Press: New Brunswick, NJ.

Lock, Margaret. 1998. "Breast Cancer: Reading the Omens." *Anthropology Today*. **14**: 8-16.

Luhmann, N. 1991. *Risk: A Sociological Theory.* De Gruyter.

_____. 1989. *Trust and Power*. John Wiley: New York.

Malakoff, David. 2000. "Suppliers: The Rise of the Mouse, Biomedicine's Model Mammal." *Science*. **288(5464):** 248 - 253

Mechanic, David. 1996. "Changing Medical Organization and the erosion of trust." *Milbank Quarterly*. **74(2):** 171-189.

Meyer, Willy. 1894. "An improved method of the radical operation for carcinoma of the breast" *Medical Record,* **46**: 746.

_____. 1918. "The advisability of totally excising both pectoral muscles in the radical operation for cancer of the breast" *Annals Of Surgery* **68**:17-26.

_____. 1920. Late results after the radical operation for cancer of the breast" *Annals of Surgery* **72(1)** : 177-180.

Milan, Albert. 1980. *Breast Self-Examination.* Liberty Publishing Co: New York.

Monette, Paul. 1988. *Borrowed Time: An AIDS Memoir*. Harcourt Brace Jovanovich: San Diego.

Montini, Teresa and Sheryl Ruzek. 1989. "Overturning an orthodoxy: the emergence of breast cancer treatment policy." *Research in Sociology of Health Care*. **8**: 3-32.

Mol, Annemarie. 2002. *The Body Multiple: Ontology in Medical Practice*. Duke University Press: Durham and London.

Morantz-Sanchez, Regina Markell. 1985. *Sympathy and Science, Women Physicians in American Medicine*. Oxford University Press: New York.

Moulin, Daniel de. 1983. *A Short History of Breast Cancer*. Boston, Martinus Nijhoff.

Nass, Sharyl; Craig Henderson, Joyce Lashof. 2001. eds. *Mammography and Beyond: Developing Technologies for the Early Detection of Breast Cancer*. National academy Press: Washington, D.C.

Olson, James S. 2002. *Bathshba's Breast: Women, Cancer and History*. The Johns Hopkins University Press: Baltimore, London.

Ong, Aiwa. 1999. "Making the Biopolitical Subject." *Social Science and Medicine*. **40(9)** 1243-1257

Paget, J. 1853. *Lectures in Surgical Pathology*. II. Reprinted in *Silvergirl's Surgery-The Breast*.

Papadopulos-Eleopulos, E., Turner, V. F., Papadimitriou, J., Page, B., Causer, D., Alfonso, H., Mhlongo, S., Miller, T., Maniotis, A. and Fiala, C. (2004). "A critique of the Montagnier evidence for the HIV/AIDS hypothesis". Med Hypotheses 63 (4): 597-601

Paterson, James. 1987. *The Dread Disease: Cancer and Modern American Culture*. Harvard University press, Cambridge Mass.

Peters, Vera. 1967. "Wedge Resection and Irradiation: An Effective Treatment in Early Breast Cancer Diagnosis." *Journal of the American Medical Association*. **200**:144-125

Pickering, Andrew. 1995. *The Mangle of Practice: Time, Agency, and Science*. The University Of Chicago Press, Chicago and London.

Pilcher, Lewis Stephen. 1903. "Operative Possibilities in Cases of Advanced Carcinoma of the Breast." *Annals of Surgery*. **38(3):** 321-335.

Porter, Dorothy. 2000. "Biological Determinism, Evolutionary Fundamentalism and the Rise of the Genoist Society." *Critical Quarterly*. **42(3)**:67-84.

_____. "Tyranny of Salvation: Historical Perspectives on Vaccination." Unpublished manuscript.

Porter, Roy. 2002. *Blood and Guts: a Short History of Medicine*. Norton Company: New York and London.

_____. 1992b. "Spreading Medical Enlightenment: The Popularization of Medicine in Georgian England, and its Paradoxes." in *The Popularization of Medicine 1650-1850*.

Porter, Roy and W. F. Bynum. 1993. *Medicine and the Five Senses*. Cambridge University Press.

Proctor, Robert. 1999. *The Nazi War on Cancer*. Princeton University Press, Princeton and Oxford.

_____. 1995. *Cancer Wars: How Politics Shapes What We Know and Don't Know about Cancer*. Basic Books: A Member of Perseus Books, L.L.C

_____. 1995 b. "The Destruction of 'Lives Not Worth Living." in Terry, Jennifer and Jacqueline Urla (Eds.) *Deviant Bodies*.

Pusztai L, Symmans FW, Hortobagyi GN. 2005. "Development of pharmacogenomic markers to select preoperative chemotherapy for breast cancer." *Breast Cancer*. **12(2):** 73-85

Rabinow, Paul. 1992. "Artificiality and Enlightenment From Sociobiology to Biosociality." In *Incorporations*. ed. Jonathan Crary and Sanford Kwinter. Zone, New York.

Riddell, Stanley, R. 2001. "Progress in cancer vaccines by enhanced self-presentation." *Proc Natl Acad Sci*. **98(16):** 8933–8935.

Risse, Guenter, 1999. *Mending Bodies, Saving Souls: a History of Hospitals*. Oxford University Press: New York.

Robbins, Guy F. ed. 1984. *Silvergirl's Surgery-The Breast*. Austin, Texas: Silvergirl. Ruge, C. Veit, J. 1881. Pathologie der Vaginalportion. Z. Gerburtshilfe, Gynakologie. 6:21. Trans and reprinted in *Silvergirl's Surgery-The Breast*

Rodman, William. 1901. "The Best Incision in the Operations for Mammary Carcinoma." *Annals of Surgery*. **34:**135-142.

Rodenhiser, G., Mann, M. 2006. "Epigenetics and human disease: translating basic biology into clinical applications." *CMAJ*. **174(3):** 341-8.

Ruge, C. Veit, J. 1881. Pathologie der Vaginalportion. Z. Gerburtshilfe, Gynakologie. 6:21.

Saunders JM. 1999. "Health problems of lesbian women." *Nurs Clin North Am*. **34(2):** 381-91

Shampo, Marc A. 1997. "Pioneers of mammography: Warren and Egan." *Mayo Clinic proceedings*. **72(1):** 32

Sontag, Susan. 1977. *Illness as Metaphor*. Farrat, Staus and Giroux: New York.

Stewart, Francis. 1915. "Amputation of the Breast by a Transverse Incision." *Annals Of Surgery* **62**: 250-251.

Stibbe, Phillip. 1918. "The internal mammary lymphatic glands." *Journal of Anatomy*, **52**:257.

Stiles, Harold. 1892. "Contributions to the anatomy of the breast. " *Edinburgh Medical Journal*. **37**: 1099. Reprinted in *Silvergirl's Surgery-The Breast*.

Strathern, M. 1991. *Partial Connections*. Rowman and Littleflied: Savage, MD.

Strauss, A. 1993. *Continual Permutations of Action*. Aldine De Gruyter: New York.

Stoppard, Miriam. 1998. *Breast Health*. DK Publishing, INC: New York, NY.

Theoharis, Sotiria. "Hyper-real Medical Insight into Flesh: Beyond Hands, Eyes, Ears and All Too Human Perspectives." Chapter 1 of Third Area.

_____. "Genes, Germs, Sins, Toxins: Remaking Illness and Disease, Rethinking the Landscape of Life and World." Chapter 2 of Third Area.

Thompson D, Easton DF. 2002. Cancer incidence in BRCA1 mutation carriers. *J Natl Cancer Inst*. 94:1358-65.

Tucker, Geoff. 2004. "Pharmacogenetics—expectations and reality: Drug response and toxicity depend on genes, environment, and behavior." *BMJ.* **329(7456):** 4–6

Turner-Warwick. 1958. "The Lymphatics of the Breast." *British Journal of Surgery.* 46: 574.

Usui, Takeshi. 2006. "Pharmaceutical Prospects of Phytoestrogens." *Endocrine Journal.* **53(1):** 7-20

Velpaeu, A . 1956. "A Treatise on the Diseases of the Breast and Mammary Region." Trans by Mitchell Henry, London, Sydenham Society. Reprinted in *Silvergirl's Surgery-The Breast.*

Venkitaraman, Ashok. 2002. "Cancer Susceptibility and the functions of BRCA 1 and BRCA 2." *Cell.* 108(2): 171-182.

Volkmann, von. 1882. *Archival Materials.* Trans and reprinted in *Silvergirl's Surgery-The Breast.*

Wagner KU. 2004. "Models of breast cancer: quo vadis, animal modeling?" *Breast Cancer Res.* **6(1):** 22-30.

Warren, J Collins. 1904. "The Operative Treatment of Cancer of the Breast." *Annals of Surgery.* **40(2):** 805-833.

_____. 1907. "Plastic Resection of the Mammary Gland." *Annals of Surgery.* **45(6):** 801-809

Weber, Max. 1946. "Religious, Rejection of the World and Their Directions." *From Max Weber: Essays in Sociology.* Gerth and Mills. eds. Oxford University Press, New York.

Williams, Simon. 1998. "Health as Moral Performance: Ritual, Transgression, and Taboo" *Health.* **2(4):**435-457.

Yadlon, Susan. (1997). "Skinny Women and Good Mothers: The Rhetoric of risk, control and Culpability in the Production of Knowledge About Beast Cancer." Feminist Studies **23:** 644-677.

Yalom, Marilyn. 1997. *A History of the Breast.* Ballantine Books: New York.

Zola, Irving Kenneth. 1991. "Bringing Our Bodies and Ourselves Back In: Reflections on a Past, Present, and Future 'Medical Sociology.'" *Journal of health and Social Behavior.* **32:**1-16.

_____. 1990. "Medicine as an institution of social control." In P. Conrad and R. Kern. *The sociology of health and illness: Critical Perspectives.* 3rd ed. St. Martin's Press: New York.

Zones, Jane. 2000. "Profits form Pain: The Political Economy of Breast Cancer." In Anne Kasper and Susan Ferguson. *Breast Cancer Society Shapes an Epidemic.* Palgrave: New York.

Zuckweiler, Becky. 1998. *Living in the Postmastectomy Body: Learning to Live in and Love Your Body Again.* Hartley and Mark Publishers.

References/ Resources

American Cancer Society. http://www.cancer.org/docroot/home/index.asp

American Association for Cancer Research. http://www.aacr.org/

Blackwell Dictionary of Social Thought. ed by William Outhwaite, Tom Bottomore, Ernest
    Gellner, Robert Nisbet, Alain Touraine. Blackwell Publishers: Oxford, UK. 1994 (1996
    reprint)

The Compact Oxford English Dictionary. Oxford University Press: Oxford, UK. 1991 (2004
    reprint)

National Cancer Institute. http://www.cancer.gov

National Library of Medicine. http://www.nlm.nih.gov/

UCSF Library. http://www.library.ucsf.edu/

Wellcome Trust. http://www.wellcome.ac.uk/

Wellcome Library http://library.wellcome.ac.uk/

Wickipedia. Free Encyclopedia. http://en.wikipedia.org/wiki/Main_Page

www.ingramcontent.com/pod-product-compliance
Lightning Source LLC
Chambersburg PA
CBHW081059290526
45795CB00006B/1913